23

JOB SATISFACTION – A READER

Job Satisfaction—
A Reader

Edited by
Michael M. Gruneberg

A HALSTED PRESS BOOK

JOHN WILEY & SONS
New York

First published in the United Kingdom 1976 by
THE MACMILLAN PRESS LTD
London and Basingstoke

Published in the U.S.A.
by Halsted Press, a Division
of John Wiley & Sons, Inc.
New York.

Printed in Great Britain

Library of Congress Cataloging in Publication Data
Main entry under title:

Job satisfaction — a reader.

Bibliography: p.
1. Job satisfaction — Addresses, essays, lectures.
I. Gruneberg, Michael M.
HF5549.5.J63J6   658.31'42   75-43852
ISBN 0-470-32911-4

To my family

Contents

Acknowledgements

I should like to acknowledge the help given to me in the preparation of this book by Dr. David Benton, Psychology Department, University College of Swansea. I should also like to thank Mrs. Maureen Rogers for her help with the typing of the book.

p. 47

Introduction

The study of job satisfaction is a relatively recent phenomenon. It can perhaps be said to have begun in earnest with the famous Hawthorne studies, conducted by Elton Mayo at the Western Electric Company in the 1920s. Those engaged in industrial psychology up to this point had been much more interested in examining the effects of physical conditions and equipment design on the productivity of individuals. Elton Mayo and his co-workers started very much in this tradition, investigating the effect of physical factors on productivity. During the course of their investigations, however, they became convinced that factors of a social nature were affecting satisfaction with the job, and productivity. The human relations school was born, which saw the function of the industrial psychologist as seeking to improve the happiness of the worker, and through this to improve productivity. The implicit assumption was, of course, that the satisfied worker produces more.

Since the Hawthorne studies there has been an enormous output of work on the nature, causes and correlates of job satisfaction. In 1969 Locke estimated that the number of studies might exceed four thousand. Since then, of course, a great many more studies have been published. Yet despite this vast output many workers, such as Locke, are dissatisfied with the progress that has been made in understanding job satisfaction, and despite the tremendous amount of information available, nothing still yields so much controversy as does the question of the nature of job satisfaction.

The traditional model of job satisfaction is that it consists of the total body of feelings that an individual has about his job. This total body of feelings involves, in effect, weighing up the sum total of influences on the job; the nature of the job itself, the pay, the promotion prospects, the nature of supervision, and so on. Where the sum total of influences gives rise to feelings of satisfaction the individual is job satisfied, where in total they give rise to feelings of dissatisfaction the individual is job dissatisfied. Improving any one of these influences will lead in the direction of job satisfaction, making less satisfactory any one of the influences will lead in the direction of job dissatisfaction.

However, what makes a job satisfying or dissatisfying does not depend only on the nature of the job, but on the expectations that individuals have of what their job should provide. Expectancy theory points to the importance of the individual's expectations of his job in determining job satisfaction. For individuals who have expectations that their job should give them opportunities for, say, challenge, a failure of the job to meet this expectation will lead to dissatisfaction compared to a situation where no such expectation is involved.

What exact expectation individuals will have of a job may vary for a large number of reasons, some deriving from social, others from individual causes. For example, the expectations that an individual has about his job may be different for males and females. Kuhlen (Part I) found females expected less from their job as teachers than did males. Foa (Part III) found that the expectations individuals had about the nature of supervision affected their satisfaction with supervision. Klein and Maher (Part IV) found expectations to vary with education; college educated managers were less satisfied with their pay than non-college educated managers, as their expectations were based on a different reference group. The study of Blood and Hulin (Part III) found expectations of individuals concerning their jobs varied according to the social conditions in which they lived. The matching of expectations and the actual job has important implications. Hackman and Lawler (1971) for example, found that only individuals who had high needs for fulfilment on the job are satisfied by having a job which provides the opportunities for such needs to be fulfilled. Admittedly, in their study, and in many others, most people seem to have higher order needs, such as those involving self-actualisation. The classical study by Walker and Guest for example (Part II) indicates the considerable alienation felt by many individuals working on a routine production-line job. This alienation was brought about by a lack of opportunity for psychological growth and development.

Although the matching of expectations to a particular job has been emphasised in many studies, Locke (1969) points out that it cannot be the whole story, and emphasises the concept of value fulfilment rather than expectation. One might well be satisfied, Locke points out, by an unexpected promotion, an unexpected rise in salary, and one might be dissatisfied with an expected dismissal. Often values and expectations will coincide, as one tends to confine what one values on the job to what one has some expectation of achieving. Satisfaction occurs when the job fulfils what one values. And just as with expectations, values will vary from group to group and between individuals within any one group.

Those proposing an expectancy theory usually regard overall job satisfaction as a function of satisfaction with the various elements of the job. In contrast to this approach is the view that the factors causing satisfaction and dissatisfaction have separate and distinct causes. Factors associated with the individual's needs for psychological growth contribute to job satisfaction. Such factors include the intrinsic nature of the job and achievement. On the other hand factors associated with job context, such as pay and supervision, when they are deficient lead to job dissatisfaction. This latter theory is associated with Frederick Herzberg and is commonly known as the two-factor theory of job satisfaction.

One main result of Herzberg's work has been the emphasis on creating conditions of psychological growth in the work environment. Herzberg's approach involves enriching the job so that the individual is not constricted by unskilled repetitive work from which he derives no satisfaction, no matter how satisfactory the contextual factors such as pay might be. Rather the job should be expected to give opportunities for decision making and the application of real skill.

Herzberg's work has come in for severe criticism recently from a number of sources. In particular a number of studies appear to show that the same factors can cause both satisfaction and dissatisfaction. Others, such as Schneider and Locke (1971), are critical of the methodology employed by Herzberg. Nevertheless there is little disagreement among theorists on the importance of the job itself as a major factor in job satisfaction for most individuals, and to this extent at least Herzberg's influence has been immense.

What then can studies of job satisfaction offer the practitioner, given the various profound differences in approach, the unresolved issues, the empirical difficulties of data collection and the sheer number of variables that affect job satisfaction? In the first place, perhaps they can offer a context of humility in approaching the problem. There is no panacea, no magic wand which will transform alienated individuals into happy, contented, hardworking, high-quality, high-quantity producers. And for all our sakes this is perhaps just as well. It is as true of job satisfaction as of any other sphere of life that one man's meat is another man's poison. Studies of job satisfaction which show that what individuals want out of a job can vary with age, sex, occupational level, social group and individual expectations, serve to emphasise that to tackle the problems of job satisfaction involves an understanding of what expectations and values individuals have, and an understanding that such expectations and values can vary from group to group, and between individuals within a group.

Nevertheless, numerous studies have shown that job satisfaction can be improved for many individuals by making fundamental changes in the nature of the job. As was previously noted, many studies such as that of Walker and Guest (Part II) have shown that deskilled repetitive jobs have an adverse effect on the satisfaction that the individual derives from his job. The studies in job enrichment reviewed by Lawler (Part II) indicate that enrichment programmes can be successful in increasing job satisfaction on the whole, and increasing the quality, if not the quantity of production. The detailed mechanics of the job restructuring involved in job enrichment is beyond the scope of this book. In general, however, Porter, Lawler and Hackman (1974) indicate three main characteristics of a motivating job. First, the job must allow a worker to feel personally responsible for a meaningful portion of his work. Second, the job must provide outcomes which are intrinsically meaningful or otherwise experienced as worth while to the individual. Third, the job must provide feedback about what is accomplished. In practice a great many manipulations have been made by practitioners under the guise of job enrichment. Locke (1975) lists the following: increased responsibility; autonomy and recognition; the development of work modules; provision of objective feedback performance; job rotation; upgrading of skills through training; the use of new tools, procedures and equipment; goal setting; the development of cohesive work teams; increased participation in decision making; pay rises; reorganisation of the work task to improve 'physical' efficiency (from a time study viewpoint).

As Locke points out, a great many things done under the rubric of job enrichment owe little to the Herzberg theory of job satisfaction, pay rises and participation being 'hygiene factors', and feedback stemming more from the theory of scientific management than from any theory of job enrichment. Nevertheless the fact that what is done under the guise of job enrichment seems often to work, is of fundamental importance to the practitioner; that it is not clear why it works is of somewhat less importance.

Studies of job satisfaction have not only shown the practitioner the way forward in terms of job change, they have highlighted the effect of job satisfaction on the matters of economic importance, such as productivity, absence and turnover. The relationship between job satisfaction and productivity is a complex one, and even though there is likely to be a relationship between certain aspects of job satisfaction and productivity, the older view of a major and direct relationship has had to be abandoned. What is considerably more clear is the relationship between the degree of job satisfaction and the extent of absence and turnover, factors which have clear and sometimes major economic effects.

This book is divided into five parts, aimed at covering the various aspects of job satisfaction which have been described above. The first part deals with the nature of job satisfaction, and includes papers both favourable to and critical of Herzberg. In addition a paper by R. Kuhlen examines the role of needs in job satisfaction.

The second part examines more closely the role of the job itself in job satisfaction, and the effect of job enlargement and enrichment on job satisfaction. The classic paper by Walker and Guest is included in this part as a highly readable account of the problems of deskilling and routine on job satisfaction. The papers by Lawler and by Alderfer give some cause for hope that despite all the problems in the study of job satisfaction, psychologists have made some contribution to methods of improvement.

The third part examines the effect of the environment on job satisfaction. As has been noted previously, social factors can have a major influence on the expectations that individuals have concerning satisfactions to be obtained from their job. These are discussed in the paper of Blood and Hulin. Among other papers in this part are those of Porter and Lawler, showing the importance of organisation structure; of Foa, showing the effects of supervision; and of England and Stein, showing the effect of occupational level on job satisfaction. The concluding paper in this part by Van Zelst suggests that where people can structure their own work-group situation this is a factor that can lead to increased job satisfaction.

The fourth part deals with individual variables that can affect job satisfaction. Among the papers included is that of Saleh and Otis which examines the effect of age, and that of Hulin and Smith which examines sex differences.

The final part includes a selection of papers which indicates the effects of job satisfaction and job dissatisfaction on important economic variables. The paper by Lawler and Porter suggests that there is indeed a relationship between job satisfaction and productivity although the relationship is not a simple one. The papers of Hulin and of Metzner and Mann indicate a relationship between job satisfaction and turnover and absence. The final paper in this part, by Orpen, indicates that there may be a relationship between job satisfaction and mental health. Only the resilience of the human organism in unpleasant situations makes the relationship between mental health and job satisfaction a relatively small one.

Given the vast output of work on job satisfaction, any selection of papers for a book of readings is incomplete. The papers in this book have, however, been selected to give as wide a coverage as possible to topics of interest to the practitioner as well as the student. For those wishing to take the topic further, a list of selected further readings is given at the end of the book. Papers in this book have been chosen which as far as possible give a clear exposition of their topic. Editing has been kept to a minimum, as it is felt that it reduces the usefulness of the reader as a reference work.

REFERENCES

Hackman, J. R. and Lawler, E. E., 'Employee Reactions to Job Character- istics', *Journal of Applied Psychology*, L V (1971) 259–86.

Herzberg, F., Mausner, B. and Snyderman B., *The Motivation to Work* (New York: Wiley, 1959).

Locke, E. A., 'What is Job Satisfaction?', *Organizational Behavior and Human Performance*, IV (1969) 309–36.

Locke, E. A., 'Personnel Attitudes and Motivation', *Annual Review of Psychology*, X X V I (1975) 457–80.

Porter, L. W., Lawler III, E. E. and Hackman, J. R., *Behavior in Organ- izations* (New York: McGraw-Hill, 1975).

Roethlisberger, F. J. and Dickson, W. J., *Management and the Worker* (Cambridge, Mass.: Harvard University Press, 1939).

Schneider, J. and Locke, E. A., 'A Critique of Herzberg's Incident Classification System and a Suggested Revision', *Organizational Be- havior and Human Performance*, V I (1971) 441–57.

PART I

The Nature of Job Satisfaction

Although the work of Frederick Herzberg has dominated the study of the nature of job satisfaction, this part presents a selection of papers to show that there are several ways of looking at the problem. The paper by R. G. Kuhlen for example, looks at job satisfaction in terms of the individual matching his personal needs to the perceived potential of the occupation for satisfying these needs. Where there is a discrepancy between an individual's needs and what the job offers, there will be dissatisfaction. To quote Kuhlen: 'One man with high achievement needs, is frustrated because he sees no future. Another with strong dominance needs, is irked by the submissiveness required of him. Both are in the same occupation, both are frustrated and dissatisfied.' It is one of Kuhlen's central points that different groups of individuals have totally different needs from their occupations, and indeed certain individuals may not require their major needs to be satisfied in a job context. One source of expectations that individuals have of their job's ability to satisfy their needs may arise from the social situation in which they find themselves. The paper by Blood and Hulin in Part III indicates the effects of social situation in this respect.

Herzberg, in his paper 'One More Time: How Do You Motivate Employees?' puts forward his famous two-factor theory of job satisfaction. In this he claims that the factors which cause job satisfaction are separate and distinct from the factors which cause job dissatisfaction. The factors causing job satisfaction, which he terms motivators, are basically high-level factors such as those relating to satisfaction with the job itself. The factors which cause job dissatisfaction (hygiene factors) are factors more concerned with conditions of work such as pay and supervision. At no time does Herzberg argue that hygiene factors will make a job satisfying when the motivators are not satisfactory, except that in the short run increases in pay may result in job satisfaction. The theory is perhaps analogous to the distinction between pleasure and pain. The absence of pain does not normally produce pleasure, although it may do in the short run when one has been suffering severe pain. On the other hand the absence of pleasure is not, of itself, painful. Herzberg, using a critical

1

incident technique, certainly provides evidence to support his position. The critical incident technique involves coding incidents when the subject either felt 'good' or 'bad' about his job. Herzberg found 'good' incidents were associated with motivators and 'bad' incidents with hygiene factors.

One problem with assessing Herzberg's theory is, as Nathan King points out, the lack of an explicit statement on the exact nature of the theory. King gives five possible versions of the theory, none of which, he argues, is unequivocally supported by the available evidence. One major problem is the potential bias in the critical incident technique, since individuals might attribute 'good' events to their own achievement and 'bad' events to outside agencies. Furthermore, a paper by Schneider and Locke (1971) is even critical about the classification system used by Herzberg in dealing with the data collected by means of the critical incident technique. They claim that Herzberg was guilty of inconsistencies in classification which alone could account for their results. For example, when the worker is praised or criticised it was classified as recognition, but when he was given credit or credit was withheld for work done, it was classified as supervision.

The other major line of argument against Herzberg is that the empirical evidence simply does not support the view that motivators are involved with satisfaction only and hygiene factors with dissatisfaction only. Locke (1975) for example in reviewing the evidence, argues that motivators are involved with both satisfaction and dissatisfaction. It does seem reasonable to conclude with Porter, Lawler and Hackman (1974) that 'all things considered, the general conceptual status of the theory must be considered highly uncertain'. In the final paper in this part Ewen and his co-workers argue that intrinsic factors, such as the job itself, are more strongly related to both overall satisfaction and overall dissatisfaction than are extrinsic factors, such as pay.

REFERENCES

Locke, E. A., 'Personnel Attitudes and Motivation', *Annual Review of Psychology*, XXVI (1975) 457–80.

Schneider, J. and Locke, E. A., 'A Critique of Herzberg's Incident Classification System and a Suggested Revision', *Organizational Behavior and Human Performance*, VI [4] (1971) 441–57.

Porter, L. W., Lawler III, E. E. and Hackman J. R., *Behavior in Organizations* (New York: McGraw-Hill, 1975)

1 Needs, Perceived Need Satisfaction Opportunities, and Satisfaction with Occupation*

RAYMOND G. KUHLEN[1]
Syracuse University

If major motives are satisfied in the context of work and career, then satisfaction with occupation should be a function of the discrepancy between personal needs and perceived potential of occupation for satisfying needs, particularly among those for whom occupation constitutes a major source of satisfaction (e.g. men rather than women), and in the instance of occupationally relevant needs, such as need achievement. The Edwards Personal Preference Schedule, a special rating scale, and a questionnaire were administered to 108 men and 95 women teachers. As predicted, discrepancy scores correlated .25 ($p < .01$) with occupational satisfaction for men, and .02 (ns) for women. Achievement need discrepancies were consistently related to occupational satisfaction. Other findings confirmed that occupation is psychologically more central for men.

It may be hypothesized that satisfaction or dissatisfaction *with* an area of life is a function of the degree to which one finds satisfaction for major needs *in* that area of living. This presumably will hold true especially among those for whom a given area of living (e.g. occupation) represents a major source of life satisfaction, and may not obtain at all in a sphere of life with which a person is little concerned even though he is participating. Schaffer (1953) has advanced a similar hypothesis with respect to work (though without the latter restriction) and has presented supporting evidence. In the area of marriage Ort (1950) has reported a correlation of —.83 between happiness and frequency with which role expectations (needs) were not satisfied.

In the present investigation, a first hypothesis was that those individuals whose measured needs are relatively stronger than the potential of the

Journal of Applied Psychology, XLVII [1] (1963) 56—64. Copyright 1963 by the American Psychological Association. Reprinted by permission.

occupation for satisfying those needs (as they perceived this potential) will tend to be frustrated and hence to be less well satisfied with their occupation. Where needs and the perceived need-satisfaction potential of the occupation are more in harmony, it was anticipated that satisfaction with occupation would be rated higher. However, since a career role tends to be primary for males and relatively secondary for females, a second hypothesis was that these relationships will hold to a greater degree among men than among women. Relevant to this hypothesis is the finding of Brayfield Wells, and Strate (1957) that job adjustment is correlated with general adjustment to a higher degree among men than among women, a finding which they attributed to the greater importance of work in the life scheme of men.

The general hypothesis of this phase of the study relates to the degree of overall satisfaction or frustration of needs experienced in the occupation. The specific needs involved are, for this hypothesis, unimportant, as long as they are vocationally relevant. One man, with high achievement needs, is frustrated because he sees no future. Another, with strong dominance needs, is irked by the submissiveness required of him. Both are in the same occupation; both are frustrated and dissatisfied. It is recognized that certain needs may not be perceived as being satisfiable in the occupational context whereas others are. Thus the satisfaction or frustration of the need for achievement would presumably bear a relationship to satisfaction with career whereas sex needs typically would not. In fact, it may be assumed that career is a major source of satisfaction for the achievement need and thus it was predicted (a third hypothesis) that satisfaction of this need would be particularly important for (i.e. more highly related to) occupational satisfaction.

METHOD
Subjects
Students in certain of the writer's graduate classes, enrolling mainly teachers-in-service, were tested in the present phase of the investigation. Of some 323 tested, complete data were available for 203 (108 men and 95 women) who were engaged in junior and/or senior high school teaching. These 203 people constituted the major sample, though numbers varied slightly from analysis to analysis (in some instances more, others less than 203) since it was desired to capitalize all the data available. The subjects were mainly in their 20s and 30s.

Procedure
The subjects were asked to respond to three instruments, administered in the following order: the Edwards Personal Preference Schedule (a measure of needs); a questionnaire which asked for ratings of satisfaction with present job and occupation, and for other information relating to job

satisfaction and plans; and an instrument entitled 'Personality Types and Occupations' which was designed to obtain estimates of the perceptions the respondents had of the need-satisfaction potential of their occupation. In some instances these instruments were administered in the same sitting, but mainly the data were collected in two separate sessions with the Edwards scale constituting the first session.

Rating of satisfaction with occupation was on an 11-point scale, with instructions to 'think of your occupation in general, not your particular job'. Similar ratings were obtained with respect to satisfaction with present position. Previous research (Johnson, 1955) has shown that ratings so obtained correlate .64 with job satisfaction scores obtained from an extensive questionnaire, and .61 with pooled ratings of teachers by colleagues as to their job satisfaction, the latter sample, however, being quite small ($N = 18$). Test-retest reliability over 3 weeks was .89 The questionnaire also contained questions inquiring as to whether or not the occupation was something they truly wanted to do or in which they planned to continue. Strong (1955, pp. 98–117) had found answers to these questions related to other evidences of satisfaction (see Table 1).

Personality Types and Occupations was the same instrument employed in a previous study (Kuhlen and Dipboye, 1959) with slight modification of directions to make it appropriate for people already employed. 'Personality types', which were actually the descriptions (or slight modifications thereof) of various needs from Edwards' (1954) test manual, were presented with instructions for the subject to rate the degree to which a person of this type would likely be satisfied or frustrated in the teaching profession.[2] In assigning such ratings he was instructed to ignore whether the type being considered would make a 'good' member of this profession, to ignore his own attitude toward this type of person, and to think of the occupation in general, not a particular school or system. An example, relating to achievement need, will illustrate this device.

Type 1. This person has a high need to achieve. He likes to do his best to accomplish tasks requiring skill and effort, to be a recognized authority, to accomplish something of a great significance, to do a difficult job well, to solve difficult problems, to be able to do things better than others, to get ahead, to be a big success.

Will this occupation offer him opportunity for satisfying experiences or will it pose frustrations? And to what degree? Circle one number to indicate your judgment.

$$-5 \quad -4 \quad -3 \quad -2 \quad -1 \quad 0 \quad +1 \quad +2 \quad +3 \quad +4 \quad +5$$

| This occupation will pose exceedingly high frustration | No special satisfactions or frustrations | This occupation will offer exceedingly high satisfactions |

Table 1 Occupational satisfaction of the teacher sample

		Men			Women	
	N	Mean occupational satisfaction	Mean job satisfaction		Mean occupational satisfaction	Mean job satisfaction
Attitude toward career						
Truly wanted to do	39	9.59	9.28	25	9.40	8.80
Approximately what wanted	49	8.47	7.90	47	8.74	7.96
Came to accept	9 }			5 }		
Would not have chosen	10 }	7.50	6.75	14 }	6.84	7.79
Dislike	1			0		
F		13.69***	11.46***		25.29***	1.93
Permanence of career						
Want to continue	53	9.17	8.85	40	9.08	8.60
No plan to change	38	8.66	8.13	34	8.47	7.68
Contemplate change	7 }			9 }		
Making effort to change	3 }	7.29	6.24	2 }	7.44	8.12
Will definitely change	7			5		
F		9.45***	11.38***		7.61***	1.40

*** $p < .01$.

6

One focus of the present study is upon the degree to which satisfaction with occupation (in this instance, teaching) is related to the discrepancy between strength of one's basic need and the perceived potential of the occupation for satisfying those needs. Discrepancies were determined in the following fashion: First, index values of 1 through 5 were assigned to indicate on the same scale (*a*) strength of needs and (*b*) perceived potential of occupation for satisfying those needs. Edwards raw scores were converted into standard scores (based on norms) before index values were assigned. The index values had the following meanings:

Index value	Edwards score	Need-satisfaction potential
1	−34	− 5, − 4
2	35−44	− 3, − 2
3	45−54	− 1, 0, + 1
4	55−64	+ 2, + 3
5	65 +	+ 4, + 5

Discrepancies were computed by subtracting the index assigned to need strengh from the index assigned to the perceived need-satisfaction potential of the occupation. Thus a person with need-strengh of 4 (between .5 and 1.5 *SD*s above the mean on Edwards norms) on achievement need who perceived need-satisfaction potential of the occupation as being at an index value of 2 (i.e. rated it − 2 or − 3 on the scale) would have a 'need-need satisfaction discrepancy' of − 2. Negative discrepancies thus identify instances of presumed probable frustration, whereas zero or positive discrepancies imply adequate or more than adequate opportunities for satisfaction in the occupation, as perceived by the particular individual.

It was predicted that negative discrepancies would be associated with low satisfaction with occupation, particularly in the instance of needs (e.g. need for achievement) which are commonly satisfied through occupation and career. In general, it was anticipated that positive discrepancies (implying ample opportunity for need satisfaction) would be associated with high satisfaction in occupation. However, it is conceivable that an occupation that offers considerable opportunity for the satisfaction of a particular need may actually be frustrating to a person low in this need, if, along with the opportunity, colleagues or superiors expect or demand a high level of motivation of the particular type. It was not anticipated that the occupation of public school teaching would be 'demanding' with respect to the type of needs here studied and analyses were not designed to reveal curvilinear relations between satisfaction with occupation and the need-need satisfaction discrepancies.

SATISFACTION WITH OCCUPATION

Generally speaking, this group of subjects was quite satisfied with their careers. Their occupational satisfaction ratings ranged from 1 to 11 for 108 males and from 3 to 11 for 95 females, with the respective medians being 8.9 and 8.8. About three-fourths of the ratings of each sex fell in the categories of 8, 9, and 10. A rating of 6 represented 'average satisfaction'.

Table 1 presents the distributions of answers to questions which might also be expected to reflect job satisfaction. It will be noted that the vast majority of both sexes (a) felt that teaching was something they truly wanted to do, or approximately so, and (b) wanted to continue in or at least had no plan to leave.[3] (However, in this sample the majority of men indicated they were contemplating changing or making an effort to change their particular *positions*.) The mean occupational satisfaction-ratings of those selecting various alternatives in this table suggest that the questions and ratings are measuring the same variable, to a degree at least.

It is to be noted, in line with the hypothesis that relationships will be less pronounced in a group for whom career has lower saliency, that there is a reliable relationship between satisfaction with *current* position and statements reflecting attitude toward career choice and expected permanency of career in the case of men, but not in the case of women. The correlation between *ratings* of satisfaction with current position and with occupation were also higher in the case of men than women, the respective r's being .62 and .36.

NEEDS, PERCEPTIONS, AND OCCUPATIONAL SATISFACTION

Table 2 contains the means and SDs for the two sexes for each of the 15 needs and for ratings as to the potential of the occupation for satisfying those needs. The Edwards raw scores were translated into standard scores according to the published norms, which have a mean of 50 and an SD of 10. Thus one can make certain comparisons of teachers with Edwards norms, if he so desires, though age and probably marital status differences make such comparisons tenuous. Compared to the norms, teachers are at about the mean in achievement need, are high in deference, low in succorance (women), high in endurance, to select examples.

The instrument devised to obtain ratings of the perceived potential of the occupation for satisfying various needs yielded especially pertinent information. Table 2 presents mean values (ratings were on an 11-point scale, -5 to $+5$) for each of 14 needs. Both sexes agreed that needs for affiliation, intraception, dominance, nurturance, and endurance might be readily satisfied in the teaching profession, but that the individuals with strong needs for autonomy, succorance, abasement, and aggression would likely be extremely frustrated. These findings would be anticipated through even a casual evaluation of the teacher's role and activities. In fact, the latter needs might be expected to be frustrated in most work situations.

However, an unanticipated finding was the marked differences in

Table 2   Mean scores of the teacher sample

Edwards PPS need subscales	Edwards score				Ratings of perception of need-satisfaction potential[a]			
	Males		Females		Males		Females	
	M	SD	M	SD	M	SD	M	SD
Ach	50.1	9.9	50.5	10.5	0.5	3.3	0.2	3.5
Def	52.9	9.3	53.1	11.0	0.7	2.8	0.5	3.2
Ord	51.1	11.8	52.1	11.7	1.8	2.8	1.2	3.2
Exh	49.3	10.4	49.7	11.3	−0.1	3.4	0.3	3.4
Aut	49.8	9.6	47.6	9.3	−2.9	2.4	−3.2	2.4
Aff	49.1	9.9	48.0	10.6	2.5	2.0	2.2	2.2
Int	49.6	10.4	51.6	9.8	3.4	1.8	2.9	2.2
Suc	48.0	9.9	46.8	10.6	−2.7	2.1	−2.6	2.4
Dom	48.5	9.8	47.6	9.3	1.7	2.8	1.0	3.0
Aba	50.0	10.0	48.8	9.9	−2.4	2.6	−3.1	2.3
Nur	50.5	9.5	49.4	10.2	3.0	1.9	3.6	1.9
Cha	49.0	11.2	50.7	10.5	−0.1	3.5	0.2	3.3
End	52.9	10.5	52.6	11.1	2.6	2.3	2.3	2.7
Het	47.6	10.5	51.4	10.8	−	−	−	−
Agg	51.7	9.3	51.0	9.7	−2.7	2.6	−3.3	2.5
N	107		91		107		91	

[a]On this rating, +5 means this occupation will be extremely satisfying to a person high in this need; −5 indicates the likelihood of extreme frustration of such a person.

perception of the need-satisfaction potential of teaching with respect to certain needs. The overall distributions of ratings are presented in Table 3 for the three needs (achievement, exhibition, and change) having the largest *SD*s.

The facts for achievement need are especially interesting. It had been anticipated that teachers would view teaching as being somewhat frustrating to individuals with strong achievement needs. But the *mean* rating suggested only that the profession would be neither especially frustrating nor satisfying. Actually the distribution of ratings is sharply bimodal. Many view teaching as extremely satisfying to the high achievement need person; many others view teaching as highly frustrating to such a person. Relatively few view it as in between. And this is true for both sexes. One can only speculate regarding the reasons for sharply divergent views. Is one group perceptive as to avenues for advancement in public education, the other not? Is one group from low socioeconomic and occupational background, and thus views the teaching profession as evidence of marked achievement, whereas the other group represents offspring of high socioeconomic or occupational level parents?

A similar tendency toward bimodality is evident in the case of

Table 3   Distribution of ratings of perceived need satisfaction of teaching

| | Type of person rated | | | | | |
| | High achievement need | | High achievement need | | High change need | |
Need-satisfaction potential ratings	Male	Female	Male	Female	Male	Female
Highly frustrating						
−5	11	14	13	12	17	12
−4	8	5	8	6	10	6
−3	13	13	14	10	14	6
−2	9	5	10	6	3	10
−1	9	3	6	3	3	4
0	0	6	6	12	7	9
+1	6	6	12	6	10	8
+2	14	9	8	9	13	8
+3	17	18	11	13	15	16
+4	17	6	10	9	12	11
+5	9	13	14	12	9	6
Highly satisfying						
Number of ratings[a]	113	98	112	98	113	96

[a]These Ns differ slightly from those reported in the preceding table. All of the data was used here, whereas the previous table is based on cases with complete data.

'exhibition'. Perhaps one group perceives the opportunities for the satisfaction of need exhibition before students, and the other is more aware of the unacceptability of such behavior on the part of a teacher in the community. In the instance of the need for change, it may be that the teachers who see opportunities for satisfaction of this need are in progressive schools while those who view teaching as frustrating to the need for change are in static schools. To be sure, though, certain kinds of people may perceive a static profession as frustrating to the need for change whereas others perceive it as offering unusual opportunities for change precisely *because* of its long-term static character.

In any event, these findings illustrate that perceptions of an occupation may vary greatly from one person to another. The need for further study of the variables that produce these contrasting perceptions is apparent.

The next analysis involved the computation of correlations between measured needs and the ratings of the need-satisfaction potential of the occupation, and between these two variables and rated occupational satisfaction. Table 4 contains the results. It will be noted that, in the data for men, reliable correlations existed between the measured need and rated need-satisfaction potential of the occupation for about half the needs, the

Table 4   Correlations among measured needs and ratings

	Correlations between					
	Need and perception		Satisfaction and need		Satisfaction and perception	
Need	Male	Female	Male	Female	Male	Female
Ach	.03	.10	−.19*	−.02	.21**	.32***
Def	.11	.14	.07	.11	−.12	−.05
Ord	.00	.16	.04	.01	−.06	−.10
Exh	.19*	.14	−.01	.08	.08	−.19
Aut	.25***	.09	−.28***	−.19	.04	.06
Aff	.15	.22*	.04	.00	−.03	.16
Int	.20*	.05	.05	.03	.03	.14
Suc	.21*	.20	−.07	−.03	−.05	.01
Dom	.27***	.06	.20*	−.12	.22*	−.05
Aba	.23*	.08	.15	−.03	−.10	−.20
Nur	.12	.10	.14	−.01	.12	−.16
Cha	.24*	−.01	−.12	.05	.16	.03
End	.05	.27**	−.11	.19	.20*	.03
Het	—	—	−.04	−.01	—	—
Agg	.11	.13	.14	−.10	.17	−.11
N	107	91	107	91	107	91

Note: All levels of confidence represent two-tailed tests, except in the case of achievement need where a one-tailed test was justified by a specific directional prediction.
* $p \leqslant .05$.
** $p \leqslant .025$.
*** $p \leqslant .01$.

highest *r* being .27 in the instance of dominance. Throughout the table one notes fewer reliable correlations for women.

Although Table 2 suggested that teachers *as a group* were average in achievement need and saw no special frustration of this need in the teaching profession, the facts in Table 4 which involve rated satisfaction as related to the raters' needs are in line with the prediction. In the case of men, those with high achievement needs tend to be dissatisfied, but those who *perceive* teaching as being potentially satisfying to the high achievement need person tend to be satisfied. In the case of women, only the latter was true. Among men, again, the data suggest that high autonomy need individuals are likely to be frustrated, and that those with high dominance needs are likely to be satisfied. Those who perceive the teaching as potentially satisfying to the high endurance need person tended to be more satisfied. Among women, only one of the 29 correlations was reliable, suggesting that for them satisfaction with

Table 5   Analysis of variance showing relationship between need for achievement and perception of the occupations potential for satisfying achievement needs versus attitude toward career and expected permanence of career

	Grouped by attitude toward career				Grouped by expected permanence of occupation			
	1 High	2 Medium	3 Low	F	1 High	2 Medium	3 Low	F
Need[a]								
Men	48.8	51.6	48.9	0.82	49.5	49.4	53.5	1.65
Women	52.0	48.1	55.3	3.19*	51.6	49.7	49.9	1
Perception[a]								
Men	6.3	7.1	4.0	3.50*	6.8	6.5	5.1	2.16
Women	7.3	5.9	5.2	2.34*	6.1	6.5	5.9	1
Number of subjects								
Men	39	49	20		53	38	17	
Women	25	47	19		40	34	16	

Note: For meaning of the groups see Table 1.
[a] Achievement.
* $p < .05$.

occupation is not so dependent upon need satisfaction as is true of men. This finding is in line with the hypothesis that such relationships will be lower among those for whom occupation has low saliency.

It will be recalled that other measures of occupational satisfaction were available in addition to the overall rating. Two questions asked that the subjects categorize themselves with respect to their attitudes toward their career and their judgments as to their permanence in the profession (see Table 1). Three groups were set up with respect to each question: those who checked Response Number 1 constituted one group; Response Number 2, the second group; and those who checked either Response Numbers 3, 4, or 5 constituted the third group. The three groups presumably varied in degree of satisfaction with the third group being least satisfied. Separate analyses of variance (simple one-way classification) were computed for each need and for each rating as to need-satisfaction potential, with the sexes separate.

This analysis was not particularly informative. Only 9 of 116 comparisons yielded reliable differences. The three that occurred (out of 58) in the case of women is the number expected by chance. These included *achievement* need in the instance of attitude toward career and perception of occupation with respect to *abasement* and *aggression* in the instance of expected permanence of career. Six were reliable among the 58 comparisons involving men. But again need for achievement seemed to be a significant variable in work satisfaction. These included need for *change* in the instance of attitude toward career and in the same classifications perception of occupation with respect to *achievement, affiliation,* and *dominance,* and in the classifications related to attitude toward career, perception with respect to *autonomy* and *change.* As Table 5 shows, in the four comparisons involving need achievement and attitude toward career (the two sexes, need and perception), two were characterized by significant *Fs.* The women who were dissatisfied had highest achievement needs, and those (both sexes, though only one reliably) who were most satisfied tended to *perceive* the occupation as potentially satisfying to the high achievement need person. No significant difference with respect to achievement need appeared when the subjects were classified according to attitude toward career.

DISCREPANCIES BETWEEN NEEDS AND NEED-SATISFACTION POTENTIAL

Although several tables of findings have already been presented the main focus of the study was the relationship between occupational satisfaction and the *discrepancy* between strength of one's needs and the perceived potential of the occupation for satisfying the particular needs.

An overall index of the degree to which the array of needs studied was viewed as being satisfiable or susceptible to frustration in the occupational context of public school teaching was computed *for each individual* by summing algebraically the discrepancies for the 14 needs (see above for description of the discrepancy score). This total index was then correlated with satisfaction-with-occupation ratings. The obtained correlations for the teacher sample of 108 men and 95 women were .25 and .02, respectively. The value for men is significantly different from zero at the .01 level of confidence (one-tailed test) while that for women obviously is not. The two correlations differ reliably at the .01 level of confidence.

This finding may be interpreted as supporting in the case of men the general hypothesis that satisfaction with occupation is a function of the degree to which one's array of needs can be satisfied in that occupation. It should be noted that the procedure employed did not ask directly the degree to which it was expected that particular needs would be satisfied or were actually satisfied *in the occupation.* One would expect higher correlations between such an index, if it could be obtained, and satisfaction with occupation than were obtained with the present index, the obtained correlation probably being somewhat attenuated by lumping together occupationally relevant and irrelevant needs. As anticipated the correlation for women was smaller than that for men, though it had been expected that this correlation also would be reliably positive. The low correlations, even for the men, may also be attributed to the probability (suggested in a previous study by Kuhlen and Dipboye, 1959) that

Table 6   Percentage of high and low occupational satisfaction groups
with favorable 'discrepancy' scores

Need	Low satisfaction (%)	High satisfaction (%)	Chi square	p
Ach				
Men	49	68	2.92	<.10 >.05
Women	48	73	4.92	<.05 >.02
Exh				
Men	57	60	.013	ns
Women	77	50	5.92	<.02 >.01
End				
Men	68	89	5.89	<.02 >.01
Women	72	88	2.74	<.10 >.05
N				
Men	37	71		
Women	39	56		

Note: This table may be read as follows: 49% of the men who fell in
the low satisfaction group had, in the case of achievement need,
discrepancy scores indicating that their rating of the need-satisfaction
potential of the occupation was equal to or greater than their need
strength (discrepancy scores of 0 or +).

teachers as a group are *not* career-minded, i.e. are not the type of people
who look to career as a major source of satisfaction.

To test the relationship of discrepancies between a specific need and
the perceived potential of the occupation for satisfying that need, the data
were dichotomized so that those individuals whose need strength equaled
or was less than the potential for satisfying that need were in one group (0
or + discrepancies) and the remainder (− discrepancies) were in the
second group. Occupational satisfaction ratings were dichotomized roughly at the median, with those with ratings of 9 and above falling in the top
groups, numbering 71 men and 56 women. The dissatisfied had ratings of
8 or below and numbered 37 men and 39 women. The data were then
classified in 2 x 2 tables and the null hypothesis tested by chi square.
Table 6 shows the findings for those three needs where significant
differences occurred for at least one of the sexes. It will be noted that the
prediction with respect to the achievement need is supported .05 level in
the case of women, but not in the case of men (p in this instance, <
.10 > .05). Thus the finding gives only tenuous support to the hypothesis,
though the differences were in the same direction for both sexes. It had
been anticipated that the stronger relationship would hold for men.

Though no specific hypotheses were formulated with respect to
endurance and exhibition, the finding is reasonable in the former. But the

excess of zero or positive discrepancy scores in the *low satisfaction* group of women in the instance of the need for exhibition is hard to explain. A possible explanation is that those who see the job as a place for gaining satisfaction of this need run into other difficulties that lower their satisfactions. But it should be noted that only 5 of 58 analyses yielded significant *F*s, and thus focusing upon these differences runs considerable risk of capitalizing chance. This would not be the case in the instance of achievement need, however, since a specific prediction was made in this instance.

DISCUSSION

The findings tend to support the general hypothesis of the study in the case of men, with respect to the array of needs, and with particular reference to the achievement need regarding which a specific prediction was made. While those correlations which were significantly different from zero were low in the case of men, correlations were generally lower for women, with only an occasional *r* reaching significance. Both the low correlations for men and the less positive findings for women are reasonable in view of the fact that as already noted, a major restriction must be placed on the hypothesis that occupational satisfaction is a function of the degree to which needs are satisfied in the occupation. This hypothesis would be expected to hold only for the people, and for occupations which attract the kind of people, who view occupation and career as a major source of need gratification; i.e. people for whom career and occupation have high 'saliency'. Other evidence (Kuhlen and Dipboye, 1959) suggests that career is less salient for teachers than for other occupational groups. Also occupation appears to be clearly a secondary role for women (i.e. not a primary source of need gratification), especially for *young* single teachers and for married teachers (Kuhlen and Johnson, 1952).

Although the present study was conducted with subjects homogeneous with respect to occupation, it would be expected that the major hypothesis relating to the array of needs would also be supported, and probably more clearly, in an occupationally heterogeneous sample. The major hypothesis does not, and need not, specify particular needs; but only that occupationally relevant 'needs' in general must be satisfied in the occupation if satisfaction is to be found. Findings which relate to the relationship of frustration or satisfaction of *particular* needs might be expected to be relatively specific to the occupation, and presumably would be suggestive of potential tension areas, worthy of attention of workers, of those selecting personnel, of supervisors in that occupation, or of those concerned with assisting young people to sound vocational decisions. In certain situations, for example, it is probably undesirable to employ people with particular need patterns. For many jobs, the ambitious man, the aggressive, dominant go-getter, may be an extremely poor choice. And not infrequently there is a conflict between the type of person needed to do a particular job and the potential of the position for satisfying fundamental career needs of the person who can do that job.

REFERENCES

Brayfield, A. H., Wells, R. V. and Strate, M. W., 'Interrelationships among Measures of Job Satisfaction and General Satisfaction', *Journal of Applied Psychology*, XLI (1957) 201–8.

Edwards, A. L., *Edwards Personal Preference Schedule* (manual) (New York: Psychological Corporation, 1954).

Johnson, G. H., 'An Instrument for the Measurement of Job Satisfaction', *Personnel Psychology*, VIII (1955) 27–38.

Kuhlen, R. G. and Dipboye, W. J., 'Motivativational and Personality Factors in the Selection of Elementary and Secondary School Teaching as a Career'. Technical report, 1959, United States Office of Education Cooperative Research Program, Washington, D. C.

Kuhlen, R. G. and Johnson, G. H., 'Changes in Goals with Increasing Adult Age', *Journal of Consulting Psychology*, XVI (1952) 1–4.

Ort, R. S., 'A Study of Role-Conflicts as Related to Happiness in Marriage', *Journal of Abnormal and Social Psychology*, XLV (1950) 691–9.

Schaffer, R. H., 'Job Satisfaction as Related to Need Satisfaction in Work', *Psychological Monographs*, LXVII [14, Whole No. 364] (1953).

Strong, E. K., Jr., *Vocational Interests 18 Years after College* (Minneapolis: University of Minnesota Press, 1955).

NOTES

1. This study was done pursuant to a contract with the Cooperative Research Branch of the Office of Education, United States Department of Health, Education, and Welfare.
2. Heterosexual needs, though included in Edwards scale, was not included in the present scale because of the disruptive influence occasioned by the humorous reaction generated by a trial form.
3. In this connection, it is of interest that only nine men and five women rated their positions as less satisfactory than the typical teaching position.

2 One More Time: How Do You Motivate Employees?*

FREDERICK HERZBERG
Professor of Psychology,
Case Western Reserve University

How many articles, books, speeches, and workshops have pleaded plaintively, 'How do I get an employee to do what I want him to do?'

The psychology of motivation is tremendously complex, and what has been unraveled with any degree of assurance is small indeed. But the dismal ratio of knowledge to speculation has not dampened the enthusiasm for new forms of snake oil that are constantly coming on the market, many of them with academic testimonials. Doubtless this article will have no depressing impact on the market for snake oil, but since the ideas expressed in it have been tested in many corporations and other organizations, it will help — I hope — to redress the imbalance in the aforementioned ratio.

'MOTIVATING' WITH KITA

In lectures to industry on the problem, I have found that the audiences are anxious for quick and practical answers, so I will begin with a straightforward, practical formula for moving people.

What is the simplest, surest, and most direct way of getting someone to do something? Ask him? But if he responds that he does not want to do it, then that calls for a psychological consultation to determine the reason for his obstinacy. Tell him? His response shows that he does not understand you, and now an expert in communication methods has to be brought in to show you how to get through to him. Give him a monetary incentive? I do not need to remind the reader of the complexity and difficulty involved in setting up and administering an incentive system. Show him? This means a costly training program. We need a simple way.

Every audience contains the 'direct action' manager who shouts, 'Kick him!' And this type of manager is right. The surest and least circumlocuted way of getting someone to do something is to kick him in the pants — give him what might be called the KITA.

Harvard Business Review, XLVI (1968) 53—62. Copyright 1968 by the President and Fellows of Harvard College; all rights reserved.

There are various forms of KITA, and here are some of them:

Negative physical KITA
This is a literal application of the term and was frequently used in the past. It has, however, three major draw-backs: (1) it is inelegant; (2) it contradicts the precious image of benevolence that most organizations cherish; and (3) since it is a physical attack, it directly stimulates the autonomic nervous system, and this often results in negative feedback — the employee may just kick you in return. These factors give rise to certain taboos against negative physical KITA.

The psychologist has come to the rescue of those who are no longer permitted to use negative physical KITA. He has uncovered infinite sources of psychological vulnerabilities and the appropriate methods to play tunes on them. 'He took my rug away'; 'I wonder what he meant by that'; 'The boss is always going around me' — these symptomatic expressions of ego sores that have been rubbed raw are the result of application of:

Negative Psychological KITA
This has several advantages over negative physical KITA. First, the cruelty is not visible; the bleeding is internal and comes much later. Second, since it affects the higher cortical centers of the brain with its inhibitory powers, it reduces the possibility of physical backlash. Third, since the number of psychological pains that a person can feel is almost infinite, the direction and site possibilities of the KITA are increased many times. Fourth, the person administering the kick can manage to be above it all and let the system accomplish the dirty work. Fifth, those who practice it receive some ego satisfaction (one-upmanship), whereas they would find drawing blood abhorrent. Finally, if the employee does complain, he can always be accused of being paranoid, since there is no tangible evidence of an actual attack.

Now, what does negative KITA accomplish? If I kick you in the rear (physically or psychologically), who is motivated? *I* am motivated; *you* move! Negative KITA does not lead to motivation, but to movement. So:

Positive KITA
Let us consider motivation. If I say to you, 'Do this for me or the company, and in return I will give you a reward, an incentive, more status, a promotion, all the quid pro quos that exist in the industrial organization', am I motivating you? The overwhelming opinion I receive from management people is, 'Yes, this is motivation'.

I have a year-old Schnauzer. When it was a small puppy and I wanted it to move, I kicked it in the rear and it moved. Now that I have finished its obedience training, I hold up a dog biscuit when I want the Schnauzer to move. In this instance, who is motivated — I or the dog? The dog wants the biscuit, but it is I who want it to move. Again, I am the one who is motivated, and the dog is the one who moves. In this instance all I did was apply KITA frontally; I exerted a pull instead of a push. When industry wishes to use such positive KITAs, it has available an incredible number and variety of dog biscuits (jelly beans for humans) to wave in front of the employee to get him to jump.

Why is it that managerial audiences are quick to see that negative KITA is *not* motivation, while they are almost unanimous in their judgment that positive KITA *is* motivation? It is because negative KITA is rape, and positive KITA is seduction. But it is infinitely worse to be seduced than to be raped; the latter is an unfortunate occurrence, while the former signifies that you were a party to your own downfall. This is why positive KITA is so popular: it is a tradition; it is in the American way. The organization does not have to kick you; you kick yourself.

MYTHS ABOUT MOTIVATION

Why is KITA not motivation? If I kick my dog (from the front or the back), he will move. And when I want him to move again, what must I do? I must kick him again. Similarly, I can charge a man's battery, and then recharge it, and recharge it again. But it is only when he has his own generator that we can talk about motivation. He then needs no outside stimulation. He *wants* to do it.

With this in mind, we can review some positive KITA personnel practices that were developed as attempts to instill 'motivation':

1. Reducing time spent at work

This represents a marvellous way of motivating people to work — getting them off the job! We have reduced (formally and informally) the time spent on the job over the last 50 or 60 years until we are finally on the way to the '6½-day weekend'. An interesting variant of this approach is the development of off-hour recreation programs. The philosophy here seems to be that those who play together, work together. The fact is that motivated people seek more hours of work, not fewer.

2. Spiralling wages

Have these motivated people? Yes, to seek the next wage increase. Some medievalists still can be heard to say that a good depression will get employees moving. They feel that if rising wages don't or won't do the job, perhaps reducing them will.

3. Fringe benefits

Industry has outdone the most welfare-minded of welfare states in dispensing cradle-to-the-grave succor. One company I know of had an informal 'fringe benefit of the month club' going for a while. The cost of fringe benefits in this country has reached approximately 25% of the wage dollar, and we still cry for motivation.

People spend less time working for more money and more security than ever before, and the trend cannot be reversed. These benefits are no longer rewards; they are rights. A 6-day week is inhuman, a 10-hour day is exploitation, extended medical coverage is a basic decency, and stock options are the salvation of American initiative. Unless the ante is continuously raised, the psychological reaction of employees is that the company is turning back the clock.

When industry began to realize that both the economic nerve and the lazy nerve of their employees had insatiable appetites, it started to listen to the behavioral scientists who, more out of a humanist tradition than from scientific study, criticized management for not knowing how to deal with people. The next KITA easily followed.

4. Human relations training

Over 30 years of teaching and, in many instances, of practicing psychological approaches to handling people have resulted in costly human relations programs and, in the end, the same question: How do you motivate workers? Here, too, escalations have taken place. Thirty years ago it was necessary to request, 'Please don't spit on the floor'. Today the same admonition requires three 'please's before the employee feels that his superior has demonstrated the psychologically proper attitudes toward him.

The failure of human relations training to produce motivation led to the conclusion that the supervisor or manager himself was not psychologically true to himself in his practice of interpersonal decency. So an advanced form of human relations KITA, sensitivity training, was unfolded.

5. Sensitivity training

Do you really, really understand yourself? Do you really, really, really trust the other man? Do you really, really, really, really cooperate? The failure of sensitivity training is now being explained, by those who have become opportunistic exploiters of the technique, as a failure to really (five times) conduct proper sensitivity training courses.

With the realization that there are only temporary gains from comfort and economic and interpersonal KITA, personnel managers concluded that the fault lay not in what they were doing, but in the employees' failure to appreciate what they were doing. This opened up the field of communications, a whole new area of 'scientifically' sanctioned KITA.

6. Communications

The professor of communications was invited to join the faculty of management training programs and help in making employees understand what management was doing for them. House organs, briefing sessions, supervisory instruction on the importance of communication, and all sorts of propaganda have proliferated until today there is even an International Council of Industrial Editors. But no motivation resulted, and the obvious thought occurred that perhaps management was not hearing what the employees were saying. That led to the next KITA.

7. Two-way communication
Management ordered morale surveys, suggestion plans, and group participation programs. Then both employees and management were communicating and listening to each other more than ever, but without much improvement in motivation.

The behavioral scientists began to take another look at their conceptions and their data, and they took human relations one step further. A glimmer of truth was beginning to show through in the writings of the so-called higher-order-need psychologists. People, so they said, want to actualize themselves. Unfortunately, the 'actualizing' psychologists got mixed up with the human relations psychologists, and a new KITA emerged.

8. Job participation
Though it may not have been the theoretical intention, job participation often became a 'give them the big picture' approach. For example, if a man is tightening 10,000 nuts a day on an assembly line with a torque wrench, tell him he is building a Chevrolet. Another approach had the goal of giving the employee a *feeling* that he is determining, in some measure, what he does on his job. The goal was to provide a *sense* of achievement rather than a substantive achievement in his task. Real achievement, of course, requires a task that makes it possible.

But still there was no motivation. This led to the inevitable conclusion that the employees must be sick, and therefore to the next KITA.

9. Employee counseling
The initial use of this form of KITA in a systematic fashion can be credited to the Hawthorne experiment of the Western Electric Company during the early 1930s. At that time, it was found that the employees harbored irrational feelings that were interfering with the rational operation of the factory. Counseling in this instance was a means of letting the employees unburden themselves by talking to someone about their problems. Although the counseling techniques were primitive, the program was large indeed.

The counseling approach suffered as a result of experiences during World War II, when the programs themselves were found to be interfering with the operation of the organizations; the counselors had forgotten their role of benevolent listeners and were attempting to do something about the problems that they heard about. Psychological counseling, however, has managed to survive the negative impact of World War II experiences and today is beginning to flourish with renewed sophistication. But, alas, many of these programs, like all the others, do not seem to have lessened the pressure of demands to find out how to motivate workers.

Since KITA results only in short-term movement, it is safe to predict that the cost of these programs will increase steadily and new varieties will be developed as old positive KITAs reach their satiation points.

HYGIENE *v* MOTIVATORS

Let me rephrase the perennial question this way: How do you install a generator in an employee? A brief review of my motivation-hygiene theory of job attitudes is required before theoretical and practical suggestions can be offered. The theory was first drawn from an examination of events in the lives of engineers and accountants. At least 16 other investigations, using a wide variety of populations (including some in the Communist countries) have since been completed, making the original research one of the most replicated studies in the field of job attitudes.

The findings of these studies, along with corroboration from many other investigations using different procedures, suggest that the factors involved in producing job satisfaction (and motivation) are separate and distinct from the factors that lead to job dissatisfaction. Since separate factors need to be considered, depending on whether job satisfaction or job dissatisfaction is being examined, it follows that these two feelings are not opposites of each other. The opposite of job satisfaction is not job dissatisfaction but, rather, *no* job satisfaction; and, similarly, the opposite of job dissatisfaction is not job satisfaction, but *no* job dissatisfaction.

Stating the concept presents a problem in semantics, for we normally think of satisfaction and dissatisfaction as opposites — i.e. what is not satisfying must be dissatisfying, and vice versa. But when it comes to understanding the behavior of people in their jobs, more than a play on words is involved.

Two different needs of man are involved here. One set of needs can be thought of as stemming from his animal nature — the built-in drive to avoid pain from the environment, plus all the learned drives which become conditioned to the basic biological needs. For example, hunger, a basic biological drive, makes it necessary to earn money, and then money becomes a specific drive. The other set of needs relates to that unique human characteristic, the ability to achieve and, through achievement, to experience psychological growth. The stimuli for the growth needs are tasks that induce growth; in the industrial setting, they are the *job content*. Contrariwise, the stimuli inducing pain-avoidance behavior are found in the *job environment*.

The growth or *motivator* factors that are intrinsic to the job are: achievement, recognition for achievement, the work itself, responsibility, and growth or advancement. The dissatisfaction-avoidance or *hygiene* (KITA) factors that are extrinsic to the job include: company policy and

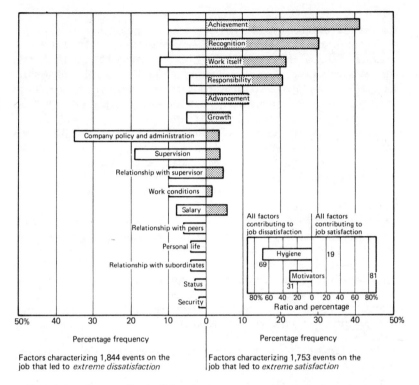

Exhibit 1   Factors affecting job attitudes, as reported in twelve investigations

administration, supervision, interpersonal relationships, working conditions, salary, status, and security.

A composite of the factors that are involved in causing job satisfaction and job dissatisfaction, drawn from samples of 1,685 employees, is shown in Exhibit 1. The results indicate that motivators were the primary cause of satisfaction, and hygiene factors the primary cause of unhappiness on the job. The employees, studied in 12 different investigations, included lower-level supervisors, professional women, agricultural administrators, men about to retire from management positions, hospital maintenance personnel, manufacturing supervisors, nurses, food handlers, military officers, engineers, scientists, housekeepers, teachers, technicians, female assemblers, accountants, Finnish foremen, and Hungarian engineers.

They were asked what job events had occurred in their work that had led to extreme satisfaction or extreme dissatisfaction on their part. Their responses are broken down in the exhibit into percentages of total 'positive' job events and of total 'negative' job events. (The figures total more than 100% on both the 'hygiene' and 'motivators' sides because often at least two factors can be attributed to a single event; advancement, for instance, often accompanies assumption of responsibility.)

To illustrate, a typical response involving achievement that had a negative effect for the employee was, 'I was unhappy because I didn't do the job successfully'. A typical response in the small number of positive job events in the Company Policy and Administration grouping was, 'I was happy because the company reorganized the section so that I didn't report any longer to the guy I didn't get along with'.

As the lower right-hand part of the exhibit shows, of all the factors contributing to job satisfaction, 81% were motivators. And of all the factors contributing to the employees' dissatisfaction over their work, 69% involved hygiene elements.

ETERNAL TRIANGLE

There are three general philosophies of personnel management. The first is based on organizational theory, the second on industrial engineering, and the third on behavioral science.

The organizational theorist believes that human needs are either so irrational or so varied and adjustable to specific situations that the major function of personnel management is to be as pragmatic as the occasion demands. If jobs are organized in a proper manner, he reasons, the result will be the most efficient job structure, and the most favorable job attitudes will follow as a matter of course.

The industrial engineer holds that man is mechanistically oriented and economically motivated and his needs are best met by attuning the individual to the most efficient work process. The goal of personnel management therefore should be to concoct the most appropriate incentive system and to design the specific working conditions in a way that facilitates the most efficient use of the human machine. By structuring jobs in a manner that leads to the most efficient operation, the engineer believes that he can obtain the optimal organization of work and the proper work attitudes.

The behavioral scientist focuses on group sentiments, attitudes of individual employees, and the organization's social and psychological climate. According to his persuasion, he emphasizes one or more of the various hygiene and motivator needs. His approach to personnel management generally emphasizes some form of human relations education, in the hope of instilling healthy employee attitudes and an organizational climate which he considers to be felicitous to human values. He believes that proper attitudes will lead to efficient job and organizational structure.

There is always a lively debate as to the overall effectiveness of the approaches of the organizational theorist and the industrial engineer. Manifestly they have achieved much. But the nagging question for the behavioral scientist has been: What is the cost in human problems that eventually cause more expense to the organization — for instance, turnover,

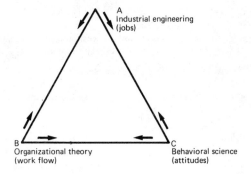

Exhibit 2   'Triangle' of philosophies of personnel management

absenteeism, errors, violation of safety rules, strikes, restriction of output, higher wages, and greater fringe benefits? On the other hand, the behavioral scientist is hard put to document much manifest improvement in personnel management, using his approach.

The three philosophies can be depicted as a triangle, as is done in Exhibit 2, with each persuasion claiming the apex angle. The motivation-hygiene theory claims the same angle as industrial engineering, but for opposite goals. Rather than rationalizing the work to increase efficiency, the theory suggests that work be *enriched* to bring about effective utilization of personnel. Such a systematic attempt to motivate employees by manipulating the motivator factors is just beginning.

The term *job enrichment* describes this embryonic movement. An older term, job enlargement, should be avoided because it is associated with past failures stemming from a misunderstanding of the problem. Job enrichment provides the opportunity for the employee's psychological growth, while job enlargement merely makes a job structurally bigger. Since scientific job enrichment is very new, this article only suggests the principles and practical steps that have recently emerged from several successful experiments in industry.

JOB LOADING
In attempting to enrich an employee's job, management often succeeds in reducing the man's personal contribution, rather than giving him an opportunity for growth in his accustomed job. Such an endeavor, which I shall call horizontal job loading (as opposed to vertical loading, or providing motivator factors), has been the problem of earlier job enlarge-ment programs. This activity merely enlarges the meaninglessness of the job. Some examples of this approach, and their effect, are:

Challenging the employee by increasing the amount of production expected of him. If he tightens 10,000 bolts a day, see if he can tighten

PRINCIPLE	MOTIVATORS INVOLVED
A. Removing some controls while retaining accountability	Responsibility and personal achievement
B. Increasing the accountability of individuals for own work	Responsibility and recognition
C. Giving a person a complete natural unit of work (module, division, area, and so on)	Responsibility, achievement, and recognition
D. Granting additional authority to an employee in his activity; job freedom	Responsibility, achievement, and recognition
E. Making periodic reports directly available to the worker himself rather than to the supervisor	Internal recognition
F. Introducing new and more difficult tasks not previously handled	Growth and learning
G. Assigning individuals specific or specialized tasks, enabling them to become experts	Responsibility, growth, and advancement

Exhibit 3   Principles of vertical job loading

20,000 bolts a day. The arithmetic involved shows that multiplying zero by zero still equals zero.

Adding another meaningless task to the existing one, usually some routine clerical activity. The arithmetic here is adding zero to zero.

Rotating the assignments of a number of jobs that need to be enriched. This means washing dishes for a while, then washing silverware. The arithmetic is substituting one zero for another zero.

Removing the most difficult parts of the assignment in order to free the worker to accomplish more of the less challenging assignments. This traditional industrial engineering approach amounts to subtraction in the hope of accomplishing addition.

These are common forms of horizontal loading that frequently come up in preliminary brainstorming sessions on job enrichment. The principles of vertical loading have not all been worked out as yet, and they remain rather general, but I have furnished seven useful starting points for consideration in Exhibit 3.

A SUCCESSFUL APPLICATION
An example from a highly successful job enrichment experiment can illustrate the distinction between horizontal and vertical loading of a job. The subjects of this study were the stockholder correspondents employed by a very large corporation. Seemingly, the task required of these carefully selected and highly trained correspondents was quite complex and challenging. But almost all indexes of performance and job attitudes were low,

and exit interviewing confirmed that the challenge of the job existed merely as words.

A job enrichment project was initiated in the form of an experiment with one group, designated as an achieving unit, having its job enriched by the principles described in Exhibit 3. A control group continued to do its job in the traditional way. (There were also two 'uncommitted' groups of correspondents formed to measure the so-called Hawthorne Effect — that is, to gauge whether productivity and attitudes toward the job changed artificially merely because employees sensed that the company was paying more attention to them in doing something different or novel. The results for these groups were substantially the same as for the control group, and for the sake of simplicity I do not deal with them in this summary.) No changes in hygiene were introduced for either group other than those that would have been made anyway, such as normal pay increases.

The changes for the achieving unit were introduced in the first two months, averaging one per week of the seven motivators listed in Exhibit 3. At the end of six months the members of the achieving unit were found to be outperforming their counterparts in the control group, and in addition indicated a marked increase in their liking for their jobs. Other results showed that the achieving group had lower absenteeism and, subsequently, a much higher rate of promotion.

Exhibit 4 illustrates the changes in performance, measured in February and March, before the study period began, and at the end of each month of the study period. The shareholder service index represents quality of

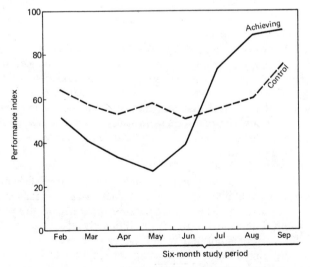

Exhibit 4   Shareholder service index in company experiment (three-month cumulative average)

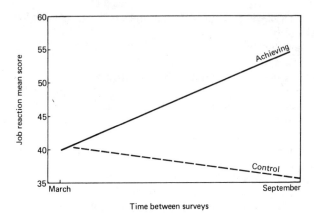

Time between surveys

Exhibit 5   Changes in attitudes toward tasks in company experiment (changes in mean scores over six-month period)

letters, including accuracy of information, and speed of response to stockholders' letters of inquiry. The index of a current month was averaged into the average of the two prior months, which means that improvement was harder to obtain if the indexes of the previous months were low. The 'achievers' were performing less well before the six-month period started, and their performance service index continued to decline after the introduction of the motivators, evidently because of uncertainty over their newly granted responsibilities. In the third month, however, performance improved, and soon the members of this group had reached a high level of accomplishment.

Exhibit 5 shows the two groups' attitudes toward their job, measured at the end of March, just before the first motivator was introduced and again at the end of September. The correspondents were asked 16 questions, all involving motivation. A typical one was, 'As you see it, how many opportunities do you feel that you have in your job for making worthwhile contributions?' The answers were scaled from 1 to 5 with 80 as the maximum possible score. The achievers became much more positive about their job, while the attitude of the control unit remained about the same (the drop is not statistically significant).

How was the job of these correspondents restructured? Exhibit 6 lists the suggestions made that were deemed to be horizontal loading, and the actual vertical loading changes that were incorporated in the job of the achieving unit. The capital letters under 'Principle' after 'Vertical loading' refer to the corresponding letters in Exhibit 3. The reader will note that the rejected forms of horizontal loading correspond closely to the list of common manifestations of the phenomenon on page 26.

Horizontal loading suggestions (rejected)	Vertical loading suggestions (adopted)	Principle
Firm quotas could be set for letters to be answered each day, using a rate which would be hard to reach.	Subject matter experts were appointed within each unit for other members of the unit to consult with before seeking supervisory help. (The supervisor had been answering all specialized and difficult questions.)	G
The women could type the letters themselves, as well as compose them, or take on any other clerical functions.	Correspondents signed their own names on letters. (The supervisor had been signing all letters.)	B
All difficult or complex inquiries could be channeled to a few women so that the remainder could achieve high rates of output. These jobs could be exchanged from time to time.	The work of the more experienced correspondents was proofread less frequently by supervisors and was done at the correspondents' desks, dropping verification from 100% to 10%. (Previously, all correspondents' letters had been checked by the supervisor.)	A
	Production was discussed, but only in terms such as 'a full day's work is expected'. As time went on, this was no longer mentioned. (Before, the group had been constantly reminded of the number of letters that needed to be answered.)	D
The women could be rotated through units handling different customers, and then sent back to their own units.	Outgoing mail went directly to the mailroom without going over supervisors' desks. (The letters had always been routed through the supervisors.)	A
	Correspondents were encouraged to answer letters in a more personalized way. (Reliance on the form-letter approach had been standard practice.)	C
	Each correspondent was held personally responsible for the quality and accuracy of letters. (This responsibility had been the province of the supervisor and the verifier.)	B,E

Exhibit 6   Enlargement *v.* enrichment of correspondents' tasks in company experiment

STEPS TO JOB ENRICHMENT

Now that the motivator idea has been described in practice, here are the steps that managers should take in instituting the principle with their employees:

1. Select those jobs in which (*a*) the investment in industrial engineering does not make changes too costly, (*b*) attitudes are poor, (*c*) hygiene

is becoming very costly, and (*d*) motivation will make a difference in performance.

2. Approach these jobs with the conviction that they can be changed. Years of tradition have led managers to believe that the content of the jobs is sacrosanct and the only scope of action that they have is in ways of stimulating people.

3. Brainstorm a list of changes that may enrich the jobs, without concern for their practicality.

4. Screen the list to eliminate suggestions that involve hygiene, rather than actual motivation.

5. Screen the list for generalities, such as 'give them more responsibility', that are rarely followed in practice. This might seem obvious, but the motivator words have never left industry; the substance has just been rationalized and organized out. Words like 'responsibility', 'growth', 'achievement', and 'challenge', for example, have been elevated to the lyrics of the patriotic anthem for all organizations. It is the old problem typified by the pledge of allegiance to the flag being more important than contributions to the country — of following the form, rather than the substance.

6. Screen the list to eliminate any *horizontal* loading suggestions.

7. Avoid direct participation by the employees whose jobs are to be enriched. Ideas they have expressed previously certainly constitute a valuable source for recommended changes, but their direct involvement contaminates the process with human relations *hygiene* and, more specifically, gives them only a *sense* of making a contribution. The job is to be changed, and it is the content that will produce the motivation, not attitudes about being involved or the challenge inherent in setting up a job. That process will be over shortly, and it is what the employees will be doing from then on that will determine their motivation. A sense of participation will result only in short-term movement.

8. In the initial attempts at job enrichment, set up a controlled experiment. At least two equivalent groups should be chosen, one an experimental unit in which the motivators are systematically introduced over a period of time, and the other one a control group in which no changes are made. For both groups, hygiene should be allowed to follow its natural course for the duration of the experiment. Pre- and post-installation tests of performance and job attitudes are necessary to evaluate the effectiveness of the job enrichment program. The attitude test must be limited to motivator items in order to divorce the employee's view of the job he is given from all the surrounding hygiene feelings that he might have.

9. Be prepared for a drop in performance in the experimental group the first few weeks. The changeover to a new job may lead to a temporary reduction in efficiency.

10. Expect your first-line supervisors to experience some anxiety and hostility over the changes you are making. The anxiety comes from their fear that the changes will result in poorer performance for their unit. Hostility will arise when the employees start assuming what the supervisors regard as their own responsibility for performance. The supervisor without checking duties to perform may then be left with little to do.

After a successful experiment, however, the supervisor usually discovers the supervisory and managerial functions he has neglected, or which were never his because all his time was given over to checking the work of his subordinates. For example, in the R & D division of one large chemical company I know of, the supervisors of the laboratory assistants were theoretically responsible for their training and evaluation. These functions, however, had come to be performed in a routine, unsubstantial fashion. After the job enrichment program, during which the supervisors were not merely passive observers of the assistants' performance, the supervisors actually were devoting their time to reviewing performance and administering thorough training.

What has been called an employee-centred style of supervision will come about not through education of supervisors, but by changing the jobs that they do.

CONCLUDING NOTE

Job enrichment will not be a one-time proposition, but a continuous management function. The initial changes, however, should last for a very long period of time. There are a number of reasons for this:

The changes should bring the job up to the level of challenge commensurate with the skill that was hired.

Those who have still more ability eventually will be able to demonstrate it better and win promotion to higher-level jobs.

The very nature of motivators, as opposed to hygiene factors, is that they have a much longer-term effect on employees' attitudes. Perhaps the job will have to be enriched again, but this will not occur as frequently as the need for hygiene.

Not all jobs can be enriched, nor do all jobs need to be enriched. If only a small percentage of the time and money that is now devoted to hygiene, however, were given to job enrichment efforts, the return in human satisfaction and economic gain would be one of the largest dividends that industry and society have ever reaped through their efforts at better personnel management.

The argument for job enrichment can be summed up quite simply: If you have someone on a job, use him. If you can't use him on the job, get rid of him, either via automation or by selecting someone with lesser ability. If you can't use him and you can't get rid of him, you will have a motivation problem.

NOTE
I should like to acknowledge the contributions that Robert Ford of the American Telephone and Telegraph Company has made to the ideas expressed in this paper, and in particular to the successful application of these ideas in improving work performance and the job satisfaction of employees.

3 Clarification and Evaluation of the Two-Factor Theory of Job Satisfaction*

NATHAN KING[1]
University of California, Berkeley

Because the two-factor theory of job satisfaction has not been explicitly stated by its proponents, various researchers have explicitly or implicitly denoted different 'theories' as the two-factor theory. Five distinct versions of the two-factor theory are explicated and evaluated. It is concluded that (a) two of these versions are invalid, as they are not supported by any empirical studies; (b) another version is invalid, as its alleged empirical support merely reflects experimenter coding biases; and (c) the validities of the remaining two versions are, at present, indeterminate, as they have not been adequately tested in studies where defensive biases inherent in certain self-report measures are eliminated. These conclusions are discussed in terms of the principle of multiple operationalism, and a method of testing the two indeterminate versions is suggested.

According to the two-factor theory of job satisfaction, the primary determinants of job satisfaction are intrinsic aspects of the job, called motivators (e.g. achievement, recognition, the work itself, responsibility, and advancement), whereas the primary determinants of job dissatisfaction are extrinsic factors, called hygienes (e.g. company policy and administration, supervision, salary, interpersonal relations with co-workers, and working conditions).

The two-factor theory originated from a study by Herzberg, Mausner, and Snyderman (1959). These investigators interviewed 203 accountants and engineers and asked them to describe specific instances when they felt exceptionally good or exceptionally bad about their jobs. Upon analyzing the content of these critical incidents, it was found that the good critical incidents were dominated by reference to intrinsic aspects of the job (motivators), while the bad critical incidents were dominated by reference to extrinsic factors (hygienes). As indicated in Table 1, this tendency was

Psychological Bulletin, LXXIV [1] (1970) 18—31. Copyright 1970 by the American Psychological Association. Reprinted by permission.

Table 1   Percentage of good and bad critical incidents in which each job factor appeared (Herzberg et al., 1959)

	Percentage[a]	
Factor	Good	Bad
Achievement (M)	41*	7
Recognition (M)	33*	18
Work itself (M)	26*	14
Responsibility (M)	23*	6
Advancement (M)	20*	11
Salary (H)	15	17
Possibility of growth (M)	6	8
Interpersonal relations — subordinate (H)	6	3
Status (H)	4	4
Interpersonal relations — superior (H)	4	15*
Interpersonal relations — peers (H)	3	8*
Supervision — technical (H)	3	20*
Company policy & administration (H)	3	31*
Working conditions (H)	1	11*
Personal life (H)	1	6*
Job security (H)	1	1
Percentage of total contributed by Ms	78	36
Percentage of total contributed by Hs	22	64

Note: Abbreviations are: M = motivator; H = hygiene.

[a]The percentages total more than 100% since more than one job factor can be mentioned in a single critical incident.

*The difference between the percentage of good and bad critical incidents is significant at the 0.1 level.

quite marked; in the reports of good critical incidents, motivators were alluded to almost four times as frequently as hygienes (78% *v.* 22%), whereas in bad critical incidents, hygienes were mentioned about twice as frequently as motivators (64% *v.* 36%).

Subsequent to the original study (Herzberg et al., 1959), a considerable number of empirical studies designed to test the validity of the two-factor theory were published, and a heated controversy has developed between supporters and critics of the theory.

It is the opinion of this writer that a major portion of the controversy stems from the lack of an explicit statement of the theory. At least five distinct versions of the two-factor theory have been stated or implied by various researchers. It is the purpose of this paper to explicate and to evaluate these various forms of the theory.

FIVE VERSIONS OF THE TWO-FACTOR THEORY
Table 2 lists five versions of the two-factor theory and an example of two types of data which might be used to support each of the different versions. The critical incident data (second column of Table 2) refer to

Table 2   Five versions of the two-factor theory of job satisfaction

Theory	Supporting data	
	Critical incident data	Correlational data
I. All motivators (Ms) combined contribute more to job satisfaction (S) than to job dissatisfaction (D), and all hygienes (Hs) combined contribute more to D than to S.	All Ms combined are mentioned proportionately more often in good critical incidents (Gs) than in bad critical incidents (Bs), and all Hs combined are mentioned proportionately more often in Bs than in Gs.	The multiple correlation (R) between the Ms and S is greater than the R between the Ms and D, and the R between the Hs and D is greater than the R between the Hs and S.
II. All Ms combined contribute more to S than do all Hs combined, and all Hs combined contribute more to D than do all Ms combined.	All Ms combined are mentioned in Gs more frequently than are all Hs combined, and all Hs combined are mentioned in Bs more frequently than are all Ms combined.	The R between Ms and S is greater than the R between the Hs and S, and the R between the Hs and D is greater than the R between the Ms and D.
III. Each M contributes more to S than to D, and each H contributes more to D than to S.	Each M is mentioned proportionately more often in Gs than in Bs, and each H is mentioned proportionately more often in Bs than in Gs.	Each M correlates more with S than with D, and each H correlates more with D than with S.
IV. Theory III holds, and in addition, each principal M contributes more to S than does any H, and each principal H contributes more to D than does any M.	The data support Theory III, and in addition, each principal M is mentioned in Gs more frequently than is any H, and each principal H is mentioned in Bs more frequently than is any M.	The data support Theory III, and in addition, each principal M correlates with S more than does any H, and each principal H corelates with D more than does any M.
V. Only Ms determine S, and only Hs determine D.	Only Ms are mentioned in Gs, and only Hs are mentioned in Bs.	Only Ms correlate with S, and only Hs correlate with D.

data of the same type as is illustrated in Table 1; whereas correlational data (third column of Table 2) might be obtained, for example, by simultaneously measuring satisfaction with each of a group of job factors, overall job satisfaction, and overall job dissatisfaction. As almost all of the relevant empirical investigations have made use of the critical incident technique, the different versions of the two-factor theory are discussed in terms of critical incident data.

Theory I

Theory I states that all motivators combined contribute more to job satisfaction than to job dissatisfaction and that all hygienes combined contribute more to job dissatisfaction than to job satisfaction. Critical incident data support Theory I if (*a*) all motivators combined are mentioned proportionately more often in good critical incidents than in bad critical incidents, and (*b*) all hygienes combined are mentioned proportionately more often in bad than in good incidents. Clearly the data of Table I meet these two requirements; motivators composed 78% of the job factors mentioned in good critical incidents compared to only 36% mentioned in bad incidents, whereas the hygienes favored the bad incidents (64% compared to 22%).

Actually, Theory I requires that critical incident data meet only one condition, as conditions *a* and *b* (see the preceding paragraph) are redundant. That is, *a* implies *b*, and *b* implies *a*. This redundancy follows from the necessity that the proportion of motivators plus the proportion of hygienes mentioned in either type of critical incident must equal one.

Let M_g denote the proportion of factors mentioned in good critical incidents which are motivators, and let H_g be the proportion which are hygienes. Similarly, define M_b and H_b, where the subscript *b* denotes bad critical incidents. In this notation, *a* states that $M_g > M_b$, and *b* states that $H_b > H_g$.

Since $M_g + H_g = 1$, and $M_b + H_b = 1$,

$$M_g > M_b \Rightarrow 1 - H_g > 1 - H_b \Rightarrow H_b > H_g.$$

That is, *a* implies *b*. The proof that *b* implies *a* is analogous.

Theory I appears to be the version of the two-factor theory adopted by Whitsett and Winslow (1967) in their review of a study by Dunnette, Campbell, and Hakel (1967). In the Dunnette et al. study, subjects used a Q-sort technique in order to assign to each of 12 job factors, a score which represented the extent to which the factor determined a good and a bad critical incident. The mean scores of the motivator and hygiene factors in the good and bad critical incidents of workers in six different occupational groups are given in Table 3. As indicated in this table, the mean motivator score was greater in good than in bad critical incidents in all six occupational groups. Also, in each occupational group, the mean hygiene

Table 3   Mean scores of motivators and hygienes in good and bad critical incidents (Dunnette et al., 1967)

Occupational group	Motivators		Hygienes	
	Good	Bad	Good	Bad
Store mangers	4.59	4.22	3.43	3.84
Sales clerks	4.37	4.17	3.63	3.68
Secretaries	4.61	4.23	3.45	3.75
Engineers and scientists	4.71	4.22	3.34	3.74
Machine equipment salesmen	4.76	4.17	3.16	3.79
Army reservists and students	4.54	4.20	3.51	3.77

score was greater in bad than in good incidents. Although this critical incident data is not of the same type as that illustrated in Table 1, the results clearly support Theory I. In their review of the Dunnette et al. (1967) experiment, Whitsett and Winslow concluded: 'We feel that the direct data of this study are supportive of the M-H theory and what the author feels is nonsupportive is a misinterpretation of the underlying structure of the M-H theory' (p. 404).

The M-H theory to which Whitsett and Winslow here referred appears to be Theory I, whereas Dunnette et al. must have been considering a 'stronger' version of the two-factor theory.

Theory II
Theory II states that all motivators combined contribute more to job satisfaction than do all hygienes combined, and conversely, that the hygienes contribute more to job dissatisfaction than do the motivators. Critical incident data support Theory II if (a) all motivators combined are mentioned in good critical incidents more frequently than are all hygienes combined, and (b) all hygienes combined appear more frequently in bad incidents than do all motivators combined. The data of Table 1 exemplify these conditions; in good critical incidents, motivators were mentioned more frequently than hygienes (78% v. 22%), whereas in bad incidents, hygienes appeared more frequently (64% v. 36%).

Unlike the critical incident data used to support Theory I, conditions a and b are here *not* redundant. For example, it is possible for all motivators combined to be mentioned more infrequently than all hygienes combined in both good *and* bad incidents.

Herzberg (1966) implied, in a review of a replication of the original study, that the 'basic' two-factor theory is Theory II. In commenting on two arrows in a chart, which illustrated the relative frequencies of motivators and hygienes in the reports of good and bad critical incidents and which indicated that the data supported Theory II, Herzberg stated: 'Once again, the two arrows shown at the bottom of the chart, indicating the divergent trends for motivators and hygiene factors, serve to verify the basic theory as these factors are involved in positive and negative job-attitude sequences' (p. 101).

Apparently the 'basic theory' is here Theory II; however, it is puzzling to this writer why Herzberg (1966), in a review of nine replications of the original study, failed to mention the fact that Theory II was supported in every one of the 15 different occupational groups studied.

In terms of critical incident data, Theory II is a stronger theory than Theory I. That is, if specific critical incident data meet the requirements of Theory II, then the data also support Theory I; however, critical incident data which support Theory I do not necessarily meet the conditions of Theory II. The proof of the first statement follows from the necessity that the proportion of motivators plus the proportion of hygienes mentioned in either type of critical incident must equal one.

Using the notation of the proof given in the section on Theory I, the requirements of Theory II are denoted as $M_g > H_g$ and $H_b > M_b$, and Theory I is supported if $M_g > M_b$ and $H_b > H_g$.

Since $M_g + H_g = 1$, and $M_b + H_b = 1$,

$M_g > H_g$ and $H_b > M_b$

$\Rightarrow M_g > .5, H_g < .5, H_b > .5$, and $M_b < .5$

$\Rightarrow M_g > M_b$ and $H_b > H_g$.

The proof of the second statement is accomplished by producing a counterexample of its negation:

Let $M_g = .8$, $H_g = .2$, $M_b = .6$, and $H_b = .4$.

This example is admissible, for the conditions $M_g + H_g = 1$ and $M_b + H_b = 1$ are satisfied. Clearly Theory I is supported, as $M_g > M_b$ and $H_b > H_g$; however, Theory II is not supported because $M_b > H_b$.

Theory III

Theory III is essentially a strong version of Theory I. instead of requiring that all motivators *combined* contribute more to job satisfaction than to job dissatisfaction, Theory III states that *each* motivator contributes more to satisfaction than to dissatisfaction (and conversely, that each hygiene contributes more to dissatisfaction than to satisfaction).

In the case of Theories I and II, where only one or two conditions are specified, it seems reasonable to conclude that a single critical incident study either supports or contradicts the particular theory depending upon whether or not the data meet the specifications indicated in Table 2. However, in the case of Theory III, where many more conditions are specified, sampling errors must be given more serious consideration. That is, one would not claim that a single critical incident study contradicted

Theory III if it did not quite meet all the conditions specified in Table 2. For example, one would not claim that the data of Table 1 exemplify a contradiction of Theory III merely because the most infrequently mentioned motivator (possibility of growth) appeared in 8% of the bad incidents and in only 6% of the good incidents. It may thus be necessary to restrict a statement of the confirmation of Theory III to collections of similar studies rather than to individual studies. It should be noted, however, that a single study might be said to contradict Theory III if, for example, a frequently mentioned motivator appeared significantly more often in bad than in good critical incidents.

On at least one occasion Herzberg implied that the basic two-factor theory is Theory II; however, in summarizing the results of nine replications of the original study, Herzberg (1966) suggested that *the* theory is Theory III:

> The chart shows that of the 51 significant differences reported for the six motivator factors, *every one* was in the predicted direction. For the 57 significant hygiene factors, 54 were in the predicted direction. In sum, then, the predictions from the theory were wrong in less than 3 per cent of the cases (p. 125).

Evidently 'the theory' is a theory which predicts that each motivator will appear proportionately more often in good than in bad critical incidents and that each hygiene will appear proportionately more often in bad than in good incidents — namely, Theory III.

Theory IV

Critical incident data support Theory IV if, in addition to supporting Theory III, each principal motivator is mentioned in good critical incidents more frequently than is any hygiene, and each principal hygiene is mentioned in bad critical incidents more frequently than is any motivator. The data illustrated in Table 1, for example, do not meet these conditions; recognition was mentioned in considerably more bad incidents than were working conditions and interpersonal relations with peers.

House and Wigdor (1967) apparently acknowledged that replications of the original experiment supported Theory III; however, in a secondary analysis of this data they criticized the two-factor theory for failing to meet the requirements of Theory IV. These investigators ranked 10 job factors according to the total number of individuals mentioning the factor in the bad critical incidents of six studies reported by Herzberg (1966). As indicated in Table 4, achievement and recognition were mentioned by more individuals than were three hygienes. House and Wigdor concluded:

> Our secondary analysis of the data presented by Herzberg (1966) in his most recent book yields conclusions contradictory to the proposition of the Two-Factor theory that satisfiers [factors appearing in good incidents] and dissatisfiers [factors appearing in bad incidents] are

Table 4   Number of individuals mentioning each of ten
job factors in the bad critical incidents of six studies
reported by Herzberg (1966) (House and Wigdor, 1967)

Factor	Frequency
Company policy & administration (H)	337
Supervision (H)	182
Achievement (M)	122
Recognition (M)	110
Working conditions (H)	108
Work itself (M)	75
Relations with superior (H)	59
Relations with peers (H)	57
Advancement (M)	48
Responsibility (M)	35

Note: Abbreviations are: M = motivator; H = hygiene

unidimensional and independent. Although many of the intrinsic aspects of jobs are shown to be more frequently identified by respondents as satisfiers, achievement and recognition are also shown to be very frequently identified as dissatisfiers. In fact, achievement and recognition are more frequently identified as dissatisfiers than working conditions and relations with the superior (p. 385).

Apparently 'the Two-Factor theory' is here a theory which requires that each principal hygiene contributes more to job dissatisfaction than does any motivator and conversely that each principal motivator contributes more to job satisfaction than does any hygiene — namely, Theory IV.

Theory V

According to Theory V, only motivators determine job satisfaction, and only hygienes determine job dissatisfaction.

Herzberg (1964) suggested Theory V in a discussion of the events leading up to the original investigation:

From a review and an analysis of previous publications in the general area of job attitudes, a two-factor hypothesis was formulated to guide the original investigation. This hypothesis suggested that the factors involved in producing job satisfaction were separate and distinct from the factors that led to job dissatisfaction (p. 3).

This 'two-factor hypothesis', which states that the factors involved in producing job satisfaction are *separate* and *distinct* from the factors leading to job dissatisfaction, clearly appears to be Theory V.

However, it is questionable whether Herzberg intended to suggest Theory V; for in referring to the results of the original experiment, Herzberg (1964) stated, 'The proposed hypothesis appears verified' (p. 4). Certainly these results (see Table 1) do not serve as verification of

Theory V. The results of the original study might possibly be interpreted as supporting Theory V if evidence indicated that the measurement errors were considerably biased in opposition to Theory V; however, evidence presented in the evaluation section indicates that the Herzberg-type experiments were biased in *favor* of Theory V.

Regardless of Herzberg's intentions, other investigators have evidently interpreted the 'two-factor hypothesis' as Theory V. For example, Lindsay, Marks, and Gorlow (1967) quoted Herzberg's statement of the hypothesis and then restated it in the following manner: 'Satisfaction(s) is a function of motivators (M) and other potential factors and/or error of measurement . . .; dissatisfaction (DS) is a function of hygienes (H) plus other potential factors and/or error of measurement' (p. 331).

EVALUATION
Irrelevant empirical studies
Many of the empirical studies which have been considered relevant to the two-factor theory are not directly relevant to the validity of the theories of Table 2.

Extensions beyond the domain of job satisfaction
The two-factor theories have been extended beyond the domain of job satisfaction. For example, Hamlin and Nemo (1962) attempted to explain differences between improved and unimproved schizophrenics in terms of a two-factor theory. Such an extension is beyond the scope of this paper.

Studies by Hinton (1968) and Levine and Weitz (1968) are ostensibly within the domain of job satisfaction. However, the job investigated in these studies was the 'job' of student, which appears to this writer to be sufficiently unlike other jobs as to warrant exclusion from consideration in this paper.

Predictions on a job satisfaction-dissatisfaction continuum
Several investigators (Ewen, Smith, Hulin, and Locke, 1966; Graen, 1968; Hinrichs and Mischkind, 1967) adopted a version of the two-factor theory which makes statements about an overall job satisfaction-dissatisfaction (S-D) continuum. More specifically, these investigators adopted a two-factor theory which states that motivators account primarily for variance on the satisfaction portion of the S-D continuum and that hygienes account primarily for variance on the dissatisfaction end of the continuum. For example, Ewen et al. (1966) grouped subjects according to their degree of satisfaction with three job factors, and then assumed that the two-factor theory predicts differences between certain groups in terms of scores on an S-D continuum. This particular version of the two-factor theory, although possibly worthy of consideration in its own right, is considerably unlike the theories of Table 2; the theories of Table 2 make statements about a job satisfaction continuum and a job dissatis-faction continuum — *not* about an S-D continuum. These studies might be

relevant to some of the theories of Table 2 if additional assumptions concerning the relationships among satisfaction, dissatisfaction, and S-D were made. However, the evaluation of such assumptions is beyond the scope of this paper. Likewise, an experiment by Lindsay et al. (1967) is here irrelevant. Lindsay et al. created descriptions of hypothetical job situations and had subjects indicate the degree of S-D inherent in each situation, thus attempting to discover how motivators and hygienes interact in determining S-D.

Studies concerning aspects of the job other than satisfaction or dissatisfaction
Several empirical studies investigated the extent to which individual job factors contributed to aspects of the job other than satisfaction or dissatisfaction. Friedlander and Walton (1964) had respondents indicate which factors operated to *keep* them with their present employer and which factors might cause them to *leave*. Similarly, Centers and Bugental (1966) had respondents indicate which three of six job factors were most important in *keeping* them on their present job. Friedlander (1966) measured the perceived importance of job factors to feelings of satisfaction *or* dissatisfaction – that is, contributions to job satisfaction and to job dissatisfaction were not measured separately; and similarly, Singh and Baumgartel (1966) had subjects rate job factors on a scale of importance *in general* – importance for job satisfaction and for job dissatisfaction were not measured separately. Although these four studies may be relevant to particular extensions of the two-factor theory, they are not directly relevant to the theories of Table 2.

Studies in which only satisfaction with individual job factors were measured
The theories of Table 2 are concerned with the relative contributions of individual job factors to overall job satisfaction and to overall job dissatisfaction. Any study which measures only satisfaction with individual job factors is not relevant, for without measures of overall job satisfaction and dissatisfaction, the relative contributions of individual factors to the overall measures cannot be determined. Such studies simply indicate what the most-liked characteristics of a specific job happen to be. Thus, studies by Friedlander' (1965) and Wolf (1967) are irrelevant. Friedlander measured only the degree of satisfaction with individual job factors, and Wolf simply had respondents indicate which aspects of a job were the most liked and which were the least liked.

Factor analytic and scaling studies
Although it may be desirable for the job factors to be factors in some factor analytic sense, the theories of Table 2 place no such restrictions on the motivators and hygienes. Thus, studies which merely consist of a

factor analysis of characteristics of a job or of a job situation (Graen, 1966; Lodahl, 1964) are here considered irrelevant. Likewise, a study by Burke (1966) is irrelevant. Burke used the unfolding technique in one dimension (Coombs, 1964) in order to determine whether or not subjects, along with Herzberg's principal job factors, could be placed on a latent unidimensional continuum so as to account for individual differences in relative preferences for job factors.

Studies lacking adequate descriptions of measures used
Four studies (Friedlander, 1963; Halpern, 1966; Malinovsky and Barry, 1965; Weissenberg and Gruenfeld, 1968) in which overall job satisfaction was purportedly measured did not clarify whether the measure used was a measure of job satisfaction or overall satisfaction-dissatisfaction (S-D). In either case, however, little information is lost by the omission of these studies. If it was S-D that was measured, the study is not directly relevant to the theories of Table 2; and if it was job satisfaction that was measured, the study is irrelevant to Theories I and III and, at most, relevant to only parts of Theories II, IV, and V, as overall job dissatisfaction was measured in none of the four studies.

Relevant empirical studies
As there appear to be no relevant empirical studies which support either Theory IV or Theory V, this evaluation is restricted to Theories I, II, and III.

Table 5 indicates whether or not each relevant empirical study supports Theories I, II, and III.

Replications of the original study
Herzberg (1966) reviewed nine studies (e.g. Herzberg, 1965; Myers, 1964; Saleh, 1964; Schwartz, Jenusaitis, and Stark, 1963) which, in toto, consist of replications of the original study in 15 different occupational groups. In two of the studies (Herzberg, 1965; Schwartz et al., 1963) an open-ended questionnaire patterned after the original interview, rather than an interview, was used. Theories I and II were supported in every one of the 15 occupational groups studied. That is (using the notation of the proof given in the section on Theory I), in each group studied, $M_g > M_b$, $H_b > H_g$, $M_g > H_g$, and $H_b > M_b$. These data, considered in toto, also support Theory III; in all replications combined, 42 hygienes and 36 motivators appeared significantly more ($p < .01$, according to Herzberg, 1966) in one type of critical incident than in the other, and of these, all the motivators and all but 3 hygienes were significant in the predicted direction.

Studies in which subjects coded the perceived determinants of their critical incidents
In the original study and in its replications, the experimenters coded the information given in the reports of critical incidents. Several critics (Ewen,

Table 5   Empirical studies relevant to the validity of Theories I, II, or III

Study	Theory I	Theory II	Theory III
Replications of the original study			
Saleh (1964)	yes	yes	
Myers (1964); 5 different occupational groups (Gps)	yes in all 5	yes in all 5	
Herzberg's (1966) review of 5 other studies; 7 Gps	yes in all 7	yes in all 7	yes[a]
Replications using a questionnaire			
Schwartz et al. (1963)	yes	yes	
Herzberg (1965)	yes	yes	
Subjects coded the perceived determinants of their critical incidents			
Friedlander (1964)	no	irrelevant	
Labiri and Srivastva (1967)			
Present job	yes	irrelevant	
Imaginary job	yes	irrelevant	no[a]
Dunnette et al. (1967); 6 Gps	yes in all 6	irrelevant	
Wernimont (1966); 2 Gps			
Forced choice	yes in both	irrelevant	
Free choice	yes in both	irrelevant	no data[b]
Correlational studies			
Hulin and Smith (1972); 2 Gps	irrelevant	irrelevant	no

[a]Considered collectively.
[b]Relevant data were evidently collected but not published.

1964; Graen, 1966; House and Wigdor, 1967) pointed out that the coding system is not completely determined by the data and a preestablished rating system, but requires additional interpretation by the experimenter. Before one can rule out the possibility of experimenter coding biases, it is necessary to consider studies in which the subjects themselves coded the perceived determinants of their reported critical incidents (subject-coded studies). Four relevant studies (Dunnette et al., 1967; Friedlander, 1964; Lahiri and Srivastva, 1967; Wernimont, 1966) fall into this category.

Friedlander (1964) had respondents indicate, on a 4-point scale, the degree to which each of 18 job factors contributed toward producing the feeling of satisfaction inherent in a good critical incident and the feeling of dissatisfaction inherent in a bad critical incident. The mean scores of each job factor in good and bad incidents are given in the first two columns of Table 6. In analyzing the data Friedlander used these mean scores; however, an alternative analysis seems more appropriate. Since the satisfaction scores were scaled independently of the dissatisfaction scores (i.e. the satisfaction scores were first determined in response to a good critical incident, and then the dissatisfaction scores were determined in response to a bad incident), the two scales are not necessarily comparable.

Table 6   A reanalysis of Friedlander's (1964) data

	Mean scores		
Job factor	Satisfaction	Dissatisfaction	Rescaled dissatisfaction
Motivators			
Promotion	2.10	1.99	2.54
Challenging assignments	3.10	2.67	3.42
Recognition	3.23	2.61	3.35
Merit increases	1.80	1.60	2.03
Achievement	3.38	2.80	3.59
Responsibility	2.84	2.01	2.57
Growth	3.38	2.19	2.80
Work itself	3.46	2.39	3.06
Use of best abilities	2.99	2.89	3.71
Hygienes			
Relations with supervisor	3.06	2.09	2.67
Relations with co-workers	2.73	1.46	1.85
Technical supervision	2.56	1.75	2.23
Working conditions	2.31	1.60	2.03
Security	2.56	1.64	2.08
Employee benefits	1.46	1.30	1.64
Home life	1.63	1.61	2.04
Work group	2.19	1.77	2.25
Management policies	2.01	2.28	2.92
Mean score of motivators	2.92	2.35	3.01
Mean score of hygienes	2.28	1.72	2.19

Assuming that the mean dissatisfaction scores represent scale values on a scale which is no stronger than an interval scale, it is admissible to transform these scores by any linear transformation. For purposes of comparison with the satisfaction scores, it thus seems most appropriate to transform the dissatisfaction scores by the unique linear transformation which yields mean scores having the same mean and variance as the satisfaction mean scores. The last column of Table 6 contains the mean dissatisfaction scores which result from applying this linear transformation to the original dissatisfaction scores, and the data are here analyzed by comparing the original satisfaction scores to the *rescaled* dissatisfaction scores.

As indicated in Table 6, the data do not support Theory I; the mean motivator score was greater in bad than in good incidents (3.01 *v.* 2.92), and the mean hygiene score was greater in good than in bad incidents (2.28 *v.* 2.19).

The data of Table 6 are irrelevant to Theory II. That is, it is inappropriate, for example, to claim that all motivators combined contributed more to good incidents than did all hygienes combined on the basis that the mean motivator score was greater than the mean hygiene score in good critical incidents (2.92 v. 2.28), for the amount of overlap among the job factors was not taken into consideration. If the set of motivators represented broad overlapping categories relative to the set of hygienes, the contribution of all motivators would be over-represented by the mean motivator score. Comparing the mean motivator score to the mean hygiene score in either type of critical incident is, in terms of correlational data, analogous to comparing the means of sets of correlation coefficients rather than multiple correlation coefficients. Correlational data (third column of Table 2), however, *are* relevant to Theory II, because the multiple correlation coefficient takes into consideration the intercorrelations (or overlap) among the factors. And the Herzberg-type critical incident studies are also relevant to Theory II, for in these studies there is no overlap among the job factors (i.e. the factors represent mutually exclusive categories).

Lahiri and Srivastva (1967) had respondents indicate, on a 10-point scale, the degree to which each of 26 job factors contributed toward satisfaction and dissatisfaction in both actual and imaginary good and actual and imaginary bad critical incidents. (In the imaginary critical incidents, subjects were asked to think of a 'best' and a 'worst' job they could imagine themselves doing.) The general methodology of this study was the same as that of Friedlander's (1964) study; and thus, Lahiri and Srivastva's data were reanalyzed in the same way as Friedlander's data. Table 7 contains the mean satisfaction and rescaled dissatisfaction scores of each job factor in the two different situations.

As indicated in Table 7, the data supported Theory I in both the present and imaginary job situations. That is, for both situations, the mean motivator score was greater in good than in bad incidents, and the mean hygiene score was greater in bad than in good incidents.

The data of Lahiri and Srivastva (and also Dunnette et al. 1967; Wernimont, 1966) are irrelevant to Theory II on the same grounds that Friedlander's (1964) data are irrelevant to Theory II.

The experiment by Dunnette et al. (1967), which is discussed in the section on Theory I, is also a subject-coded study. In describing both a good and a bad critical incident, the Q-sort items representing job factors were sorted into a 7-point quasi-normal distribution. Thus, the scores representing contributions of job factors to good incidents are comparable to the scores derived from the reports of bad incidents, and unlike the studies of Friedlander (1964) and Lahiri and Srivastva (1967), it is unnecessary to rescale the mean scores. As indicated in Table 3, Theory I was supported in all six occupational groups studied

Wernimont (1966) constructed 50 pairs of positive items describing good critical incidents and 50 pairs of negative items describing bad incidents. One member of each pair represented a motivator, the other represented a hygiene, and the members of each pair were equated in terms of social desirability. The respondents were first required to indicate which member of each pair most closely described a good or a bad critical incident

Table 7   A reanalysis of Lahiri and Srivastva's (1967) data

	Mean scores			
	Present job		Imaginary job	
Job factor	Satis-faction	Rescaled dissatis-faction	Satis-faction	Rescaled dissatis-faction
Motivators				
Recognition	6.32	6.68	7.97	8.33
Challenging assignments	6.59	6.06	7.73	7.38
Growth	6.09	6.98	7.88	8.44
Achievement	7.03	6.47	8.68	7.74
Liking for the work	7.00	6.30	8.76	7.78
Accomplishment	7.65	6.02	8.21	7.96
Use of best abilities	7.18	5.96	8.53	8.11
Responsibility	8.00	5.79	8.68	7.45
Autonomy	6.35	6.10	7.29	8.68
Promotion	4.59	8.05	7.53	8.52
Prestige	6.91	6.82	8.18	8.64
Work itself	6.35	6.22	8.53	8.00
Status	6.73	6.88	8.26	8.15
Hygienes				
Relations with co-workers	6.82	5.30	8.09	7.20
Superior's help	6.12	7.36	7.41	7.96
Friendliness of superior	7.15	6.98	7.12	7.76
Technical competence of superior	5.44	6.82	7.47	7.65
Salary	4.94	7.91	7.38	8.56
Security	7.29	6.13	8.29	7.34
Working conditions	6.53	4.63	7.62	7.26
Benefits	6.47	5.69	7.53	7.57
Fairness of authority	6.12	6.33	7.91	8.58
Freedom of expression	5.79	6.47	7.76	8.42
Work group	5.12	5.96	7.03	7.36
Managerial policies	5.12	8.69	6.59	8.27
Home life	8.00	5.11	8.82	6.16
Mean score of motivators	6.68	6.49	8.17	8.09
Mean score of hygienes	6.22	6.41	7.62	7.70

(forced choice situation), and they were then asked to go back over the items and indicate the 10 items which were the most descriptive of each type of critical incident (free choice situation). The data were analyzed separately for two different occupational groups — engineers and accountants. Theory I was supported in both occupational groups in both the forced choice and free choice situation. That is, in all four situations, motivator items were selected more often in good than in bad incidents, and hygiene items were selected more often in bad than in good incidents.

If Theory III is valid, one would not expect to find incorrect predictions made for the *same* job factors in all occupational groups. (Definition

Table 8　Success of predictions based on Theory III in studies where subjects coded the perceived determinants of their critical incidents

Job factor	Friedlander (1964)	Lahiri and Srivastva (1967)		Dunnette et al. (1967) (6 groups)	Wernimont (1966), forced choice (2 groups)	Total
		Present	Imaginary			
Motivators						
Achievement	−	+	+	6+	2+	10+, 1−
Recognition	−	−	−	5−, 1+	2−	10−, 1+
Work itself	+	+	+	6+	2+	11+
Responsibility	+	+	+	6+	2+	11+
Advancement	−	−	−	6−	2−	11−
Hygienes						
Company policy and administration	+	+	+	5+, 1−	2+	10+, 1−
Supervision	−	+	+	5+, 1−	2+	9+, 2−
Working conditions	−	−	−	6+	2−	6+, 5−
Relations with superior	−	−	+	5+, 1−	no data[a]	6+, 3−
Relations with peers	−	−	−	6−	no data[a]	9−

Note: A plus sign signifies a correct prediction, and a minus sign indicates an incorrect prediction.
[a]Relations with superior and relations with peers were grouped into a single category — interpersonal relations.

of an incorrect prediction for a job factor: if a motivator, the mean score in bad incidents is greater than the mean score in good incidents; and if a hygiene, the mean score in good incidents is greater than the mean score in bad incidents.) That is, if incorrect predictions are due entirely to sampling errors, one would expect the errors to be randomly distributed among the different job factors. However, as indicated in Table 8, recognition, advancement, and relations with peers were *consistently* linked to incorrect predictions. Thus, the results of the subject-coded studies contradict Theory III, indicating that the support given to Theory III by the Herzberg-type studies merely reflects experimenter coding biases.

Correlational studies
In both the Herzberg-type studies and the subject-coded studies, the determinants of satisfaction and dissatisfaction were measured by direct self-report. While the very nature of satisfaction and dissatisfaction may require that these constructs be measured by a self-report technique, it is neither necessary nor desirable that the *determinants* of satisfaction and dissatisfaction be measured by direct self-report. As emphasized by several critics (Dunnette et al., 1967; House and Wigdor, 1967; Vroom, 1964), the use of these self-report measures permits an explanation of the results solely in terms of defensive biases inherent in such measures. For example, even though the subjects accurately report the determinants of critical incidents, the recall of the incidents may be selective so that those good incidents which happen to be recalled tend to be biased toward those incidents which were due to one's own efforts (motivators) as opposed to those incidents which were due to the efforts of others (hygienes).

In correlational studies, the extent to which job factors contribute toward satisfaction and dissatisfaction is not determined by self-report but is inferred from the correlations between measures of satisfaction with individual job factors and measures of overall satisfaction and dissatisfaction. Thus, in order to eliminate the possible defensive biases of the measures used in critical incident studies, correlation studies should be considered.[2] Although correlational data may not be sufficient to permit a determination of the causal relationships stated in the theories of Table 2, certainly correlational support is a necessary requirement.

One correlational study (Hulin and Smith, 1967) is relevant. Hulin and Smith measured satisfaction with each of the five job factors of the Job Description Index (JDI); (Smith, 1967). In addition, overall job satisfaction was measured on one-fourth of the subjects, overall job dissatisfaction was measured on another one-fourth of the subjects, and a measure of overall satisfaction-dissatisfaction (S-D) was obtained on the remaining half of the subjects, where the overall measures consisted of variations of the General Motors Faces Scale (Kunin, 1955).[3] Since the theories of Table 2 do not make statements about an S-D continuum, data from only half the respondents are directly relevant.

Table 9   Correlations between satisfaction with each of five job factors and measures
of overall job satisfaction and overall job dissatisfaction (Hulin and Smith, 1967)

	Males		Females	
Job factor	Satisfaction	Dissatisfaction	Satisfaction	Dissatisfaction
Motivators				
Work itself	.68*	.44	.45	.43
Promotion	.40	.38	.46	.14
Hygienes				
Pay	.39	.24	.12	.18
Supervision	.53*	.25	.31	−.03
Co-workers	.48*	.13	.20	−.08

*The difference between the correlation with satisfaction and with dissatisfaction
is significant at the .05 level.

The correlations between satisfaction with each of the five job factors
and the two relevant overall measures are given in Table 9. In the male
group, the two hygienes, supervision and co-workers, correlated significantly more with overall satisfaction than with overall dissatisfaction.
However, these differences may be partially explained by possible differences in the reliabilities of the satisfaction and dissatisfaction measures.
That is, if the dissatisfaction measure is much less reliable than the
satisfaction measure, the hygienes might be expected to correlate more
with satisfaction than with dissatisfaction, even though Theory III is valid.
Certainly this possibility should be considered, especially since Hulin and
Smith mentioned that the variability of scores on the dissatisfaction
measure was considerably less than the variability on the satisfaction
measure. As the reliabilities of the overall satisfaction and dissatisfaction
measures are not known, it is not possible to obtain a reasonable estimate
of the 'true' correlations. However, as shown in Table 10, if the largest
conceivable discrepancy between the reliabilities of the overall measures
was assumed, the two hygienes, supervision and co-workers, would still
correlate considerably higher with satisfaction than with dissatisfaction. It
is thus concluded that the results of this study contradict Theory III.
    Since Hulin and Smith considered only five of Herzberg's principal job
factors, this study is irrelevant to Theories I and II; Theories I and II
contain statements about the effects of all motivators combined and all
hygienes combined.

Conclusion
In considering all relevant empirical studies, the following conclusions
seem justified:
    1. Theory III, being supported by the Herzberg-type studies but not by
the subject-coded studies, merely reflects experimenter coding biases.
    2. Theory I, although being supported by both the Herzberg-type

Table 10   Correlations of Table 9 'corrected' for
attenuation so as to support Theory III as much as
possible

Job factor	Males	
	Satisfaction	Dissatisfaction
Motivators		
Work itself	.68	.66
Promotion	.40	.57
Hygienes		
Pay	.39	.36
Supervision	.53	.38
Co-workers	.48	.20

Note: The correlations are 'corrected' for the
attenuation of one variable under the assumption that
the reliability of the overall satisfaction measure was 1
and that the reliability of the overall dissatisfaction
measure was .44 — the highest observed correlation
between overall dissatisfaction and any other variable
(work itself).

studies and the subject-coded studies, has not been adequately tested in studies where the determinants of satisfaction and dissatisfaction were measured by techniques other than direct self-report. It is thus possible that Theory I merely reflects defensive biases inherent in such self-report measures.

3. Theory II has not been adequately tested in studies other than the Herzberg-type critical incident studies. It is thus possible that Theory II merely reflects experimenter coding biases or defensive biases inherent in self-report measures.

The relationship between these conclusions and the principle of multiple operationalism (Garner, Hake, and Eriksen, 1956; Webb, Campbell, Schwartz, and Sechrest, 1966) should be noted. According to the principle of multiple operationalism, a hypothesis is validated only if it is supported by two or more different methods of testing, where each method contains specific idiosyncratic weaknesses, but where the entire collection of methods permits the elimination of all alternative hypotheses. The application of this principle to Theories I, II, and III indicates that none of these theories have been validated. In the case of Theory III, three distinct methods, each containing different weaknesses, were used: Herzberg-type studies, subject-coded studies, and a correlational study. And two alternative hypotheses were considered: (*a*) the support given Theory III by the Herzberg-type studies is due not to the validity of Theory III but to experimenter coding biases; and (*b*) this support is due to defensive biases inherent in the self-report measures used. Neither did all three types of studies support Theory III nor were the two alternative hypotheses eliminated. In the case of Theory I, only the Herzberg-type studies and the subject-coded studies were used. Although both types of studies supported Theory I and although the alternative hypothesis analogous to hypothesis *a* was eliminated, these studies did not eliminate the alternative hypothesis analogous to hypothesis *b*. Likewise, Theory II was not validated, for neither of the two alternative hypotheses were eliminated.

SUGGESTIONS FOR FUTURE RESEARCH

The preceding section indicates a major gap in the relevant empirical studies — namely, studies which are relevant to Theories I and II and in which the determinants of satisfaction and dissatisfaction are measured by techniques other than direct self-report. It is thus suggested that correlational studies patterned after the study by Hulin and Smith (1967) be performed. However, three exceptions to the Hulin and Smith design should be made: (*a*) Satisfaction with each of Herzberg's principal motivators and hygienes, rather than with only the five JDI factors, are measured, (*b*) the use of a measure of overall dissatisfaction which is possibly more reliable than the measure used by Hulin and Smith, and (*c*) the calculation of the multiple correlation coefficients indicated in Table 2.

In both types of critical incident studies (Herzberg-type studies and subject-coded studies) there appeared to be no differences among different occupational groups in terms of the support given Theories I, II, and III; however, this similarity may merely reflect a similarity of defense mechanisms rather than a similarity of determinants of job satisfaction. It is thus desirable that subsequent correlational studies consider relatively homogeneous occupational groups separately, for it may be found that Theory I or II is valid for specific occupational groups.

REFERENCES

Burke, R. J., 'Are Herzberg's Motivators and Hygienes Unidimensional?', *Journal of Applied Physiology*, L (1966) 317–21.

Centers, R. and Bugental, D. E., 'Intrinsic and Extrinsic Job Motivations among Different Segments of the Working Population', *Journal of Applied Psychology*, L (1966) 193–7.

Coombs, C. H., *A Theory of Data* (New York: Wiley, 1964).

Dunnette, M. D., Campbell, J. P. and Hakel, M. D., 'Factors Contributing to Job Satisfaction and Job Dissatisfaction in Six Occupational Groups', *Organizational Behavior and Human Performance*, II (1967) 143–74.

Ewen, R. B., 'Some Determinants of Job Satisfaction: A Study of the Generability of Herzberg's Theory', *Journal of Applied Psychology*, XLVIII (1964) 161–3.

Ewen, R. B., Smith, P. C., Hulin, C. L. and Locke, E. A., 'An Empirical

Test of the Herzberg Two-Factor Theory', *Journal of Applied Psychology*, L (1966) 544–50.

Friedlander, F., 'Underlying Sources of Job Satisfaction', *Journal of Applied Psychology*, XLVII (1963) 246–50.

Friedlander, F., 'Job Characteristics as Satisfiers and Dissatisfiers', *Journal of Applied Psychology*, XLVIII(1964) 388–92.

Friedlander, F., 'Relationships between the Importance and the Satisfaction of Various Environmental Factors', *Journal of Applied Psychology*, XLIX (1965) 160–4.

Friedlander, F., 'Importance of Work versus Non-Work among Socially and Occupationally Stratified Groups', *Journal of Applied Psychology*, L (1966) 437–41.

Friedlander, F. and Walton, E., 'Positive and Negative Motivations toward Work', *Administrative Science Quarterly*, IX (1964) 194–207.

Garner, W. R., Hake, H. W. and Eriksen, C. W., 'Operationism and the Concept of Perception', *Psychological Review*, LXIII (1956) 149–59.

Graen, G. B., 'Motivator and Hygiene Dimensions for Research and Development Engineers', *Journal of Applied Psychology*, L (1966) 563–6.

Graen, G. B., 'Testing Traditional and Two-Factor Hypotheses Concerning Job Satisfaction', *Journal of Applied Psychology*, LII (1968) 366–71.

Halpern, G., 'Relative Contributions of Motivator and Hygiene Factors to Overall Job Satisfaction', *Journal of Applied Psychology*, L (1966) 198–200.

Hamlin, R. M. and Nemo, R. S., 'Self-Actualization in Choice Scores of Improved Schizophrenics', *Journal of Clinical Psychology*, XVIII (1962) 51–4.

Herzberg, F., 'The Motivation-Hygiene Concept and Problems of Manpower', *Personnel Administration*, XXVII [1] (1964) 3–7.

Herzberg, F., 'The Motivation to Work among Finnish Supervisors', *Personnel Psychology*, XVIII (1965) 393–402.

Herzberg, F., *Work and the Nature of Man* (Cleveland: World Publishing Company, 1966).

Herzberg, F., Mausner, B. and Snyderman, B., *The Motivation to Work*, 2nd ed. (New York: Wiley, 1959).

Hinrichs, J. R. and Mischkind, L. A., 'Empirical and Theoretical Limitations of the Two-Factor Hypothesis of Job Satisfaction', *Journal of Applied Psychology*, LI (1967) 191–200.

Hinton, B. L., 'An Empirical Investigation of the Herzberg Methodology and Two-Factor Theory', *Organizational Behavior and Human Performance*, III (1968) 217–38.

House, R. J. and Wigdor, L. A., 'Herzberg's Dual-Factor Theory of Job Satisfaction and Motivation: A Review of the Evidence and a Criticism', *Personnel Psychology*, XX (1967) 369–89.

Hulin, C. L. and Smith, P. A., 'An Empirical Investigation of Two

54 *The Nature of Job Satisfaction*

Implications of the Two-Factor Theory of Job Satisfaction', *Journal of Applied Psychology*, L I (1967) 396–402.

Kunin, T., 'The Construction of a New Type of Attitude Measure', *Personnel Psychology*, V I I I (1955) 65–77.

Lahiri, D. K. and Srivastva, S., 'Determinants of Satisfaction in Middle-Management Personnel', *Journal of Applied Psychology*, L I (1967) 254–65.

Levine, E. L. and Weitz, J., 'Job Satisfaction among Graduate Students: Intrinsic versus Extrinsic Variables', *Journal of Applied Psychology*, L I I (1968) 263–71.

Lindsay, C. A., Marks, E. and Gorlow, L., 'The Herzberg Theory: A Critique and Reformulation', *Journal of Applied Psychology*, L I (1967) 330–9.

Lodahl, T. M., 'Patterns of Job Attitudes in Two Assembly Technologies', *Administrative Science Quarterly*, V I I I (1964) 482–519.

Malinovsky, M. R., and Barry, J. R., 'Determinants of Work Attitudes', *Journal of Applied Psychology*, X L I X (1965) 446–51.

Myers, M. S., 'Who Are Your Motivated Workers?', *Harvard Business Review*, X L I I [1] (1964) 73–88.

Saleh, S. D., 'A Study of Attitude Change in the Preretirement Period', *Journal of Applied Psychology*, X L V I I I (1964) 310–12.

Schwartz, M. M., Jenusaitis, E. and Stark, H., 'Motivational Factors among Supervisors in the Utility Industry', *Personnel Psychology*, X V I (1963) 45–53.

Singh, T. N. and Baumgartel, H., 'Background Factors in Airline Mechanics' Work Motivations: A Research Note', *Journal of Applied Psychology*, L (1966) 357–9.

Smith, P. C., 'The Development of a Method of Measuring Job Satisfaction: The Cornell Studies', in *Studies in Personnel and Industrial Psychology*, ed. E. A. Fleishman (Homewood, Ill.: Dorsey Press, 1967).

Vroom, V. H., *Work and Motivation* (New York: Wiley, 1964).

Weissenberg, P. and Gruenfeld, L. W., 'Relationship between Job Satisfaction and Job Involvement', *Journal of Applied Psychology*, L I I (1968) 469–73.

Wernimont, P. F., 'Intrinsic and Extrinsic Factors in Job Satisfaction', *Journal of Applied Psychology*, L (1966) 41–50.

Whitsett, D. A. and Winslow, E. K., 'An Analysis of Studies Critical of the Motivator-Hygiene Theory', *Personnel Psychology*, X X (1967) 391–415.

Webb, E. J., Campbell, D. T., Schwartz, R. D. and Sechrest, L., *Unobtrusive Measures: Nonreactive Research in the Social Sciences* (Chicago: Rand McNally, 1966).

Wolf, M. G., 'The Relationship of Content and Context Factors to Attitudes toward Company and Job', *Personnel Psychology*, X X (1967) 121–32.

NOTES

1. The author is especially grateful to Charles L. Hulin and Milton R. Blood for reading earlier versions of this paper and providing helpful comments.
2. It should be noted that in correlational studies, not only are defensive biases eliminated, but also, the assumption (implicit in the critical incident studies) that the determinants of critical incidents are identical to the determinants of less-than-critical incidents is not made. However, it is the opinion of the writer that this second distinction between correlational and critical incident studies is much less crucial than the defensive bias distinction.
3. This description of the Hulin and Smith study is actually incomplete. However, the omitted portion of the study is not directly relevant, for it is essentially concerned with predictions on an S-D continuum.

4 An Empirical Test of the Herzberg Two-Factor Theory*

ROBERT B. EWEN
New York University
PATRICIA CAIN SMITH
Bowling Green State University
CHARLES L. HULIN
University of Illinois
EDWIN A. LOCKE
American Institutes for Research, Washington Office

Results of an empirical test of the Herzberg 2-factor theory of job satisfaction are reported. A number of hypotheses for which the Herzberg theory and traditional unidimensional theory make different predictions were tested using a sample of 793 male employees from various jobs. The intrinsic variables ('satisfiers') were the work itself and promotions, and the extrinsic variable ('dissatisfier') was pay. Neither the Herzberg theory nor the traditional theory was supported by the data. Instead, results indicate that intrinsic factors are more strongly related to both overall satisfaction and overall dissatisfaction than the extrinsic factor, pay, and suggest that functioning of the extrinsic variable may depend on the level of satisfaction with the intrinsic variables. It was concluded that the concepts of 'satisfiers' and 'dissatisfiers' do not accurately represent the manner in which job-satisfaction variables operate.

The two-factor theory of job satisfaction proposed by Herzberg, Mausner, and Snyderman (1959) several years ago has occasioned considerable controversy. Briefly, this theory states that certain variables in the work situation ('satisfiers') lead to overall job satisfaction, but play an extremely small part in producing job dissatisfaction; while other variables

Journal of Applied Psychology, L [6] (1966) 544–50. Copyright 1966 by the American Psychological Association. Reprinted by permission.

('dissatisfiers') lead to job dissatisfaction but do not in general lead to job satisfaction. The Herzberg study cited the factors of work itself, responsibility, and advancement as the major satisfiers, and company policy and administration, supervision (both technical and interpersonal relationships), working conditions, and pay as the major dissatisfiers. These findings are, of course, in direct opposition to the traditional idea that if the presence of a variable in the work situation leads to job satisfaction, then its absence will lead to job dissatisfaction, and vice versa. These findings also contradict the findings of Herzberg, Mausner, Peterson, and Capwell (1957) based on an extensive review of the literature; for example, compare Herzberg et al. (1957, p. 48) with Herzberg et al. (1959, p. 81).

Research relevant to the Herzberg (1959) theory has produced conflicting results. On the positive side, Schwartz, Jenusaitis, and Stark (1963), using supervisory personnel in public utility industries, supported Herzberg's findings. Myers (1964), using employees on five different industrial jobs, also replicated Herzberg's results. Similarly Dysinger (1965), using civilian scientists and engineers in various Army research and development (R&D) installations, supported Herzberg's results using an incident check-list technique rather than an interview technique. Saleh (1964) also claimed to have supported the Herzberg hypothesis, although (as he observed) the results were not entirely clear-cut. Also, Herzberg (1965) replicated his earlier findings using a sample of Finnish supervisors.

All these studies, however, had in common the fact that they used the same recall method: subjects (Ss) first recalled instances of previous satisfaction and dissatisfaction and then described or checked the events which they perceived as leading up to or causing each instance. Inasmuch as Ewen (1964) and Dunnette and Kirchner (1965, pp. 152–3) among others have pointed out possible drawbacks of this method (e.g. selective bias in recall and projection of individual failure onto external sources), and since Hardin (1965) has reported evidence which makes studies which rely upon retrospective accounts of satisfaction extremely suspect, replications, obtained by this method alone cannot be regarded as giving unequivocal support to the Herzberg theory. A different method was used by Halpern (1965) who had Ss rate their 'best-liked job' on four 'satisfiers' and four 'dissatisfiers' as well as overall satisfaction. He found that the scores on the satisfiers correlated more highly with overall satisfaction than the scores on the dissatisfiers. Unfortunately, this study did not deal with the other half of the theory (dissatisfaction) at all.

On the negative side, Wernimont and Dunnette (1964) compared results using the Herzberg method to results using a forced-choice checklist method of indicating the causative factors in satisfaction and dissatisfaction. Using engineers and accountants as Ss, they found that with the forced-choice method, the satisfiers were endorsed more often to account for *both* satisfying and dissatisfying situations. On the other hand, in the free-choice situation the results replicated those obtained by Herzberg, thus supporting the notion that a free-choice situation may encourage bias in recall. A unique variation on the Herzberg method was used by Lindsay (1965). Instead of having his Ss (employees of an R & D company) *first* recall affective incidents and *then* their alleged causes, he had Ss *first* think of job factors (e.g. success experiences, company policy changes) and *then* the attitudes these experiences produced; in other words, the exact reverse of the Herzberg order. Using one satisfier (achievement) and one dissatisfier (company policy) Lindsay found that the satisfier accounted for three times as much variance in overall job satisfaction as the dissatisfier (i.e. it produced both more satisfaction and more dissatisfaction than the dissatisfier), thus agreeing with Wernimont and Dunnette's (1964) findings using the forced-choice format. Friedlander (1964) came to the same conclusion using still a different method. He had Ss rate the importance of various factors as to their perceived importance in producing satisfaction and dissatisfaction. Again the 'satisfiers' (e.g. achievement, recognition) were rated more important than the 'dissatisfiers' in producing *both* satisfaction and dissatisfaction.

In a factor-analytic study, Friedlander (1963) did not obtain a general intrinsic and a general extrinsic factor as the Herzberg theory would suggest. Instead, factors of social and technical environment, intrinsic self-actualizing work, and recognition through advancement were obtained. Ewen (1963, 1964) investigated a sample of approximately 1,000 life insurance agents and found that various job factors did not for the most part act in the manner predicted by the Herzberg theory. Dunnette (1965) studied samples of executives, sales clerks, secretaries, scientists and engineers, salesmen, and army reserves and supervision students, and concluded that the two-factor theory was an oversimplification. He stated that job satisfaction was multidimensional, and the same factors were able to contribute to both satisfaction and dissatisfaction. Graen (1965) performed a factor analysis using groups of engineers and found that Herzberg's a priori satisfaction dimensions did not emerge as clear factors. He therefore concluded that a priori theorizing is no substitute for empirical verification insofar as determining the factors of job satisfaction is concerned. Malinovsky and Barry (1965) investigated a sample of blue-collar workers and found that, contrary to the Herzberg theory, both satisfiers and dissatisfiers were positively related to job satisfaction.

There exist several straightforward hypotheses for which the Herzberg two-factor theory and the traditional unidimensional theory make diametrically opposed predictions. By subjecting these hypotheses to empirical tests, it should be possible to obtain evidence which will provide an indication as to the relative merits of the two theories. These hypotheses are enumerated below.

Hypothesis 1

Suppose there is one group of employees which is neutral (neither satisfied nor dissatisfied) with regard to the alleged satisfiers, and a second group which is dissatisfied with these alleged satisfiers. Suppose further that both groups are equated regarding their satisfaction with the alleged dissatisfiers. The Herzberg theory would predict that the two groups would be equal in overall job satisfaction, since being dissatisfied with the satisfiers is assumed to be no worse than being neutral with regard to the satisfiers — dissatisfaction with satisfiers should not lead to job dissatisfaction. However, the traditional theory would predict that the first group (neutral with regard to the satisfiers) would be more satisfied than the second group (dissatisfied with regard to the satisfiers), since this theory postulates that dissatisfaction with any variable tends to lead to overall job dissatisfaction.

This hypothesis may be tested independently three times with the data. Three separate groups can be formed, matched on degree of satisfaction with the dissatisfiers: a group dissatisfied with dissatisfiers (Group A), a group neutral with regard to the dissatisfiers (Group B), and a group satisfied with the dissatisfiers (Group C). Within each group can be compared those who are neutral on the satisfiers with those who are dissatisfied with the satisfiers. The Herzberg theory would predict no difference between these subgroups, whereas the traditional theory would predict those neutral on the satisfiers would be more satisfied than those dissatisfied on the satisfiers. The three tests of Hypothesis 1 will be called Tests 1A, 1B, and 1C, the letters corresponding to the above groups.

Hypothesis 2

A parallel hypothesis may be made for the effects of the dissatisfiers. This time satisfaction with the satisfiers is held constant by selecting three separate groups: a group dissatisfied with the satisfiers (Group A), a group neutral with regard to the satisfiers (Group B), and a group satisfied with the satisfiers (Group C). The Herzberg theory would predict no difference within each group between those neutral with regard to the dissatisfiers and those satisfied with the dissatisfiers. The traditional theory would predict a significant difference between the two subgroups. Again the three tests of the hypothesis will be called 2A, 2B, and 2C with the letters corresponding to the above groups.

Hypothesis 3

The Herzberg theory would predict that being dissatisfied with a dissatisfier should lead to greater overall dissatisfaction than being dissatisfied with a satisfier. Traditional theory would predict no such difference. Thus, suppose there are the following two groups: Group A is dissatisfied with the satisfiers and neutral with regard to the dissatisfiers, and Group B is neutral with regard to the satisfiers and dissatisfied with the dissatisfiers. The Herzberg theory would predict that Group A would show higher overall job satisfaction than Group B, while the traditional theory would not predict any difference between the two groups.

Hypothesis 4
Similarly, the Herzberg theory would predict that being satisfied with a satisfier should lead to greater overall satisfaction than being satisfied with a dissatisfier. Thus, suppose there are the following two groups: Group A is satisfied with the satisfiers and neutral with regard to the dissatisfiers, and Group B is neutral with regard to the satisfiers and satisfied with the dissatisfiers. The Herzberg theory would predict that Group A would show higher overall satisfaction than Group B, while traditional theory would not predict any difference between the two groups.

The purpose of the present paper is to test the various hypotheses stated above. Job-satisfaction instruments other than the one used in the Herzberg study will be used so as to avoid the possibility (Ewen, 1964) that the critical incidents method used in the Herzberg study affects the nature of the obtained results.

METHOD
Subjects
Briefly, the original sample from which these Ss were drawn consisted of 1,978 males, randomly selected from the lists of employees 35 years of age and older (25 in one company) in 21 'units'. These units had been selected to form a sample of industrial and business organizations (local) employing 50 or more persons, stratified so as to obtain widely different sizes and policies. The sample of Ss varied greatly according to job level, age, educational background, experience, place of employment, and other relevant characteristics. For details of the sample, see Kendall (1963). As will be explained below, only 793 of these S s were suitable for use in the tests of the various hypotheses.

Instruments
In view of its extensive validation, the Job Descriptive Index (JDI) developed at Cornell University (Hulin, Smith, Kendall and Locke, 1963; Kendall, Smith, Hulin and Locke, 1963; Locke, Smith, Hulin and Kendall, 1963; Locke, Smith, Kendall, Hulin and Miller, 1964; Macaulay, Smith, Locke, Kendall and Hulin, 1963; Smith, 1963; Smith and Kendall, 1963) was used as the measure of job satisfaction. Vroom (1964) has called this measure 'without doubt the most carefully constructed measure of job satisfaction in existence today' (p. 100). The JDI is an adjective checklist dealing with five areas of the job: the work itself, supervision, people, pay, and promotions. While the JDI does not deal with all of the satisfiers and dissatisfiers used in the Herzberg study, it was considered

preferable to other instruments which while measuring more factors were of less well-substantiated validity.

The General Motors Faces Scale (Kunin, 1955) was used as the measure of overall job satisfaction. This measure is a one-item graphic scale, consisting of six faces varying from a large smile to a large frown. The S is asked to check the face which most closely represents his feelings toward his job-in-general. This particular scale has not been validated, but faces scales for particular job-satisfaction dimensions have previously shown good discriminant and convergent validity (Locke et al., 1964).

Procedure
The JDI assesses five aspects of job satisfaction: the work itself, pay, promotional opportunities and policies, co-workers, and supervision. Inasmuch as the co-workers variable was neither a major satisfier nor a major dissatisfier in the Herzberg study, this variable was excluded from the analysis. The supervision variable was also excluded since the JDI does not distinguish between such factors as recognition given by the supervisor (supposedly a satisfier) and the technical aspects of supervision (supposedly a dissatisfier). Thus, three factors remained: the work itself and promotions, supposedly satisfiers; and pay, supposedly a dissatisfier.

From the original sample of 1,978 Ss, the groups defined by the various hypotheses were formed. Only those Ss were used whose general level of satisfaction on the two satisfiers was approximately equal. Were this not done (e.g. if Ss were included who were satisfied with regard to the work itself but dissatisfied with regard to promotions), it would not be possible to form meaningful conclusions about the hypotheses. That is, the effects of one of the satisfiers might or might not be cancelled out by opposite effects of the other satisfier. By equating for satisfaction on the two satisfiers (work itself and promotions), this problem was eliminated. A fairly large number of Ss differed with regard to satisfactions concerning the two satisfiers. When these were eliminated, a total of 837 remained. One group of 44 Ss (those satisfied with the satisfiers and dissatisfied with the dissatisfier) was not used in any of the tests. Thus, the final number of Ss was 793.

In order to determine which Ss were satisfied, which Ss were neutral, and which Ss were dissatisfied with each of the variables in question, it was necessary to determine neutral points for each JDI scale. This had been done in a previous study (Ewen, 1965). The procedure involved obtaining data for two groups of workers (not those used in the present study), consisting of JDI scores and Faces Scale scores for each of the five components (work, supervision, people, pay, and promotions). For each JDI scale and corresponding Faces Scale, a linear-regression analysis was carried out, and the neutral point of any JDI scale was taken to be the point on the regression line that corresponded to the neutral face on the Faces Scale. This was done separately for each of the two groups, and the results of the two groups were in high agreement. Any *S* with a score within five points above or below the neutral point on a JDI scale was taken to be neutral with regard to the component measured by that scale.

RESULTS
The results of the various tests are shown in Table 1. The data regarding Tests A, B, and C of Hypothesis 1 clearly support the traditional theory and argue against the Herzberg theory. The results indicate that dissatisfaction with the satisfiers (work itself and promotions) *does* lead to overall dissatisfaction. That is, groups neutral with regard to the satisfiers showed significantly higher overall satisfaction than those dissatisfied with the satisfiers. The results were highly significant in all three cases, indicating that the same conclusion holds whether we consider people who are dissatisfied with the dissatisfier (pay), neutral with regard to the dissatisfier, or satisfied with the dissatisfier. In each case, those neutral with regard to the satisfiers showed significantly higher overall job satisfaction than those dissatisfied with the satisfiers.

The data regarding Tests A and B of Hypothesis 2 support the Herzberg theory and argue against the traditional theory. That is, being satisfied with the dissatisfier led to no more overall satisfaction than being neutral with regard to the dissatisfier for those *S*s who were either dissatisfied or neutral with regard to the satisfiers. However, the data concerning Test C support the traditional theory rather than the Herzberg theory. That is, for people who are satisfied with the satisfiers, being satisfied with the dissatisfier led to greater overall satisfaction than being neutral with regard to the dissatisfier.

The data regarding Hypothesis 3 do not support either theory. The Herzberg theory predicts that being dissatisfied with a dissatisfier should lead to more overall dissatisfaction than being dissatisfied with a satisfier. However, the data indicate that the opposite is true. Being dissatisfied with the satisfiers led to more overall dissatisfaction than being dissatisfied with the dissatisfier. The traditional theory would not predict any difference between these two groups. The data regarding Hypothesis 4, on the other hand, support the Herzberg theory. Being satisfied with a satisfier led to more overall satisfaction than being satisfied with a dissatisfier.

DISCUSSION
It is clear that the present results taken as a whole do not provide clear support for either the Herzberg theory or for the traditional theory. Some of the results favor one theory while other results favor the other theory.

Though the results may appear to be contradictory, a logical explanation does exist. All of the various results form a consistent pattern if it can be assumed that the satisfiers used in this study, the work itself and promotions, are more potent variables than the dissatisfier, pay. Thus, the results concerning Hypothesis 1 indicate that the satisfiers can serve as strong sources of dissatisfaction (as well as strong sources of satisfaction).

Table 1 Predictions made by the Herzberg theory and the traditional theory and results concerning these predictions

Hypothesis	Test	Group	Satisfaction with		Overall satisfaction		Predictions[c]		t	Theory supported
			Satisfiers	Dissatisfiers	N	$\bar{X}$	H	T		
1	A	1	D[a]	D	71	1.77[b]	1 = 4	1 < 4	3.69**	T
		4	N	D	20	2.95				
1	B	2	D	N	29	2.24	2 = 5	2 < 5	4.38**	T
		5	N	N	28	3.54				
1	C	3	D	S	33	2.33	3 = 6	3 < 6	4.30**	T
		6	N	S	47	3.32				
2	A	2	D	N	29	2.24	2 = 3	2 < 3	<1	H
		3	D	S	33	2.33				
2	B	5	N	N	28	3.54	5 = 6	5 < 6	<1	H
		6	N	S	47	3.32				
2	C	8	S	N	94	3.71	8 = 9	8 < 9	3.70**	T
		9	S	S	471	4.11				
3		2	D	N	29	2.24	4 < 2	4 = 2	2.21*	?
		4	N	D	20	2.95				
4		6	N	S	47	3.32	6 < 8	6 = 8	1.95*	H
		8	S	N	94	3.71				

Note: Group 7, which consisted of subjects satisfied with the satisfiers and dissatisfied with the dissatisfier, was not used in any of the tests of the hypotheses. The N for this group was 44, and the mean overall satisfaction was 3.52.

[a]D = dissatisfied; N = neutral; S = satisfied.
[b]High mean scores indicate high overall job satisfaction.
[c]H = Herzberg theory; T = traditional theory.
*$p < .05$.
**$p < .001$.

The results concerning Hypothesis 2 indicate that satisfaction with pay is insufficient to significantly increase overall satisfaction if satisfaction with the more potent variables, the satisfiers, is at a low or neutral level. However, for those who are satisfied with the satisfiers, satisfaction with pay can increase overall satisfaction. The results concerning Hypotheses 3 and 4 indicate that satisfaction with the satisfiers leads to greater overall satisfaction than satisfaction with the dissatisfier, while dissatisfaction with the satisfiers leads to greater overall dissatisfaction than dissatisfaction with the dissatisfier. This interpretation supports the previous findings of Friedlander (1964), Lindsay (1965), and Wernimont and Dunnette (1964) that intrinsic factors are the most important sources of both satisfaction and dissatisfaction.

It must be kept in mind that the present study dealt with only three of a large number of factors that affect job satisfaction. Variables other than the work itself, promotions, and pay play a part in producing overall satisfaction and dissatisfaction. Also, the theory that the intrinsic factors are the most important variables was formulated after the results were in. A careful reading of the previous research should have indicated to us the desirability of explicitly testing this theory; but nevertheless the fact remains that the present study was not specifically designed with the intention of testing this theory.

In spite of the above limitations, the present results taken in conjunction with those of Friedlander (1964), Halpern (1965), Lindsay (1965), and Wernimont and Dunnette (1964) strongly suggest that the intrinsic factors are in fact the most potent factors in the work situation in terms of their relationship to overall job satisfaction. The results of the present study suggest that the manner in which the extrinsic factors operate may depend on the level of satisfaction with the intrinsic factors. This latter finding is only tentative, however, inasmuch as only one extrinsic factor (pay) was used in the present study.

It should be noted that traditional theory in no way precludes the possibility of some areas of job satisfaction being more potent than other areas. In fact, it would be rather startling if all areas were equally potent. The unidimensionality of the intrinsic variables in the present study clearly supports traditional theory. The next question is whether intrinsic variables are simply more potent than extrinsic variables, or (as the present results suggest may be the case) whether the functioning of the extrinsic variables depends on the level of satisfaction with the intrinsic variables. If subsequent research indicates that the latter is the case, a modification of traditional theory would be in order.

Further research is necessary to determine the generality of the present results. The question arises as to whether the present findings will be replicated in new situations, and at all job levels, whether or not these findings hold up when sources of job satisfaction other than those used in this study are used, and whether the way in which job-satisfaction variables operate is related to such variables as age, tenure, and job level.

The weight of the evidence to date indicates that the concepts of 'satisfiers' and 'dissatisfiers' are misleading and do not accurately indicate the way in which job-satisfaction variables affect overall job satisfaction. If the results of the present study prove to be of general applicability, the functioning of the various factors might better be described by such terms as 'primary satisfaction variables' (i.e. those variables which are strong sources of both overall satisfaction and overall dissatisfaction) and 'secondary satisfaction variables' (i.e. those variables the nature of whose operation depends on the level of satisfaction with the primary satisfaction variables). For the present, however, the 'intrinsic' and 'extrinsic' classifications would appear to be preferable to the 'satisfier-dissatisfier' terminology.

REFERENCES

Dunnette M. D., 'Factor Structures of Unusually Satisfying and Unusually Dissatisfying Job Situations for Six Occupational Groups'. Paper read at the Midwestern Psychological Association, Chicago, April 1965.

Dunnette, M. D. and Kirchner, W. K., *Psychology Applied to Industry*, (New York: Appleton-Century-Crofts, 1965).

Dysinger, D. W., 'Motivational Factors Affecting Civilian Army Research and Development Personnel'. Report AIR-D-95-5/65-TR, American Institutes for Research, Pittsburgh, 1965.

Ewen, R. B., 'Some Determinants and Correlates of Job Satisfaction', Unpublished master's thesis, University of Illinois, 1963.

Ewen R. B., 'Some Determinants of Job Satisfaction: A Study of the Generality of Herzberg's Theory', *Journal of Applied Psychology*, XLVIII (1964) 161–3.

Ewen R. B., 'Weighting Components of Job Satisfaction'. Unpublished doctoral dissertation, University of Illinois, 1965.

Friedlander, F., 'Underlying Scores of Job Satisfaction', *Journal of Applied Psychology*, XLVII (1963) 246–50.

Friedlander, E., 'Job Characteristics as Satisfiers and Dissatisfiers', *Journal of Applied Psychology*, XLVIII (1964) 388–92.

Graen, G. B., 'The Differential Perceptions of Work Motivations by High and Low Job Satisfied Engineers'. Paper read at the Midwestern Psychological Association, Chicago, April 1965.

Halpern, G., 'Relative Contribution of Motivator and Hygiene Factors to Overall Job Satisfaction', *Research Bulletin* 65–34 (Princeton, N.J.: Educational Testing Service, 1965).

Hardin, E., 'Perceived and Actual Change in Job Satisfaction', *Journal of Applied Psychology*, XLIX (1965) 363–7.

Herzberg, F., 'The Motivation to Work among Finnish Supervisors', *Personnel Psychology*, XVIII (1965) 393–402.

Herzberg, F., Mausner, B., Peterson, R. O. and Capwell, D. F., *Job Attitudes: Review of Research and Opinion* (Pittsburgh: Psychological Service of Pittsburgh, 1957).

Herzberg, F., Mausner, B. and Snyderman, B. B., *The Motivation to Work* (New York: Wiley, 1959).

Hulin, C. L., Smith, P. C., Kendall, L. M. and Locke, E. A., 'Cornell Studies of Job Satisfaction: II. Model and Method of Measuring Job Satisfaction', Cornell University, 1963. (Mimeo)

Kendall, L. M., 'Canonical Analysis of Job Satisfaction and Behavioral, Personal Background, and Situational Data'. Unpublished doctoral dissertation, Cornell University 1963.

Kendall, L. M., Smith, P. C., Hulin C. L. and Locke E. A., 'Cornell Studies of Job Satisfaction: IV. The Relative Validity of the Job Descriptive Index and Other Methods of Measurement of Job Satisfaction', Cornell University, 1963. (Mimeo)

Kunin T., 'The Construction of a New Type of Attitude Measure', *Personnel Psychology*, VIII (1955) 65–77.

Lindsay, C. A., 'Job Satisfaction: An Examination and Test of a Modification of the Herzberg Theory'. Unpublished doctoral dissertation, Pennsylvania State University, 1965.

Locke, E. A., Smith P. C., Hulin, C. L. and Kendall, L. M., 'Cornell Studies of Job Satisfaction: V. Scale Characteristics of the Job Descriptive Index', Cornell University, 1963. (Mimeo)

Locke, E. A., Smith, P. C., Kendall, L. M., Hulin, C. L. and Miller, A. M., 'Convergent and Discriminant Validity for Areas and Methods of Rating Job Satisfaction', *Journal of Applied Psychology*, XLVIII (1964) 313–19.

Macaulay, D. A., Smith, P. C., Locke, E. A., Kendall, L. M. and Hulin, C. L., 'Cornell Studies of Job Satisfaction: III. Convergent and Discriminant Validity for Measures of Job Satisfaction by Rating Scales', Cornell University, 1963. (Mimeo)

Malinovsky, M. R. and Barry, J. R., 'Determinants of Work Attitudes', *Journal of Applied Psychology*, XLIX (1965) 446–51.

Myers, M. S., 'Who Are Your Motivated Workers?', *Harvard Business Review*, XLII (1964) 73–88.

Saleh, S. D., 'A Study of Attitude Change in the Pre-Retirement Period', *Journal of Applied Psychology*, XLVIII (1964) 310–12.

Schwartz, M. M., Jenusaitis, E. and Stark, H., 'Motivational Factors among Supervisors in the Utility Industry', *Personnel Psychology*, XVI (1963) 45–53.

Smith, P. C., 'Cornell Studies of Job Satisfaction: I. Strategy for the Development of a General Theory of Job Satisfaction', Cornell University, 1963. (Mimeo)

Smith, P. C. and Kendall, L. M., 'Cornell Studies of Job Satisfaction: VI. Implications for the Future', Cornell University, 1963. (Mimeo)

Vroom, V. H., *Work and Motivation* (New York: Wiley, 1964).

Wernimont, P. F. and Dunnette, M. D., 'Intrinsic and Extrinsic Factors in Job Satisfaction'. Paper read at Midwestern Psychological Association, St. Louis, May 1964.

PART II

Job Satisfaction and the Nature of the Job Itself

The first paper in this part is the classic study by Walker and Guest, showing the effects of mass production technology on satisfaction with the job. In particular Walker and Guest highlight the point that conveyer belt technology causes feelings of anonymity and boredom, and a general dissatisfaction with work. They suggest one remedy in the form of job enlargement, giving individuals a greater number of operations to perform. Herzberg, in his paper, had advocated job enrichment rather than job enlargement. Job enlargement involved only a horizontal increase in the number of different operations performed. Herzberg argues that this is just more of the same soul-destroying work and claims that only by allowing the job to give opportunities for psychological growth, through vertical enrichment, is motivation likely to be increased. Vertical enlargement involves giving employees greater opportunities to utilise their decision-making abilities. It is described more fully in the paper by Lawler, who also evaluates research on the subject. The paper of Alderfer is an example of a job enlargement study. The papers presented in this part make abundantly clear the importance of the job itself as a major factor in job satisfaction.

5 The Man on the Assembly Line*

CHARLES R. WALKER and ROBERT H. GUEST

There are a lot of good things about my job. The pay is good. I've got seniority. The working conditions are pretty good for my type of work. But that's not the whole story. . . . You can't beat the machine. They have you clocked to a fraction of a second. My job is engineered, and the jigs and fixtures are all set out according to specifications. The foreman is an all right guy, but he gets pushed, so he pushes us. The guy on the line has no one to push. You can't fight that iron horse. — *Worker on an assembly line, interviewed by the authors.*

Machines alone do not give us mass production. Mass production is achieved by both machines *and* men. And while we have gone a long way toward perfecting our mechanical operations, we have not successfully written into our equation whatever complex factors represent man, the human element. — *Henry Ford II, in a talk before the American Society of Mechanical Engineers, shortly after he was made President of the Ford Motor Company.*

The principal social and psychological problems connected with mass production and human nature have been stated many times and in many different forms. Their importance in an age of advancing technology is hardly in dispute. The question has become rather: What shall we do about them?

Here are a few of the common problems. Since individuals react very differently to industrial occupations, what are the personality characteristics of those who adjust quickly to — and appear to thrive on — mechanically paced and repetitive jobs? What, on the other hand, are the personality characteristics of those who suffer mentally and physically on such jobs — and who therefore tend to perform them badly? Can the adjustment problem, in other words, be solved by selection? Or is the modern work environment simply *wrong* for the normal human being?

Or to take an engineering and management approach: In the present state of the mechanical arts, what part of a worker's skill and power can the engineer build into a machine? What must he leave out? Precisely how and to what extent in the most mechanized sectors of our economy does the human equation still affect quantity and quality?

Or again, granted that the principles of mass production such as breakdown of jobs into their simplest constituent parts are sound and vital to efficient manufacture, have we yet found how to combine these principles with equally well authenticated principles of human behavior?

Or taking still another approach, if a man spends a third of his life in direct contact with a mass-production environment, why should we not consider important (to him and to society) the hours of living time he spends inside the factory — as important and valuable, for example, as the product he produces which is consumed outside the factory? We talk of a high standard of living, but frequently we mean a high standard of consumption. Man consumes in his leisure, yet fulfills himself not only in his leisure but in his work. Is our mass-production work environment making such fulfillment more difficult?

A short way to sum up these and a great many more questions is: To what degree can — or should — men be 'adjusted' to the new environment of machines, and to what degree is it possible to adjust or rebuild that environment to fit the needs and personalities of men?

NEED FOR SYSTEMATIC STUDY
Despite the tremendous contributions of mass-production methods to the productiveness of the economic system under which we live, and notwithstanding the fact that editors, philosophers, and propagandists have long speculated and written about the beneficent or injurious effects of highly mechanized jobs on human behavior, there has been singularly little systematic effort to discover 'whatever complex factors represent man, the human element' in the mass-production method as such. The relatively small number of studies which have been made of assembly-line and other types of repetitive work have been mostly laboratory experiments, not explorations of experience in actual industrial plants.

A notable exception is the series of monographs which for some 25 years have been published from time to time under the auspices of the British Medical Council on the effects of mechanization and the repetitive job on productivity and *mental* fatigue. Even these, however, have only touched occasionally on the subject of assembly lines, and have never at all — to the best of our knowledge — dealt specifically with that advanced sector of a mass-production economy, the final assembly line of a plant making a large, complex product like automobiles.

Survey of automobile assembly plant
For these reasons the authors undertook two years ago an exploratory survey of a modern automobile assembly plant.[1] This is intended as the first of a series of studies designed to define more clearly the several

'human equations' involved in assembly work, to prepare and sharpen tools of research, and to look for proximate and empirical answers to the more acute practical problems posed for men and management.

In this article we shall emphasize how an assembly line looks and feels to the men who work on it, rather than its importance to the engineers who designed it, the executives who manage it, or the public who buys its product.

In order to preserve the anonymity of those who freely supplied information — managers, workers, and union leaders — the plant in question has been called Plant X. Over a period of months 180 workers were interviewed in their homes about all phases of their life on 'the line'. These workers constituted a substantial — and representative — sample of the total number of productive workers in the plant.

Nearly 90% of the men working at Plant X came from jobs where the pace of work was not machine-governed in a strict sense, and from jobs over 72% of which were not repetitive. In short, the area from which they were recruited had few mass-production factories. One might say, then, that these men were like the majority of workers who in the past 30 years have made the transition from occupations characteristic of the first industrial revolution to work environments characteristic of a mass-production era. Their attitudes should be all the more revealing.

Most people, in thinking about an assembly line and the workers on it, focus only on the effect of the line on what a man does hour by hour, even minute by minute, with his mind and his muscles. Any serious study of the human effects of the mass-production method, however, must extend its field of vision. For the method not only impinges directly on a man's immediate or intrinsic job but molds much of the character of the in-plant society of which he is a part, including both his relations with his fellow workers and his relations with management. Accordingly we shall discuss the impact of the mass-production method not only directly but indirectly on human nature.

Definition of mass-production methods

But what is the 'mass-production method'? We must have a definition if our discussion and our findings are to be understandable.

Although the methods of mass production or, more accurately and specifically for our purposes, the methods of *progressive manufacture* have been defined and discussed in different ways by different writers, it is agreed by nearly everyone that these methods derive from at least two fundamental and related ideas: (*a*) standardization and (*b*) inter-changeability of parts.

Given these basic ideas, plus the accurate machining methods which make them applicable to manufacture, Ford was able to work out and apply the three following additional 'principles' of progressive manufacture: (*c*) the orderly progression of the product through the shop in a series of planned operations arranged so that the right part always arrives at the right place at the right time; (*d*) the mechanical delivery of these parts and of the product as it is assembled to and from the operators; and (*e*) a breakdown of operations into their simple constituent motions.[2]

Let us look now at how these principles translate themselves into job characteristics from the standpoint not of the engineer but of the man on the assembly line. In the first place, most automobile assembly jobs are *mechanically paced* (especially those on the main line). In the second place, since the engineer has broken the jobs down into simple and separate elements and assigned only a few to each man, they are clearly *repetitive*. Among other characteristics of most jobs are these: they have a low skill requirement, permit work on only a fraction of the product, severely limit social interaction, and predetermine for nearly every worker any use he may make of tools and methods.

Taken together, automobile assembly-line jobs exemplify all these characteristics, but not every job exemplifies all of them. Put another way, in spite of many common characteristics, automobile assembly jobs are far from being equal — either as to the quantity or quality of job content or as to the satisfaction or dissatisfaction which workers derive from them. They differ both in the number of the several assembly-line characteristics they exemplify and in the degree of impact of any one characteristic. An understanding of this point must mark the beginning of any serious inquiry into the relation of human behavior to assembly-line work.

ATTITUDE TOWARD JOBS
But that is enough of making distinctions. Now let the men on the assembly line tell us themselves about their jobs, and tell us also what they like and what they do not like about them. Here are six jobs by way of illustration: two on the main moving line, one off the main line but on a moving conveyer, one off the main line and not on a moving conveyer, one repair job on the line, and one utility job on the line. These six will illustrate at least the principal differences in human impact of mass-production assembly-line jobs. (It should be remembered, however, that these six are not representative of the distribution of jobs in the whole plant, where one-half the jobs are on the *main moving assembly line*. Specifically the distribution of jobs in our sample was as follows: main assembly line, 86; subassembly on moving belt, 28; subassembly not on moving belt, 38; repairmen, 14; utility men, 11; and other, 3).

On the main moving line
Here is the way the assembler of the baffle windbreaker in the trim department describes his job:

As the body shell moves along the line, I start putting on a baffle windbreaker (two fenders fit on it) by putting in four screws. Then I put nine clips at the bottom which hold the chrome molding strip to the body. On another type of car there is a piece of rubber which fits on the hood latch on the side and keeps the hood from rattling. I drill the holes in the rubber and metal and fit two screws in. Also I put four clips on the rubber in the rear fender. On another type of body I put the clips on the bottom molding, and in the trunk space I put two bolts which hold the spare tire clamp. I repeat these things all the time on the same types of car.

How does this man's job measure up in terms of some of the characteristics we have mentioned, particularly pace and repetitiveness?

To begin with, the job is on the main line and the worker rides along on the conveyer, completing his cycle of operations in less than two minutes while the conveyer is moving over a distance of about 30 feet. He then walks to his starting point and begins over again. In short, his pace is directly determined by the moving belt. On the other hand, he is sometimes able to work back up the line and so secure a breather for himself.

The job is clearly repetitive, but there is some element of variety since between five and ten operations are required to complete the job cycle. There are also different models to be worked on. Comparing the repetitiveness of this job with that of other assembly jobs, it is somewhere in the middle range — far less repetitive than a single-operation job and far more repetitive than the job of a repairman.

Similarly, in the matter of skill it is in the middle as assembly-line jobs go. Because of the number of parts handled, learning time is slightly longer than that for many assembly jobs. The worker reported that it took him a month to do the job properly. As for the expenditure of physical energy, it is a light job.

Also on the main moving line

Or consider the job of the worker who installs toe plates and who performs operations typical of short-cycle, on-the-main-line jobs: 'I put in the two different toe plates. They cover the holes where the brake and clutch pedals are. I am inside the car and have to be down on the seat to do my work. On one kind of car I put in the shift lever while another man puts in the toe plates.'

While doing his job this man rides along in the car and must complete the job before he is carried too far. After finishing his work cycle he returns to his station, climbs into another car, and begins another installation. Thus his pace is strictly governed by the moving line. This particular worker told the interviewer that he did not mind the pace.

Such a job which demands but two operations in a two-minute cycle is highly repetitive. Only slight variety is introduced when the man installs a shift lever instead of a toe plate on certain cars.

The job demands very little skill and has a learning period of just two days. Although the worker gets in and out of cars 20 or 30 times an hour, his expenditure of physical energy on the actual assembly operation is slight.

Off the main line but on a moving conveyer
The job of a seat-spring builder is typical of those off the main line but on a moving belt:

> I work on a small conveyer which goes around in a circle. We call it a merry-go-round. I make up zig-zag springs for front seats. Every couple of feet on the conveyer there is a form for the pieces that make up the seat springs. As that form goes by me, I clip several pieces together, using a clip gun. I then put the pieces back on the form, and it goes on around to where other men clip more pieces together. By the time the form has gone around the whole line, the pieces are ready to be set in a frame, where they are made into a complete seat spring. That's further down the main seat cushion line. The only operation I do is work the clip gun. It takes just a couple of seconds to shoot six or eight clips onto the spring, and I do it as I walk a few steps. Then I start right over again.

This job is clearly paced by a moving conveyer quite as much as if it were on the main line. A comment by the worker regarding his previous job emphasized the point: 'I liked the piecework system on my old job. If I wanted to stop for a few minutes, I could. You can't do that here.'

As for variety, there is none. The job is highly repetitive, consisting of one set of operations repeated every few seconds on a part which is standard for all models.

The skill requirement is minimum. This worker gave two days as his learning time, with a few days more 'in order to do it like I do it now'.

As for physical energy, the job would probably be rated as light since the worker guides an automatic hand gun. But there is considerable fatigue because the worker performs the operation standing up.

The worker's over-all estimate of the job is typical. As to what he liked about the job, he mentioned good pay, steady work, and good working hours — in that order of priority. As to what he disliked, he said that he could not set his own pace, that he did not have interesting work, and that his job was physically tiring.

Off the main line but not on a moving conveyer
We turn to a blower-defroster assembler who works off the main line and not on a moving belt:

> I work at a bench on blower defrosters. The blowers come in two parts. I take one part and attach the blower motor to it. I then connect the fan to the motor shaft. Then I take the other half on the air pipe and put two

parts together with fourteen screws. I test the motor to see if it works, and if it does, I put in a fifteenth screw which grounds it to the pipe. The materials are brought to me and put in a pile by a stock chaser. After I finish, I put each assembled blower on one of six shelves.

Here is an example of a job where pace is only indirectly determined by the main line. The worker must keep his shelves stocked with a supply of blower defrosters, but he has some choice of pace in doing so. He may work fast and 'build up a bank', then slow down and take a breather. Or he may choose to work quite steadily. The demands of the stock-chaser who brings him materials and takes away the finished assembly are the determinants of his work pace, rather than the moving conveyer.

There is not much variety since there are only three operations. However, a slight variation is introduced through differences in models. The worker called his job completely repetitive but said he did not mind it.

His job operations require a minimum of skill: 'I learned it in a couple of hours, though it took me about a week to get up speed'. He does not move around, and the materials he handles are light, so very little physical energy is demanded.

Summing up his job, this worker gave good bosses, good pay, and good working conditions as his first three reasons for liking the job. He mentioned only one thing he disliked: 'I cannot do different things'.

Repairman
Here is a job description by a repairman in the car-conditioning section of the chassis department:

> I work in a pit underneath the final line. The cars move along over the pit. On the previous assembly operations, the inspectors for the under parts of the car have indicated where parts were missing or damaged or not properly attached. There are any number of things which can be wrong, and they are usually different for each car. Sometimes we have a run of the same thing which we have to work on until they get at the bug earlier in assembly operations. The shock absorbers may be bad, gas line in wrong, brake lines or spring attachments off. I fix whatever I see checked by the inspector. The others in the pit do the same thing. I just work down the line until I get it cleared up. Sometimes I have to work down a long way on one thing. Other times it's just a simple problem on a number of different things.

This worker is on the main line, but his pace is not strictly governed by the moving conveyer. 'We don't feel the pressure of the line since we don't have to do just one thing in a given area and length of time'.

The variety the job offers is derived from the nature of the work.

'There are any number of things which can be wrong, and they are usually different for each car. . . . There is something different all the time'.

As for skill, the job as repairman requires manual skill and mechanical experience. A garage repairman's job would be a good preparation. (The man whose job description is given here had, in fact, worked as a repairman in a garage before coming to Plant X.)

The job varies between light and medium-heavy work, with the expenditure of physical energy called for changing appreciably from job to job and from day to day.

The worker's personal satisfaction with his job was clear. He gave as three reasons for liking the job: 'I can set my own pace, I have good working conditions, and I have steady work'. He also commented favorably on being able to 'use my brains', 'do different things', and 'choose how the job is to be done'.

Utility man

A utility man in the chassis department describes his job as follows:

> I work on the whole length of that part of the chassis line beginning with motor drop up to where the wheels are mounted. My job is to fill in wherever I am needed. A man might be absent or away from the job or may need help on the job.
>
> We start where the motor is lowered onto the frame (motor mount). The clutch assembly is installed and hooked up. Then the exhaust system is attached and the bolts tightened. The clutch assembly bolts and the motor mount bolts are also tightened. In the next area on the line the brake chambers are filled and bled.
>
> Off to the side, the subassembly men put the steering column together. The steering post and the Pittman arm assembly are put in. Further down the line, men put in air cleaners and inject hydraulic fluid for the transmission.
>
> Next, the brakes are tested and the clutch linkage hooked up. The bumper brackets are put on; a serial number is attached next; and then the bumper brackets are tightened up. Finally, the chassis is sprayed, mounted on wheels, and moved on toward body drop. All in all, about 28 men work on these jobs, each man with his own special operation. I go on each of these jobs, depending on where I am needed most. It is different each day. Some of the jobs are hard to learn, so when I take over one on which I haven't had much experience, it's hard to keep up. I have been learning how to do the work ever since I've been in the plant. I can never learn everything because new changes are always being made.

The pace of this utility man's work, since it is on the main line, is as strictly governed as that of any assembly worker. In certain ways he may feel the pressure more acutely than some of those for whom he substitutes, since he has less practice on any single job than its regular holder.

To compensate him, however, there is plenty of variety, for, as he points out, he shifts about among 28 different jobs. Notice how in describing his many tasks this utility man gives a very clear account of a whole segment of assembly operations in the chassis department.

Notice, too, the character of a utility man's skill. It is the sum of many little skills of many repetitive jobs. The learning time is six months to a year. The worker said: 'Sometimes I walk up and down checking the line. I ask questions of the different men. I rarely stay on the same job more than a couple of days.' That his job is not easy is suggested by an additional comment: 'Some days you feel like learning, other days you don't. On jobs that take time to learn, you get disgusted because it's hard to keep up. A utility man, when on a job, has more trouble keeping up than the regular man.'

This man mentioned good pay, steady work, and good bosses as the three main reasons for liking his job, in that order. Other items bearing on the immediate job which he liked were 'having interesting work, having to use my brains, doing many different things', as in the case of the repairman, and also 'talking with others'. He had only one complaint about the job: that it was 'physically tiring'.

Summary of attitudes toward jobs

In all of this classification of the automobile assembly workers' jobs, we have clearly been concerned not with an engineering analysis but with factors which have an effect on satisfaction or dissatisfaction with the immediate job. Mechanical pace, repetitiveness, minimum skill require- ment, and the other factors were all found reflected in attitudes and feelings.

These examples underline some of the commonest facts and feelings which are part of the daily experience of the productive worker in an assembly plant. To recall a few:

1. Contrary to popular belief, all jobs on an assembly line are not alike, either in skill, variety, learning time, or the degree of satisfaction or dissatisfaction which they offer the average wage earner.

2. There are definite ways on certain jobs to get a break or a breather, such as 'working back up the line', or 'bank building'.

3. There is a general, though not a unanimous, desire to move from highly paced jobs to jobs which are less highly paced and 'off the line'.

4 It is evident from the statements of the six workers — which for illustrative purposes we have selected from 180 — that other factors such as good pay, a good foreman, and a secure job must be considered in appraising the total index of a worker's satisfaction or dissatisfaction.

MAJOR REACTIONS OF WORKERS

Looking over the range of factors connected with their immediate jobs by all the men interviewed, we see that the two which were given greatest prominence were (a) mechanical pacing and (b) repetitiveness.

To mechanical pacing
We asked no direct attitude questions on the first and central characteristic of any automobile assembly plant — the moving conveyer — but nearly every worker expressed his opinions about it when describing his job, when talking about the company, or at some other point in the interview. These free-association comments on pace as governed by the moving conveyer showed that: (1) A large majority of the workers regarded the moving line or belt as an undersirable feature of the job. (2) A small minority expressed themselves as enjoying the excitement of the moving line.

Following are typical comments of workers who were highly critical of the line:

'The bad thing about assembly lines is that the line keeps moving. If you have a little trouble with a job, you can't take the time to do it right.'

'On the line you're geared to the line. You don't dare stop. If you get behind, you have a hard time catching up.'

'The line speed is too great. More men wouldn't help much. They'd just expect more work out of an individual. There's an awful lot of tension.'

'I don't like rushing all the time. . . . I don't mind doing a good day's work, but I don't like to run through it.'

'The work isn't hard; it's the never-ending pace. . . . The guys yell "hurrah" whenever the line breaks down. . . . You can hear it all over the plant.'

In contrast, a minority liked the challenge and excitement of keeping up with the line:

'I do my job well. I get some satifaction from keeping up with a rapid-fire job. On days when the cars come off slowly, I sometimes get bored.'

'I get satisfaction from doing my job right and keeping up with the line.'

'It makes you feel good . . . when the line is going like hell and you step in and catch up with it.'

To repetitiveness
Turning now to the job characteristic, repetitiveness, our findings are that: (1) A majority of the workers were critical of the repetitive character of their jobs. (2) A minority preferred the repetitive character of their work or were indifferent to it. (3) A large number of workers compared on-the-line jobs unfavorably with off-the-line jobs, because off-the-line jobs offered more variety.

We found we were able to correlate the number of operations a man performed (which can serve as a rough measure of repetitiveness) with expressions of interest or lack of interest in his job. The number of operations performed on any given job was determined not by direct questioning but by analysis of the job descriptions. The workers, however, were asked directly: 'Would you say your job was very interesting, fairly interesting, not at all interesting?' The correlation with number of operations was as follows:

Operations performed	Very or fairly interesting	Not very or not at all interesting
1	19	38
2–5	28	36
5 or more	41	18

In the column of workers giving a positive rating to 'interest', the number of workers increases as the number of operations increases. In other words, there is a tendency for interest in work to vary directly with the number of operations performed.

Following are typical comments of those men who were critical of the repetitive nature of their jobs:

'I dislike repetition. One of the main things wrong with this job is that there is no figuring for yourself, no chance to use your brain. It's a grind doing the same thing over and over. There is no skill necessary.'

'I'd rather work for a small company any day. They're interested in doing good work, and they are willing to allot enough time for it. The assembly line is no place to work, I can tell you. There is nothing more discouraging than having a barrel beside you with 10,000 bolts in it and using them all up. Then you get a barrel with another 10,000 bolts, and you know every one of those 10,000 bolts has to be picked up and put in exactly the same place as the last 10,000 bolts.'

'I'd like to do different things on this job. I get bored. It's the same thing all the time. Cars always coming down the line endlessly every time I look up.'

'I would like to perform different operations, but I do the same thing all the time. I always know what I'm going to do when I come in. There's nothing to look forward to like there was on my old job.'

'The monotony is what I don't like. It's pretty noisy, but you get used to that. I'd never get used to the monotony. I dislike the plant for this reason.'

'It's not a matter of pace. It's the monotony. It's not good for you to get so bored. I do the same thing day after day; just an everlasting grind.'

'The job gets so sickening — day in and day out plugging in ignition wires. I get through with one motor, turn around, and there's another motor staring me in the face.'

A minority of workers who declared that they were indifferent to or preferred doing the same thing over and over again commented as follows:

'I keep doing the same thing all the time, but it doesn't make any difference to me.'

'Repeating the same thing you can catch up and keep ahead of yourself. I like the routine. You can get in the swing of it.'

'We do the same thing all the time, but I don't mind it really.'

'I like doing the same thing all the time. I'd rather stay right where I am. When I come in in the morning, I like to know exactly what I'll be doing.'

'I like to repeat the same thing, and every car is different anyway. So my job is interesting enough.'

Explanation of why this minority group either preferred or was indifferent to the factor of repetitiveness in contrast to the majority of workers in our sample would appear to lie in the pattern of their individual personalities. An investigation of the psychological characteristics of men who react this way is clearly suggested. We sought but found no other unique characteristics in the group as regards education, age, or any of the other categories of information we used.

EFFECT OF HUMAN EQUATION
In the introductory paragraphs of this article we reviewed some of the typical questions on which it was hoped research into the human equation of assembly-line work might throw light, including some of special interest to both the production manager and the engineer: What part of a worker's skill and power can the engineer build into a machine? What must he leave out? Precisely how and to what extent in the most mechanized sectors of our economy does the human equation still affect quantity and quality?

Influence of workers on quality
So far as assembly lines go, there is still a widespread belief on the part of *outsiders* that the machine has completely taken over and that on mechanized conveyer-line jobs the individual has no influence on quality. There is also a belief widely held by *insiders* (employers and production managers) that, even though the quality of individual performance on a mechanized job may still be important for the final product, the average worker no longer cares or gets satisfaction from doing a good job.

In Plant X, both beliefs were shown to be unfounded.

As many as 79 men in the sample of 180 felt that it was difficult to sustain the kind of quality performance which was expected of them or which they themselves wanted to sustain. To most of the 79 *this was a discouraging and negative feature of the job.*

About half the workers felt it was possible to do the kind of quality job expected of them. Few of these workers, however, had jobs which were strictly line-paced. Rather they included mostly repairmen, utility men, workers on off-line jobs, or men on the line who had longer time cycles or greater freedom to move up and down the line. Typical comments among this group were:

'No time limit is set on my job, so I can do it right. I get satisfaction out of really fixing a job. I can usually get this, but sometimes the company doesn't want the cars fixed as well as I'd like to.'

'I get satisfaction and quality because I have time to complete my job right.'

'I never let a car go by with my number on it unless it is done right. Maybe some of the men on the line don't get quality.'

'You can take time to get quality. It's not like on the line when you have to rush so much. And I get satisfaction. It makes me feel good when I put out a good day's work and get no kickbacks.'

The effects of poor-quality work on job satisfaction were reflected in many of the comments of men on conveyer-paced jobs:

'The cars come too fast for quality. It's quantity instead of quality. I'm doing the best I can, but could do a neater job slower.'

'On an assembly line you just do it once; if it's wrong, you have no time to fix it. I get no satisfaction from my work. All I do is think about all the things that went through wrong that should have been fixed. My old job was nothing like this.'

'I try to do quality work, but I'm too rushed. This keeps me from getting pleasure from the work. They say "haste makes waste", and they're getting plenty of both.'

'I'd rather do less work and do it right. How can you get quality when they don't give you time? The "quality" signs they have mean nothing.'

These comments tend to show that the characteristics or components of the assembly man's immediate job do have a significant bearing upon the quality of the product, and that mass production restricts rather than eliminates the 'human factor' as a determinant of quality for any given part or for the total product. Most workers were conscious of this fact. For a substantial number, inability to put out quality was a source of irritation while putting out quality was a source of job satisfaction.

CONSTRUCTIVE MEASURES BY MANAGEMENT
Are there any measures that management can take to modify on-the-job conditions of work in the interest of greater efficiency and of increased satisfaction for the individual operator?

One answer to this question may be sought in the elements of satisfaction or of compensation which some workers already found in their jobs. To begin with, it should be remembered that there was a minority of workers who preferred or were indifferent to repetitiveness and mechanical pacing. Presumably by improved methods of recruiting and selection this minority could be increased. Then there was a number of men who found their immediate jobs on and off the line satisfying — actually all the repairmen and utility men interviewed with one exception. The only measures needed here are protective — to make sure that the content of these jobs is not diluted.

This still leaves the majority of the production workers. Here the clue to constructive action lies in the fact that many of them reacted favorably to particular features of their jobs:

1. Social interaction breaking the monotony.
2. Enough operations on their particular jobs to give variety.
3. Opportunity to work back up the line and get a breather.
4. Opportunity to build up a bank and get a breather.
5. Opportunity to alternate one set of operations with another set of a substantially different character.
6. Opportunity to alternate jobs with other workers within the same section.
7. A long time cycle encompassing a larger number of operations than usual and of a more interesting character.

A practical directive for management would appear to be exploration of the possibility of extending these and other desirable features, so that more assembly men could share in them. The degree of that extension would necessarily vary with the special circumstances — physical and organizational — of individual plants, and with the ingenuity of management; but there would be few plants where something could not be done in this direction.

Detailed discussion of such measures is beyond the scope of this article, but the tenor of our thinking may be indicated by reference to two of the seven features to which Plant X workers reacted favorably.

Job rotation
Take Number 6 — alternation of jobs between workers, a technique often called 'rotation'. At Plant X we were struck with the unusually high degree of job satisfaction expressed by the members of one work group under a particular foreman. With the permission and encouragement of their foreman, the men were working under a system of job rotation. It was to this system that the members of the group ascribed their relatively high

job satisfaction. And to the same system the section foreman owed in part a smoothly running and efficient work unit. Top plant management is now encouraging a more wide-spread application of this practice.

In connection with any system of job rotation the question immediately comes to mind: Since it requires some effort to learn several jobs instead of one, will not the worker — unless he is exceptional — object? Many managers seem to find it difficult to get workers to change jobs frequently.

The best answer to this question about worker resistance is the pragmatic one. In certain sectors on the line at Plant X rotation *is* working. Moreover, in the other industries and on other types of assembly lines the practice of rotation is steadily gaining ground. For most people learning to do something new is hard work, and it is only undertaken when an adequate reward is held out. For a considerable number of assembly-line workers the rewards of variety and of possessing a repertory of skills will be sufficient.

Of course, some resistance to an experiment in rotation is to be expected. The key to the situation lies, we suggest, in the word 'experiment'. Where rotation has been successfully installed on other types of assembly lines, it has usually been started as an experiment, with management guaranteeing to the work group or to any single individual a return to stationary assignments if desired — and rarely have the workers wished to return.

Another question is: Will the work be done as well or as fast under job rotation? The answer for the Plant X section which practices it is an affirmative. For other work groups in other industries with which the authors are familiar, the answer has also been 'yes'. Of course there are work situations where job rotation appears either altogether impractical or less efficient. But always the real test is in the over-all and long-term performance of the group. Gains in quality and a drop in turn-over or absenteeism may balance some decrease in output, if it occurs.

Job enlargement

Or consider Number 7 — a long-time cycle encompassing a larger number of operations than usual and of a more interesting character, sometimes called 'job enlargement'. Here is a concept and a practice that has proved successful in decreasing monotony without impairing efficiency in certain sectors of other industries. We here suggest that it be introduced experimentally into automobile assembly work.

Job enlargement is simply the recombining of two or more separate jobs into one. Certain plant managers in other industries have been finding that a law of diminishing returns applies to the subdivision of jobs and that a recombination of certain fractured parts has increased efficiency. This points toward a lengthening of time cycles. Job enlargement in the sense in which we suggest it does not mean turning automobile assembly back into the hands of master mechanics with one worker assigned to the assembly of one car. It does mean paying greater attention to psychological and social variables in the determination of time cycles and, by the same token, paying more attention to the *content* of individual jobs.

To one unfamiliar with assembly-line work experience, the difference between a job with five operations and a job with ten, or between a job taking two minutes to perform and a job taking four minutes, might seem a matter far too trivial to concern anyone. Our data have shown that this is not true. Management has a vital interest in such matters; the proper assignment of time cycles throughout an assembly plant will make an important difference in the efficiency of the plant. As for the worker, one of the most striking findings of this study is the psychological importance of even minute changes in his immediate job experience.

At the risk of oversimplication, the point may be summarized this way: Other things being equal, the difference between a satisfied and a dissatisfied worker may rest on whether he has a ten-operation or a five-operation job.

RELATIONSHIP AMONG WORKERS

Another place to look for possibilities of improvement is in the area of indirect influences — the impact of mass production methods on the plant's social structure. Ever since the early studies of Elton Mayo, it has been widely accepted that the character of the 'work group' frequently exercises a decisive influence on a worker's efficiency — not to mention on his satisfaction on the job. How did the technology of the automobile assembly line affect the grouping of men at Plant X?

Most workers are located along the 'main line' according to the particular manpower requirements of each segment of the assembly process. Each operator works in a limited area completing his own operations independently of others as the car is carried by the conveyer down the line. A particular individual may talk with the men immediately around him, but these men cannot be said to comprise a bona fide work group in the usual sense of the term. Take as an illustration the polishing line. Exhibit 1 shows in diagrammatic form an actual interaction pattern of a left-front-door polisher, Worker E.

The ten men from A to J comprise a work group of which Worker E is a part, and he has some social contact with all the other nine. His really close contacts, however, are only with C, D, F and G. Note that these four workers comprise a group — *but only from E's point of view*. As to the social relationship pattern of G, his immediate group would consist of E, F. H and I; it would not include C and D, who were clearly members of E's group. Further variations occur, for example, when a line makes a bend or loop and brings men in different sections closer together. Thus each man, because of the nature of conveyer operations, has a slightly different circle of associates from that of the man next to him. So it goes along the entire stretch of a line, a line well over two miles long.

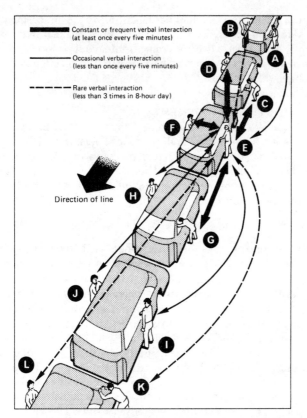

Exhibit 1   Social interaction pattern of typical main assembly line worker — polisher paint department

In our interviews these men exhibited little of what the sociologist would call 'in-group awareness'. Rarely, for example, did they talk about 'our team' or 'our group' or 'the men in our outfit'. Instead, the following remark was typical: 'I've been here over a year, and I hardly know the first names of the men in the section where I work'.

In sharp contrast, however, to the majority of line workers, a minority — principally off-line operators — worked on bona fide teams or crews; that is, they were members of a close working group, were functionally interdependent, and frequently assisted their fellows or exchanged operations with them. On charting the interaction pattern of such groups it was found that the frequency of conversational exchange was high and constant for nearly all members of the group. Of greater significance, the group exhibited a marked *esprit-de-corps* not found among the bulk of line operators.

It is clear that the present technology of an automobile assembly line limits social interaction and does not lend itself to the arrangement of men in bona fide teams or crews. It is suggested, however, that in the design of *new* plants, and at periods of retooling or of layout revisions, an effort be made to maximize the opportunities for social interaction and for team relationships.

RELATIONS WITH MANAGEMENT

Still another area of social relationships — that of worker to supervisor — is crucial to an intelligent understanding of social organization.

The formal organizational structure of the various production departments in Plant X was similar to that found in many plants. In interviews with workers we came to know the quality of relationship between workers and supervisors.

Foremen

Qualitative comments by the men about their foremen suggested a relatively informal and friendly relationship on the part of the majority. The average foreman had from 15 to 25 men under him, and talking between worker and foreman was generally frequent, friendly, and informal. The sort of remarks one hears about any good foreman were also heard here, as for example: 'Our foreman is a real good guy. We're lucky. If he got into trouble, the whole department would back him right up.'

There were criticisms of foremen, but usually these were not directed at the individual. Rather they were aimed at the 'line' and the role the foreman had to play with reference to the line. As one man said: 'After all, the foreman has to be a pusher, and nobody likes to be pushed. He's got to hold his job. If he doesn't push, somebody else will get his job.'

Often men exonerated foremen for 'pushing' since they recognized that the compulsion of line production was not the fault of the foremen. One man put it this way: 'I guess you'd say the foreman gets along with the men. But they don't need a foreman. *The line is the foreman.* You have to keep up with the line.'

Higher supervisors

An interesting finding which came out of the study was the relationship, or lack of it, between workers and management above the foreman level. The 180 men in our sample were asked to indicate contacts with supervisors in their department at the general foreman and department-head levels. Only 59 reported that they talked with their general foreman as often as once a week; 15 put it at one to three times a month; and 88 said less than once a month. Contact between workers and upper departmental supervisors was even less, with 70% saying they spoke with their department heads less than once a month. (Departments ranged in size from 200 to 400.)

It is significant in this connection that in a steel fabricating plant which we recently studied the workers talked far more frequently with supervisors above the foreman level. There the nature of the process and the high degree of worker skills made for a closer relationship. It was an everyday experience to find a superintendent in charge of 400 men talking with an individual worker or group of workers. He did this because the technical and skilled judgment of the individual worker was important in the production process.

On the automobile assembly line, on the other hand, because of the high degree of mechanization and fractional assembly there appears to be less need for supervisors to discuss production matters with individual workers. Management relies on the judgment of the engineer, not the worker. Thus the basic factor which determines the rate and quality of worker-supervisor interaction is the technology of mass production.

IMPACT ON WAGE STRUCTURE
Not the least important secondary effect of the mass-production method has been its impact on the wage structure. A leveling of workers' skills has inevitably resulted in a narrowing of differentials between wage grades, in contrast to industries where the latest mass-production methods have not been applied. For example, in the steel fabricating plant which we investigated — a seamless tube mill — the differential between the rates of the lowest and of the highest paid workers was over a dollar an hour. At Plant X, however, the differential between the lowest paid and the highest paid was around 10 cents for the major categories of production workers, and over half the workers in the production departments received exactly the same hourly wage.

It is obvious that changes in skill levels and in wage categories affect what the wage administrator calls the 'system of job progression'. Before the application of mass-production methods most industries had many well-defined steps in their ladders of promotion. Mass-production methods, while often raising the general level of wages and bringing other benefits, have knocked out a good many rungs in these promotion ladders. To turn again to the steel mill for contrast: there were as many as seven or eight steps from laborer to roller, each one associated with progressively higher wages, skills, and prestige.

This system of promotion, with its connotations of growth, incentive, and progress, has beeen weakened or virtually eliminated on the assembly line. Almost any assembly worker can — and some do — say: 'There are hundreds of jobs like mine, not much better, not much worse. The differences are so slight — or seem so slight to management — that I am interchangeable.' Consequently, to escape a resulting sense of anonymity as much, perhaps, as to escape monotony, the average worker at Plant X does not aspire to climb into another slightly better production job, but rather into a utility man's job or a repairman's job or out of production altogether, where he can be recognized, and where also he can recognize himself, as an individual.

Most of the benefits of the mass-production method are obvious and have often been celebrated. If we are to continue to enjoy them and to expand and refine the method, we should understand more fully its impact on the traditional organization of industry. Surely the problems as well as the promises of mass production are worthy of study.

CONCLUSION

It is obviously impossible in a single article to do more than sketch some of the problem areas in the broad field of relations between mass production and human nature. Concerning the direct impact of the method on the individual we made a few empirical suggestions and tried to point out at least one direction in which management might seek practical solutions.

But what can be said about the *indirect* impact of mass production on human nature through the character of work groups, the wage structure, and the promotion system? In a negative sense, at least, all these phenomena appear to be related: At Plant X they tended to increase the workers' sense of anonymity within the production enterprise of which they were functional parts. In fact, one way to express the net result of these several influences might be to say that little sense of membership in a common work community existed. (Our evidence showed that to some extent membership in the union gave the worker the feeling of personal identity and 'belonging' which neither the shop nor relations with management supplied.)

It seems to us significant that the average worker appeared to be oppressed by this sense of anonymity *in spite of the fact that he declared himself well satisfied with his rate of pay and the security of his job.* The answer to this problem in the most general terms would appear to be a program designed to re-create the sense *and also* the reality of a bona fide work community. And for such a program to be successful we believe that both union and management would have to agree on the measures to be taken.

A comment by a man on the line will suggest the nature of the problem more clearly than many paragraphs of exposition:

There is a different feeling in this plant. It's much bigger than people around here have ever seen. It's just like the kid who goes up to a grown-up man and starts talking to him. There doesn't seem to be a friendly feeling. At the plant I used to work in there was a different feeling. Everyone spoke to everyone else. . . . Nobody goes to other departments in this plant. The understanding could be better — happier and much easier. Here a man is just so much horsepower.

Perhaps the human needs in Plant X are merely an expression in more explicit terms of the needs of our industrial civilization. The problem of reintegrating the several faculties of man into a significant unity presents itself in many fields — in industry, science, and government, to name but three — in an age of overspecialization

It is striking that throughout the survey of Plant X both union and management agreed with the authors that the more basic problems to be explored were not those connected with a particular plant, industry, or corporation. Rather they were problems related to technological and organizational trends common to modern industry. Both agreed that modern American civilization as we know it rests upon mass-production principles quite as much as upon the natural resources of the United States. The attitude of both, therefore, was a simple and heartening one: *Since these problems exist, let us get all the facts we can. In time we shall be able to solve them.*

As Saint-Exupéry, the French aviator and author, wrote:

The Machine is not an end. . . . It is a tool. . . . like the plough.

If we believe that it degrades Man, it is possibly because we lack the perspective for judging the end results of transformations as rapid as those to which we have been subjected. What are two hundred years in the history of the Machine when compared with two hundred thousand years in the history of Man? We have scarcely established ourselves in this country of mines and of central electricity. It is as if we had hardly begun to live in the new house that we have not yet finished building. Everthing has changed so rapidly around us: human relations, conditions of work, customs. . . . Every step in our progress has driven us a little further from our acquired habits, and we are in truth pioneers who have not yet established the foundations of our new country.[3]

NOTES
1. The full details of this survey are published in book form: *The Man on the Assembly Line* (Cambridge, Mass.: Harvard University Press, 1952).
2. This is a rephrased and slightly more explicit statement of the three principles of mass production as set down in 'Mass Production' by Henry Ford in the *Encyclopaedia Britannica*, 14th ed., Vol. 15, pp. 38–9.
3. Antoine de Saint-Exupéry, *Terre des Hommes* (Paris: Gallimard, 1939) p. 58.

6 Job Design and Employee Motivation*

EDWARD E. LAWLER III
Yale University

The psychological literature on employee motivation contains many claims that changes in job design can be expected to produce better employee job performance. Very few of these claims, however, are supported by an explanation of why changes in job design should be expected to affect performance except to indicate that they can affect employee motivation. Thus, I would like to begin by considering the WHY question with respect to job design and employee performance. That is, I want to focus the reasons for expecting changes in job design to affect employee motivation and performance. Once this question is answered, predictions will be made about the effects on performance of specific changes in job design (e.g. job enlargement and job rotation).

A THEORY OF MOTIVATION
Basic to any explanation of why people behave in a certain manner is a theory of motivation. As Jones (1959) has pointed out, motivation theory attempts to explain 'how behavior gets started, is energized, is sustained, is directed, is stopped and what kind of subjective reaction is present in the organism'. The theory of motivation that will be used to understand the effects of job design is 'expectancy theory'. Georgopoulos, Mahoney, and Jones (1957), Vroom (1964) and others have recently stated expectancy theories of job performance. The particular expectancy theory to be used in this paper is based upon this earlier work and has been more completely described elsewhere (e.g. Lawler and Porter, 1967; Porter and Lawler, 1968). According to this theory, an employee's motivation to perform effectively is determined by two variables. The first of these is contained in the concept of an effort-reward probability. This is the individual's subjective probability that directing a given amount of effort toward performing effectively will result in his obtaining a given reward or positively valued outcome. This

---

*Personnel Psychology, XXII (1969) 426–35. Reprinted by permission.

effort-reward probability is determined by two subsidiary subjective probabilities: the probability that effort will result in performance and the probability that performance will result in the reward. Vroom refers to the first of these subjective probabilities as an expectancy and to the second as an instrumentality.

The second variable that is relevant here is the concept of reward value or valence. This refers to the individual's perception of the value of the reward or outcome that might be obtained by performing effectively. Although most expectancy theories do not specify why certain outcomes have reward value, for the purpose of this paper I would like to argue that the reward value of outcomes stems from their perceived ability to satisfy one or more needs. Specifically relevant here is the list of needs suggested by Maslow that includes security needs, social needs, esteem needs, and self-actualization needs.

The evidence indicates that, for a given reward, reward value and the effort-reward probability combine multiplicatively in order to determine an individual's motivation. This means that if either is low or nonexistent then no motivation will be present. As an illustration of this point, consider the case of a manager who very much values getting promoted but who sees no relationship between working hard and getting promoted. For him, promotion is not serving as a motivator, just as it is not for a manager who sees a close connection between being promoted and working hard but who doesn't want to be promoted. In order for motivation to be present, the manager must both value promotion and see the relationship between his efforts and promotion. Thus, for an individual reward or outcome the argument is that a multiplicative combination of its value and the appropriate effort-reward probability is necessary. However, an individual's motivation is influenced by more than one outcome. Thus, in order to determine an individual's motivation it is necessary to combine data concerned with a number of different outcomes. This can be done for an individual worker by considering all the outcomes he values and then summing the products obtained from multiplying the value of these outcomes to him by their respective effort-reward probabilities.

According to this theory, if changes in job design are going to affect an individual's motivation they must either change the value of the outcomes that are seen to depend upon effort, or positively affect the individual's beliefs about the probability that certain outcomes are dependent upon effort. The argument in this paper is that job design changes can have a positive effect on motivation, because they can change an individual's beliefs about the probability that certain rewards will result from putting forth high levels of effort. They can do this because they have the power to influence the probability that certain rewards will be seen to result from good performance, not because they can influence the perceived probability that effort will result in good performance. Stated in Vroom's language, the argument is that job design changes are more likely to affect the instrumentality of good performance than to affect the expectancy that effort will lead to performance.

Before elaborating on this point, it is important to distinguish between two kinds of rewards. The first type are those that are extrinsic to the individual. These rewards are part of the job situation and are given by others. Hence, they are externally-mediated and are rewards that can best be thought of as satisfying lower order needs. The second type of rewards are intrinsic to the individual and stem directly from the performance itself. These rewards are internally-mediated since the individual rewards himself. These rewards can be thought of as satisfying higher order needs such as self-esteem and self-actualization. They involve such outcomes as feelings of accomplishment, feelings of achievement, and feelings of using and developing one's skills and abilities. The fact that these rewards are internally-mediated sets them apart from the extrinsic rewards in an important way. It means that the connection between their reception and performance is more direct than is the connection between the reception of externally-mediated rewards and performance. Hence, potentially they can be excellent motivators because higher effort-reward probabilities can be established for them than can be established for extrinsic rewards. They also have the advantage that for many people rewards of this nature have a high positive value.

Job content is the critical determinant of whether employees believe that good performance on the job leads to feelings of accomplishment, growth, and self-esteem; that is, whether individuals will find jobs to be intrinsically motivating. Job content is important here because it serves a motive arousal function where higher order needs are concerned and because it influences what rewards will be seen to stem from good performance. Certain tasks are more likely to arouse motives like achievement and self-actualization, and to generate, among individuals who have these motives aroused, the belief that successful performance will result in outcomes that involve feelings of achievement and growth. It is precisely because changes in job content can affect the relationship between performance and the reception of intrinsically-rewarding outcomes that it can have a strong influence on motivation and performance.

There appear to be three characteristics which jobs must possess if they are to arouse higher order needs and to create conditions such that people who perform them will come to expect that good performance will lead to intrinsic rewards. The first is that the individual must receive meaningful feedback about his performance. This may well mean the individual must himself evaluate his own performance and define the kind of feedback that he is to receive. It may also mean that the person may have to work on a whole product or a meaningful part of it. The second is that the job must be perceived by the individual as requiring him to use abilities that he values in order for him to perform the job effectively. Only if an individual feels that his significant abilities are being tested by a job can feelings of accomplishment and growth be expected to result from good performance. Several laboratory studies have in fact shown that, when people are given tasks they see as testing their valued abilities, greater motivation does appear (e.g. Alper, 1946; French, 1955). Finally, the individual must feel he has a high degree of self-control over setting his own goals and over defining the paths to these goals. As Argyris (1964) points out, only if this condition exists will people experience psychological 'success' as a result of good performance.

Thus, it appears that the answer to the *why* question can be found in the ability of job design factors to influence employees' perceptions of the probability that good performance will be intrinsically rewarding. Certain job designs apparently encourage the perception that it will, while others do not. Because of this, job design factors can determine how motivating a job will be.

JOB DESIGN CHANGES

Everyone seems to agree that the typical assembly line job is not likely to fit any of the characteristics of the intrinsically-motivating job. That is, it is not likely to provide meaningful knowledge of result, test valued abilities, or allow self-control. Realizing this, much attention has been focused recently on attempts to enlarge assembly line jobs, and there is good reason to believe that enlarging assembly line jobs can lead to a situation where jobs are more intrinsically motivating. However, many proponents of job enlargement have failed to distinguish between two different kinds of job enlargement. Jobs can be enlarged on both the horizontal dimension and the vertical dimension. The horizontal dimension refers to the number and variety of the operations that an individual performs on the job. The vertical dimension refers to the degree to which the job holder controls the planning and execution of his job and participates in the setting of organization policies. The utility man on the assembly line has a job that is horizontally but not vertically enlarged, while the worker who Argyris (1964) suggests can participate in decision making about his job while he continues to work on the assembly line, has a vertically but not a horizontally-enlarged job.

The question that arises is, what kind of job enlargement is necessary if the job is going to provide intrinsic motivation? The answer, that is suggested by the three factors that are necessary for a task to be motivating, is that jobs must be enlarged both vertically and horizontally. It is hard to see, in terms of the theory, why the utility man will see more connection between performing well and intrinsic rewards than will the assembly line worker. The utility man typically has no more self-control, only slightly more knowledge of results, and only a slightly greater chance to test his valued abilities. Hence, for him, good performance should be only slightly more rewarding than it will be for the individual who works in one location on the line. In fact, it would seem that jobs can be over-enlarged on the horizontal dimension so that they will be less motivating than they were originally.

Excessive horizontal enlargement may well lead to a situation where meaningful feedback is impossible, and where the job involves using many additional abilities that the worker does not value. The worker who is allowed to participate in some decisions about his work on the assembly line can hardly be expected to perceive that intrinsic rewards will stem from performing well on the line. His work on the line still is not under his control, he is not likely to get very meaningful feedback about it, and his valued abilities still are not being tested by it. Thus, for him it is hard to see why he should feel that intrinsic rewards will result from good performance.

On the other hand, we should expect that a job which is both horizontally and vertically enlarged will be a job that motivates people to perform well. For example, the workers Kuriloff (1966) has described, who make a whole electronic instrument, check and ship it, should be motivated by their jobs. This kind of job does provide meaningful feedback, it does allow for self-control, and there is a good chance that it will be seen as testing valued abilities. It does not, however, guarantee that the person will see it as testing his valued abilities since we don't know what the person's valued abilities are. In summary, then, the argument is that if job enlargement is to be successful in increasing motivation, it must be enlargement that affects both the horizontal and the vertical dimensions of the job. In addition, individual differences must be taken into consideration in two respects. First and most obviously, it must only be tried with people who possess higher order needs that can be aroused by the job design and who, therefore, will value intrinsic rewards. Second, individuals must be placed on jobs that test their valued abilities.

Let me now address myself to the question of how the increased motivation, that can be generated by an enlarged job, will manifest itself in terms of behavior. Obviously, the primary change that can be expected is that the individual will devote more effort to performing well. But will this increased effort result in a higher quality work, higher productivity, or both? I think this question can be answered by looking at the reasons we gave for the job content being able to affect motivation. The argument was that it does this by affecting whether intrinsic rewards will be seen as coming from successful performance. It would seem that high quality work is indispensable if most individuals are to feel they have performed well and are to experience feelings of accomplishment, achievement, and self-actualization. The situation is much less clear with respect to productivity. It does not seem at all certain that an individual must produce great quantities of a product in order to feel that he has performed well. In fact, many individuals probably obtain more satisfaction from producing one very high quality product than they do from producing a number of lower quality products.

There is a second factor which may cause job enlargement to be more likely to lead to higher work quality than to higher productivity. This has to do with the advantages of division of labor and mechanization. Many job enlargement changes create a situation in which, because of the losses in terms of machine assistance and optimal human movements, people actually have to put forth more energy in order to produce at the pre job enlargement rate. Thus, people may be working harder but producing less. It seems less likely that the same dilemma would arise in terms of work quality and job enlargement. That is, if extra effort is devoted to quality after job enlargement takes place, the effort is likely to be translated into improved quality. This would come about because the machine assistance and other features of the assembly line jobs are more of an aid in bringing about high productivity than they are in bringing about high quality.

THE RESEARCH EVIDENCE
There have been a number of studies that have attempted to measure the effects of job enlargement programs. These were examined to determine if the evidence supports the contention stated previously that both horizontal and vertical job enlargement are necessary if intrinsic motivation is to be increased. Also sought was an indication of whether the effects of any increased motivation was more likely to result in higher quality work than in high productivity.

In the literature search, reports of ten studies where jobs had been enlarged on both the horizontal and the vertical dimensions were found. Table 1 presents a brief summary of the results of these studies. As can be seen, every study shows that job enlargement did have some positive effect since every study reports that job enlargement resulted in higher quality work. However, only four out of ten studies report that job enlargement led to higher productivity. This provides support for the view that the motivational effects produced by job enlargement are more likely to result in higher quality work than in high productivity.

There are relatively few studies of jobs enlarged only on either the horizontal or the vertical dimension so that it is difficult to test the

Table 1

Research study	Higher quality	Higher productivity
Biggane and Stewart (1963)	Yes	No
Conant and Kilbridge (1965) Kilbridge (1960)	Yes	No
Davis and Valfer (1965)	Yes	No
Davis and Werling (1960)	Yes	Yes
Elliott (1953)	Yes	Yes
Guest (1957)	Yes	No
Kuriloff (1966)	Yes	Yes
Marks (1954)	Yes	No
Rice (1953)	Yes	Yes
Walker (1950)	Yes	No

prediction that both kinds of enlargement are necessary if motivation is to be increased. There are a few studies which have been concerned with the effects of horizontal job enlargement (e.g. Walker and Guest, 1952), while others have stressed its advantages. However, most of these studies have been concerned with its effects on job satisfaction rather than its effects on motivation. None of these studies appears to show that horizontal enlargement tends to increase either productivity or work quality. Walker and Guest, for example, talk about the higher satisfaction of the utility men but they do not report that they work harder. Thus, with respect to horizontal job enlargement, the evidence does not lead to rejecting the view that it must be combined with vertical in order to increase production.

The evidence with respect to whether vertical job enlargement alone can increase motivation is less clear. As Argyris (1964) has pointed out, the Scanlon plan has stressed this kind of job enlargement with some success. However, it is hard to tell if this success stems from people actually becoming more motivated to perform their own job better. It is quite possible that improvements under the plan are due to better overall decision making rather than to increased motivation. Vroom (1964) has analyzed the evidence with respect to the degree to which participation in decision making per se leads to increased motivation. This evidence suggests that vertical job enlargement can lead to increased motivation when it leads to the employees' committing themselves to higher production goals.

Perhaps the crucial distinction here is whether the participation involves matters of company policy or whether it involves matters directly related to the employees' work process. Participation of the former type would seem much less likely to lead to increased motivation than would participation of the latter type. Thus, it seems to be crucial to distinguish between two quite different types of vertical job enlargement, only one of which leads to increased motivation. Considered together, the evidence suggests that, of the two types of job enlargement, vertical is more important than horizontal. Perhaps this is because it can lead to a situation in which subjects feel their abilities are being tested and where they can exercise self-control even though horizontal enlargement does not take place. Still, the evidence, with respect to situations where both types of enlargement have been jointly installed, shows that much more consistent improvements in motivation can be produced by both than can be produced by vertical alone.

SUMMARY
It has been argued that, when a job is structured in a way that makes intrinsic rewards appear to result from good performance, then the job itself can be a very effective motivator. In addition, the point was made that, if job content is to be a source of motivation, the job must allow for meaningful feedback, test the individual's valued abilities, and allow a great amount of self-control by the job holder. In order for this to happen, jobs must be enlarged on both the vertical and horizontal dimensions. Further, it was predicted that job

enlargement is more likely to lead to increased product quality than to increased productivity. A review of the literature on job enlargement generally tended to confirm these predictions.

REFERENCES

Alper, Thelma G., 'Task-orientation vs. Ego-orientation in Learning and Retention', *American Journal of Psychology*, XXXVIII (1946) 224–38.

Argyris, C., *Integrating the Individual and the Organization* (New York: Wiley, 1964).

Biggane, J. F. and Stewart, P. A., *Job Enlargement: A Case Study*. Research Series No. 25, Bureau of Labor and Management, State University of Iowa, 1963.

Conant, E. H. and Kilbridge, M. D., 'An Interdisciplinary Analysis of Job Enlargement: Technology, Costs, and Behavioral Implications', *Industrial and Labor Relations Review*, XVIII (1965) 377–95.

Davis, L. E. and Valfer, E. S., 'Intervening Responses to Changes in Supervisor Job Designs', *Occupational Psychology*, XXXIX (1965) 171–89.

Davis, L. E. and Werling, R., 'Job Design Factors', *Occupational Psychology*, XXXIV (1960) 109–32.

Elliot, J. D., 'Increasing Office Productivity through Job Enlargement', in *The Human Side of the Office Manager's Job*. A.M.A. Office Management Series, No. 134, New York, 1953, 5–15.

French, Elizabeth G., 'Some Characteristics of Achievement Motivation', *Journal of Experimental Psychology*, L (1955) 232–6.

Georgopoulos, B. S., Mahoney, G. M. and Jones, M. N., 'A Path-goal Approach to Productivity', *Journal of Applied Psychology*, XLI (1957) 345–53.

Guest, R. H., 'Job Enlargement: A Revolution in Job Design', *Personnel Administration*, XX (1957) 9–16.

Jones, M. R. (ed.), *Nebraska Symposium on Motivation* (Lincoln, Nebr.: Nebraska University Press, 1959).

Kilbridge, M. D., 'Reduced Costs through Job Enlargement: A Case', *Journal of Business*, XXXIII (1960) 357–62.

Kuriloff, A. H., *Reality in Management* (New York: McGraw-Hill, 1966).

Lawler, E. E. and Porter, L. W., 'Antecedent Attitudes of Effective Managerial Performance', *Organizational Behavior and Human Performance*, II (1967) 122–42.

Marks, A. R. N., 'An Investigation of Modifications of Job Design in an Industrial Situation and Their Effects on Some Measures of Economic Productivity'. Unpublished Ph.D. dissertation, University of California, Berkeley, 1954.

Porter, L. W. and Lawler, E. E., *Managerial Attitudes and Performance* (Homewood, Ill.: Irwin-Dorsey, 1968).

Rice, A. K., 'Productivity and Social Organization in an Indian Weaving Shed', *Human Relations,* VI (1953) 297–329.

Vroom, V. H., *Work and Motivation* (New York: Wiley, 1964).

Walker, C. R., 'The Problem of the Repetitive Job', *Harvard Business Review,* XXVIII (1950) 54–9.

Walker, C. R. and Guest, R. H., *The Man on the Assembly Line* (Cambridge, Mass.: Harvard University Press, 1952).

7 Job Enlargement and the Organizational Context*

CLAYTON P. ALDERFER
Yale University

The purpose of this paper is to report some findings from a job enlargement project carried out in a manufacturing organization over a period of three years. The paper basically has four parts. The first part deals with a review of the literature concerning the impact of job enlargement on employee attitudes. The second part describes the nature of the particular project. The third part reports the findings concerning the particular job enlargement project. The fourth part will present an analysis of the impact of the total organizational context on this particular job enlargement project.

REVIEW OF THE LITERATURE

A number of different investigators have reviewed the literature on job enlargement projects. From those reviews one can make a number of generalizations about the attitudes associated with job enlargement. The first generalization is that overall job satisfaction tends to be higher in enlarged jobs than in non-enlarged jobs. The second generalization is that the meaningfulness of the job tends to be higher in the enlarged job than in the more routine kind of blue-collar job. There is another attitude dimension, however, which is not as clearly understood. It concerns the impact of job enlargement on interpersonal relationships. Some reviewers have concluded that job enlargement tends to improve interpersonal relationships while others have reached the opposite conclusion.

Friedmann (1961, p. 47), for example, reported one study in which, as a result of job enlargement, the entire framework of communication and interaction was altered. Foremen began to discuss their problems directly with workers whose status and prestige increased as a consequence. In another experiment, described by Friedmann (1961, p. 52), the functions of supervisors were enlarged to include hiring employees, forming budgets, initiating changes, and directly handling complaints and grievances.

*Personnel Psychology, XXII (1969) 418—26. Reprinted by permission.

Other writers have suggested that job enlargement can be viewed as an alternative to working directly on improving interpersonal relationships. Guest (1957) suggested that human relations programs fail to improve morale, quality, and turnover because management fails to look at the nature of work itself. Davis (1966) suggested that human relations programs dealing with personal relationships and supervision are 'mere palliatives'. Changes in job design and organization are to be preferred.

However, in another job enlargement project, severe interpersonal problems were reported (Whyte, 1955). On an incentive-based assembly line operation women employees were allowed to control the speed of the line. As a result, their overall job satisfaction went up as did their pay. But repercussions throughout the plant also followed. Irritation grew between superintendent and foreman, engineers and foreman, and superintendent and engineers. Eventually the experiment was halted. The foreman and six of the eight girls participating in the enlargement left the organization.

Whyte's report is not fully congruent with the work reported by the other writers. His account suggests that job enlargement may not result in only desirable outcomes. The failure which he reports implies that the larger organizational context plays a key role in the results of job enlargement projects. A similar point will follow from the results of the present study.

THE JOB ENLARGEMENT PROGRAM

This job enlargement program was begun at the same time that the company introduced a new product and a new system of technology. The new product was an improved version of the same kind of product that they had been manufacturing for a number of years. The technology, as well, was the same order as had been used previously, but this technology added a number of significant improvements to the other types already present in the plant. The manufacturing operation was basically a continuous process system. Materials entered the system at the beginning and proceeded through a complex series of operations and different kinds of machines, emerging at the end as a finished product ready to be shipped to a sales outlet. The jobs which were enlarged concerned those people who had primarily responsibility for watching and tending the machines through which the developing product moved.

The organization in which this experiment was carried out prided itself in being concerned not only with the economic growth and well being of the organization but also with the kind of lives that the people who worked in the organization experienced while they were at work. In company literature one often found reference to the first and second goals of the organization. The first goal was to manufacture a good product which met consumer needs. The second goal was to provide a useful and meaningful work life for the employees. The very fact that there was a job enlargement program testifies to the commitment which the organization held toward its second goal. It is not uncommon, of course, for organizations to give only lip service to similar kinds of goals such as helping an employee to have a meaningful work life. But this organization was different from many in that it invested considerable time and energy in developing programs which were designed to help the employee have a more creative and self-fulfilling experience at work.

When the job enlargement program was being designed and this work was known among behavioral scientists, a number asked to be included in order to study the program. However, the organization chose to do the job enlargement program with essentially inside people and, therefore, many of the controls which might have been instituted had there been a behavioral scientist in the project from the outset were not included. One such control, of course, would have been random assignment of the employees to the enlarged jobs rather than specifically selecting people for these jobs. However, the organization members chose not to assign people randomly to these jobs, but rather to select carefully the employees who would participate in the enlargement experiment. Their goals in this selection were to get those they felt were the best possible blue-collar workers in the job enlargement project. Because a whole new technological system was introduced in the plant concurrently with the job enlargement program, the employees who worked on this project were physically separated from those who worked on other kinds of similar work in the plant.

Having taken considerable time and expense to select people for the job enlargement program, the organization then developed an educational program for these people. It is possible to consider three parts of the educational program. The first part consisted of a series of courses in which the employees were given the equivalent of additional high level high school courses in a number of areas, such as mathematics, physics, and chemistry. The second area of training concerned the kind of technical training that was needed for operating the newer more complicated machinery which the new technological process brought into the organization. The third kind of training concerned work in the area of interpersonal relationships. There was not nearly as much time spent with the interpersonal training as with the others, and there was some mention by both managers and educators in the organization that gave one the impression that the training in interpersonal relationships did not go smoothly and, indeed, may have caused problems for both enlargement people and for their supervision.

The new job itself, while similar to other machine-tending jobs in the organization, had a number of new features. First, as already indicated, the technical complexity of the newer machinery was higher than that present in existing machines. In addition, there were a number of what might be termed 'staff duties' which were associated with the new jobs. These staff duties included some jobs in the areas of accounting, personnel, and scheduling.

RESULTS FROM THE STUDY

The first results pertain to determining some of the psychological properties of the new jobs as they were evaluated, not by the job holders, but by other members of the organization. These 'company experts' were asked to rate some thirty jobs in the organization along a number of different dimensions. The jobs rated included many more than just the enlarged jobs and their analogous counterparts in the organization. From these ratings one could conclude that, as perceived by people who do not hold the jobs, the enlarged jobs differed from the analogous machine -tending jobs in having a higher requirement for technical competence, more opportunities for innovation, a greater variety of duties, a longer time until decision results were known, and in requiring more ability to deal effectively with people. These ratings, which were made by four experts who were not actually holding the enlarged jobs, showed a very high degree of agreement with each other. Thus, one can say that the enlarged jobs were significantly and substantially more complex than similar machine-tending jobs in the organization, as seen by company experts. It is also true that the employees holding the enlarged jobs received a higher rate of pay than their counterparts in other positions in the organization.

The next question concerns how the people who held the jobs themselves experienced their work. To answer this question, a job attitude questionnaire was administered throughout the organization, covering employees who held the least challenging jobs all the way along the job complexity dimension up through four levels of management. This attitude questionnaire had items pertaining to a number of different kinds of need satisfaction presented in the form of a seven-point Likert scale. Three needs will be the focus of attention in comparing the enlarged with the regular machine-tending jobs.

The first dimension was satisfaction with pay. The attitude scale which measured pay satisfaction had seven different items, some of them dealing with absolute pay satisfaction and others with relative or comparative pay satisfaction. Items in the questionnaire were factor-analyzed accordingly by the principal components method and rotated by the varimax procedure. One of the factors which emerged could rather clearly be labeled satisfaction with pay. Two items which loaded on the pay satisfaction factor were:

(1). 'Compared to the rates for similar work here my pay is good.'
(2). 'My pay is adequate to provide for the basic things in life.'

When the pay satisfaction between those employees with the older machine-tending jobs was compared with those of the enlarged machine-tending jobs, the people with the enlarged jobs tended to have significantly higher satisfaction with pay. This finding is not surprising since those with the enlarged jobs actually had higher rates of pay.

Another attitude scale had items which were designed to determine the degree to which an employee felt he was using his skills and abilities on the job and learning new things from his work experience. This scale had twelve items and also formed a clearly identifiable factor when the attitude items were factor-analyzed. Two samples from the scale were:

1. 'I have an opportunity to use many of my skills at work.'
2. 'This job has helped me to see some talents I never knew I had.'

The employees who held the enlarged jobs showed very significantly higher satisfaction with use of their skills and abilities.

The third attitude scale concerned satisfaction with respect from superiors. This scale, which also formed a factor, contained items such as:

1. 'It's easy to talk to my boss about my job.'
2. 'My boss will play one person against another.' (On the second item, disagreement was scored as satisfaction.)

The results indicate that the people holding the enlarged jobs tended to have significantly *lower* satisfaction with respect from superiors than the people holding the analogous unenlarged jobs.

To summarize the findings comparing the new, enlarged jobs with analogous but unenlarged jobs, one could say that those with the enlarged jobs tend to have higher satisfaction with pay and higher satisfaction with opportunities to use skills and abilities and lower satisfaction with respect from superiors.

It will be recalled that more than just the new and traditional maching-tending jobs were studied in this investigation. Therefore, it was of interest to examine the attitude patterns across the whole range of jobs in this manufacturing organization. This study has been carried out at some length and is recorded in detail elsewhere (Alderfer, 1967).

A summary of the major findings covering the wider range of jobs is as follows: First, satisfaction with pay was essentially constant over the whole range of jobs investigated; therefore, it was not a function of job complexity, even though the absolute pay received was a function of job complexity. Second, satisfaction with use of skills and abilities tended to increase as a function of job complexity. Third, satisfaction with respect from superiors tended to decrease as a function of job complexity. Thus, we can conclude that, over the full range of job complexity examined in this study, the patterns found in just comparing the newer enlarged jobs with the traditional machine-tending jobs were found to hold for two types of need satisfaction.

IMPACT OF THE ORGANIZATIONAL CONTEXT
Another variable which was found to be related to satisfaction with respect from superiors was seniority. The longer the person had been with the organization, the lower was his satisfaction with respect from

superiors. When this relationship was examined adjusting for job complexity, it still tended to be true. Thus, even though there was a tendency for job complexity to be positively associated with seniority, this did not in itself account for the fact that satisfaction with respect from superiors tended to decrease as a function of seniority. However, there was also a relationship between seniority and satisfaction with use of skills and abilities; the latter tended to increase as a function of seniority. However, when this relationship was adjusted for the effect of seniority varying with job complexity, the relationship between satisfaction with use of skills and abilities and seniority with job complexity adjusted by analysis of co-variance tended to indicate no relationship between satisfaction with use of skills and abilities and seniority. Therefore, one can conclude that satisfaction with use of skills and abilities was a function only of job complexity and not of seniority, while satisfaction with respect from superiors was a function both of job complexity and of seniority. Thus, one important dimension of the organizational context was isolated. Therefore, the lower satisfaction with respect from superiors found in enlarged jobs may have been due both to the jobs being more complex technically and to being part of an organizational context in which superior-to-subordinates relations seemed to decay with time.

In some ways the job enlargement experiment was designed to speed up the growth of a person within the organization. Certainly one meaning of growth is to increase one's rank in the organization. The data showed that this certainly tended to be true since the more complex jobs tended to have higher pay and more varied and challenging job duties. In addition, however, it turned out that the more complex jobs also tended to have lower satisfaction with respect from superiors. It can be suggested from these results that speeding up the growth process with job enlargement, in this organization, also had the effect of increasing the difficulties which the people in the enlarged jobs tended to have with their superiors. Therefore, in this organization with its particular context, the job enlargement was a mixed blessing and not a universal benefit to the employees.

One should be cautious in generalizing these results, because there were characteristics of this organization which may not fit all or even many other organizations. Just two of these variables will be mentioned briefly. The first is that it was an organization that was very successful economically. It had experienced quite rapid growth over the ten years preceding the time in which the study reported here was carried out. During this time of rapid growth, there were many opportunities for advancement for people at all levels in the organization. As a result, the investigator found advancement very much on the minds of most employees. They were frequently thinking about how they could better themselves in order to move up in the hierarchy. This kind of expectation would put additional strain on superior-to-subordinate relationships.

We must recall also that the more complex jobs had higher require- ments for being able to deal effectively with people. Continuous process technology is not necessarily characteristic of all settings where job enlargement has been implemented. It was present in this particular organization, but one characteristic of continuous process technology is that it puts a high demand for interdependency among employees in order to have a coordinated system. This need for coordination would seem to require more interpersonal skills on the part of both superiors and subordinates. The data reported by Whyte (1955), showing the failure of a much simpler job enlargement project, also were taken from a continuous process system.

We have, therefore, results from more than one project which suggest that under certain conditions job enlargement may be a mixed blessing. It seems particularly important to take account of the larger organizational context when job enlargement is contemplated. While job enlargement does, indeed, seem to be a way to make work meaningful, it takes place in a setting in which other people may be involved. To make the results of job enlargement even more beneficial, we must give more than passing attention to the interpersonal aspects of the change.

REFERENCES

Alderfer, C. P., 'An Organizational Syndrome', *Administrative Science Quarterly*, XII (1967) 440—60.

Davis, L. E., 'The Design of Jobs', *Industrial Relations*, VI (1966) 21—45.

Friedmann, Georges, *The Anatomy of Work* (Glencoe, Ill.: Free Press, 1961).

Guest, R. H., 'Job Enlargement — A Revolution in Job Design', *Personnel Administration*, XX (1957) 9—16.

Whyte, W. F., *Money and Motivation* (New York: Harper and Brothers, 1955).

PART III

Job Satisfaction and Environmental Factors

In this part papers are presented which cover a wide range of variables shown to affect individuals' job satisfaction. The paper of England and Stein shows that job satisfaction varies according to occupational level and whether an individual is a blue or white collar worker. The paper of Schwab and Wallace considers factors related to satisfaction with pay. As Schwab and Wallace point out, employees' satisfaction with pay should be of particular importance to organisations if for no other reason than that pay constitutes one of the major costs of business. Of great interest in their paper is the finding that pay by performance proved less satisfying than pay by time. They suggest that incentive systems are likely to disrupt the social system and this leads to feelings of inequity and dissatisfaction.

The paper by Porter and Lawler examines the effect of organisational structure on job satisfaction. 'Flat' structures are less complex structures with a maximum of administrative decentralisation compared to 'tall' structures, where there are a large number of administrative levels. Porter and Lawler found no overall difference in satisfaction for one structure compared to the other, although this to some extent depends on the size of the organisation. For small organisations satisfaction was greater in 'flat' organisations, but the position is reversed for large organisations. However, different structures affected different needs. Flat organisations helped to fulfil self-actualisation needs to a greater extent than did tall organisations.

The paper by Foa indicates the relationship between the supervisor and job satisfaction. He found that 'a stern attitude on the part of the supervisor goes together with lower satisfaction of the worker' but that attitudes to supervision vary with individuals' expectations concerning the nature of supervision.

The paper by Blood and Hulin serves to point out further that social factors affect the expectations that individuals have of their job, and therefore the satisfactions they are likely to derive. Industrialised, heterogeneous, metropolitan conditions are likely to foster alienation from middle-class values for industrial workers. Highly skilled jobs which have undergone enlargement may not appeal to such individuals, and Blood and Hulin cite evidence suggesting just this. Certainly research in this field has

107

indicated that job satisfaction cannot be divorced from the social situation in which people live.

The final paper in this part also shows the effects of social factors on job satisfaction. Van Zelst's study shows that where people can structure their own work groups on the basis of mutual attraction it can result 'in increased satisfaction on the part of the worker and greater financial returns on the part of management'.

8 Relation of Workers' Expectation to Satisfaction with Supervisor*

URIEL G. FOA
Israel Institute of Applied Social Research and Tel Aviv University

A number of investigations, carried out at the Survey Research Center of the University of Michigan, have shown a consistent relationship between certain patterns of supervisory behavior and workers' satisfaction (Kahn and Katz, 1953).

The findings of the present study,[1] which deals with Israeli workers, seem to confirm the conclusions reached at the University of Michigan: a stern attitude on the part of the supervisor goes together with lower satisfaction of the worker. When the worker's expectation, with regard to the behavior of the supervisor, is also considered, a different picture is, however, revealed: a certain supervisory attitude might lead to different levels of worker's satisfaction, according to whether such an attitude conforms or not with the expectation of the worker.

PROCEDURE

The data to be reported here represent part of a wider study[2] of the seagoing personnel of an Israel shipping company, and refer to the officers and crews of 18 ships.

Each subject, officer or member of the crew, was administered a questionnaire which included Guttman scales (Stouffer et al., 1950) on the following topics:

(a) Need for formal discipline on board the ship.
(b) Satisfaction with the ships' officers (crew only).

Here are the questions included in each scale:

Discipline
Do you think that a most strict discipline is always necessary on board ship?

* *Personnel Psychology*, X (1957) 161–8. Reprinted by permission.

1. A strict discipline on board ship is indispensable
2. Discipline on board ship is necessary
3. Discipline on board ship is desirable
4. Strict discipline is not necessary
5. Strict discipline is not at all necessary

Discipline on board ships requires that work should be carried out as instructed by the officers without any refusal at all. Do you think this requirement is right?

1. Definitely right, etc.

Do you think that the seamen should carry out any work, if so instructed by the officers?

1. Definitely yes; always, etc.

Satisfaction with officers

Are you satisfied with the attitude of the officers toward the seamen on your ship?

1. Always very satisfied
2. Almost always satisfied
3. Sometimes satisfied, and sometimes not
4. In many cases I am not satisfied
5. I am not at all satisfied

Do you think that the usual attitude of the officers on board your ship ensures good relationship between them and the seamen?

1. Definitely ensures, etc.

Do you think the fact that officers do not adopt the right attitude, prevents the establishment of good labor relations on board your ship?

1. Definitely does not prevent, etc.

Do you think that the attitude of the officers toward seamen on board your ship could be defined as snobbish?

1. Definitely not, etc.

The scalability of the two areas proved satisfactory. This also suggests fair reliability since, in the Guttman scale, reproducibility is a lower bound for reliability (Stouffer et al., 1950, p. 305).

The median score of the attitude toward discipline was computed for the whole population of respondents. Then the median score for the crew of each ship was also calculated and compared with the general median. Thus the ships were divided into two groups: ships with crews expecting more than an average degree of discipline; and ships with crews expecting less than an average degree of discipline. Let us call the expectation of the first type of crew 'authoritarian' and the expectation of the second type 'permissive'. Within each group the procedure was repeated with the officers. Thus the ships of each type of crew were again divided into two groups: ships with officers requiring more than an average degree of discipline, this is officers with 'authoritarian' attitude and ships with officers requiring less than an average degree of discipline, officers with

Table 1 Percentage distribution of scores (scale scores), on the discipline scale, for officers and men

Rank of respondents	Permissive							Authoritarian		Total Percentage	Absolute
	1	2	3	4	5	6	7	8	9		
Officers	—	—	—	—	1	7	31	29	32	100	99
Men	1	2	3	7	17	29	24	17		100	351
Both	1	2	2	6	14	30	25	20		100	450

'permissive' attitude. In conclusion the 18 ships were divided into four groups according to the degree of discipline required by the officers and the degree of discipline expected by the crews.

The next step was to find out whether the proportion of crewmen satisfied or dissatisfied with their officers varies significantly among the four groups. For this purpose the satisfaction attitude was dichotomized at the zero point of the intensity function (Stouffer et al., 1950, p. 213ff.).

RESULTS

The percentage distribution of the scores on the Discipline Scale is presented in Table 1, for officers and men separately, and for both combined.

As it could be expected, the officers are in favor of discipline more than the men. We may dichotomize the distribution between score 7 and 8, approximately at the median point. This leaves 55% of the respondents on the 'permissive' side of the scale and 45% of them on the 'authoritarian' side. A full 61% of the officers, and only 41% of the men, hold an 'authoritarian' attitude toward discipline.

The frequency distribution of the sailors on the scale of satisfaction with officers is given in Table 2. The zero point of this scale is in score 5:

Table 2 Percentage distribution of scores on the scale of satisfaction with officers for 'permissive' and 'authoritarian' men

Expectation of men toward discipline	Scores of satisfaction scale											Total	
	Dissatisfied				Zero point		Satisfied					Percentage	Absolute
	1	2	3	4	5	6	7	8	9	10	11		
Permissive	3	7	13	10	14	13	12	11	8	6	3	100	199
Authoritarian	3	2	4	5	10	12	8	21	9	13	13	100	136
Both	3	5	10	8	12	13	10	15	8	9	7	100	335

Note: The slight differences in the totals of the various tables are due to the omission of 'no answer'.

Job Satisfaction and Environmental Factors

Table 3 Satisfaction with officers of authoritarian and permissive men belonging to different types of crew

Prevailing expectation of crew	Expectation of men	Percentage satisfied with officers	Number of men in group
Authoritarian	Authoritarian	87	40
	Permissive	81	27
Permissive	Authoritarian	75	95
	Permissive	52	170
Both	Both	65	332

approximately three quarters of the frequencies of score 5 falls on the 'dissatisfied' side and the remaining quarter on the 'satisfied' side of the scale. Therefore 65% of the men are satisfied with the behavior of their officers. Among sailors with authoritarian expectation 78% are satisfied, as compared with 56% only among the sailors with permissive expectation.

Sailors with permissive expectation are more likely to be satisfied when they belong to a prevailing authoritarian crew, than to a permissive one. Table 3 shows that 81% of the permissive sailors, in an authoritarian crew, are satisfied, as against 52% in a permissive crew. This difference of 29% is significant, as we learn from Table 4. Authoritarian sailors, however, are nearly equally satisfied in either a permissive or an authoritarian crew.

In a crew where permissive expectations prevail, authoritarian sailors tend to be more satisfied than their mates with permissive expectations. The difference in satisfaction between authoritarian and permissive sailors, both belonging to a permissive crew, is 23% and it is significant, as shown by the χ^2 test[3], reported in Table 4.

When the expectations of the crew are mainly authoritarian, permissive sailors belonging to it are nearly as satisfied as authoritarian sailors. Thus authoritarian expectations, either of the individual sailor, or of the crew to which he belongs, seem to be conducive to higher satisfaction of the sailor.

We come now to the main point of this paper: the effects on satisfaction of the interaction between the predominant attitude of the officers and the prevailing expectation of the crew. The relevant findings

Table 4 Significance of differences in satisfaction when either crew's or sailor's expectations are kept constant

Constant	Difference between	χ^2	P value (approx.)
Crew: authoritarian	Authoritarian and permissive sailors	.57	.50
Crew: permissive	Authoritarian and permissive sailors	13.4	<.001
Sailor: authoritarian	Authoritarian and permissive crew	2.7	.10
Sailor: permissive	Authoritarian and permissive crew	8.3	<.01

Table 5   Percentage of sailors satisfied with ship officers by type of officers' attitude and crew's expectation prevailing aboard ship

Prevailing officers' attitude	Prevailing crew's expectation	Percentage of satisfied sailors	Number		
			Sailors	Officers	Ships
Authoritarian	Authoritarian	84	51	16	3
	Permissive	55	191	54	8
Permissive	Authoritarian	93	15	3	1
	Permissive	73	60	20	6
Both	Both	65	317	93	18

are reported in Table 5. Table 6 summarizes the result of the test of significance[3] of the differences in the satisfaction of the various groups.

It will be recalled that the four groups were obtained by comparing the median discipline score of the officers and of the men, in each ship, with the general median for all the respondents. The number of officers and sailors in the various groups is widely different because of the skewness of the distribution of the discipline scores. (See Table 1.)

When the officers are authoritarian, crews with prevailing authoritarian expectations are much more satisfied than crews with permissive expectations. The difference, 29%, is significant. Also significant is the difference, of 18%, between the satisfaction of crews with permissive expectations, respectively under authoritarian and permissive officers: those last are more satisfied. On the other hand when the officers are permissive, the expectation of the crew does not produce a significant difference in satisfaction. The same happens when the crew holds authoritarian expectations: the attitude of the officers does not change significantly the satisfaction of the men.

Thus the attitude of the officers is decisive when the crew expects permissiveness. The expectation of the crew is decisive when the officers tend to be authoritarian. On the average sailors under permissive officers tend to be significantly more satisfied than sailors under authoritarian officers.

Table 6   Significance of differences in satisfaction when either officers' attitudes or crew's expectations are kept constant

Constant	Difference between	χ^2	P value (approx.)
Officers: authoritarian	Authoritarian and permissive crews	14.12	<.001
Officers: permissive	Authoritarian and permissive crews	2.73	.10
Crews: authoritarian	Authoritarian and permissive officers	.74	.40
Crews: permissive	Authoritarian and permissive officers	5.98	<.02

CONCLUSION

Three factors have been discussed which contribute, under certain conditions, to determine the satisfaction of the sailor, namely:

1. The expectation of the sailor with regard to the behavior of the officers.
2. The prevailing expectation of the crew, to which the sailor belongs, with regard to the same behavior.
3. The prevailing attitude of the officers toward discipline.

Sailors with authoritarian expectation, or sailors belonging to a crew with such an expectation, are more likely to be satisfied with whatever behavior the officers might adopt. Officers with a permissive attitude are more likely to have satisfied men, no matter what the sailors' expectation is.

The results seem to indicate that, in the analysis of the relationship between supervisor and worker, one should consider the expectation of the worker as well as the attitude of the supervisor. An attempt to construct a broadened framework for investigating both aspects of the relationship has been described elsewhere (Foa, 1955, 1957).

In practice, it seems desirable, in order to increase satisfaction, to assign workers with permissive expectations to permissive supervisors or to groups where most workers have authoritarian expectations. Authoritarian supervisors should preferably be in charge of workers with prevailing authoritarian expectations. Permissive supervisors can team up with either type of worker; authoritarian workers with either type of supervisor.

REFERENCES

Foa, U. G., 'The Foreman—Worker Interaction: A Research Design', *Sociometry*, XVIII (1955) 226—44.

Foa, U. G., 'A Test of the Foreman—Worker Relationship', *Personnel Psychology*, IX (1957) 469—86.

Kahn, R. L. and Katz, D., 'Leadership Practices in Relation to Productivity and Morale', in *Group Dynamics: Research and Theory*, ed. D. Cartwright and Z. Zander (Evanston, Ill.: Row, Petersen and Co., 1953).

Stouffer, S., Guttman, L. et al., *Measurement and Prediction* (Princeton, N.J.: Princeton University Press, 1950).

NOTES

1. This study is part of a program of research, on human factors in production, supported by the Ford Foundation.
2. This project was supervised by Mr. Moshe Sandberg of the Israel Institute of Applied Social Research.
3. The advice received from Dr. Louis Guttman, on the procedure for testing the significance of the data, is gratefully acknowledged.

9 Correlates of Employee Satisfaction with Pay[*]

DONALD P. SCHWAB
Associate Professor of Personnel and Industrial Relations,
University of Wisconsin, Madison

MARC J. WALLACE, JR
Assistant Professor of Administrative Science and
Industrial Relations, University of Kentucky

Of the many aspects of job satisfaction investigated in recent years, satisfaction with pay appears to be most deserving of additional study. Employee satisfaction with pay should be of particular importance to organizations if for no other reason than that pay constitutes a substantial — often the major — cost of doing business. Despite its importance, however, considerable controversy has surrounded discussions of satisfaction with pay, and only recently have we begun to learn something about the personal and organizational factors associated with pay satisfaction.

This study[1] examines six personal and organizational correlates of pay satisfaction of both male and female nonexempt employees in a large firm manufacturing durable consumer goods. In general, the results indicate that although satisfaction with pay is related to several of the observed variables, the vast majority of the variance in pay satisfaction is not explained with the variables used in this study. Based on these results, additional variables worth investigating are suggested for future research.

RESEARCH ON PAY SATISFACTION

A major source of the controversy over the meaning of pay satisfaction has resulted from the conflicting positions put forth by various behavioral scientists. Herzberg, for example, has maintained that pay can lead only to feelings of dissatisfaction (i.e. pay is a 'hygienic factor' in the work environment).[2] The evidence seems to support Herzberg only to the extent that we know pay is a major source of dissatisfaction.[3] However,

Industrial Relations, XIII (1974) 78—89. Reprinted by permission.

the evidence clearly does not support the hypothesis that pay (or other so-called hygienes) operates only as a dissatisfier.[4]

An apparently more defensible view holds that pay satisfaction should be regarded as a continuous variable ranging from positive (satisfied) to negative (dissatisfied) feelings. Discrepancy theories of satisfaction such as Locke's and Porter's posit that satisfaction is a function of the employee's comparison of what exists on his job with what he seeks on the job.[5] Pay satisfaction results when existing pay corresponds to desired pay; dissatisfaction increases as the two diverge. Equity theories proposed by Adams, Jacques, and Patchen also view pay satisfaction as a unidimensional continuum possessing both positive and negative values.[6]

Efforts focusing on the correlates of pay satisfaction have centered around various individual and organizational variables. Lawler has reviewed a substantial amount of this literature.[7] (This review and a model he has proposed based on both discrepancy and equity theory are explicated in Appendix A.) Unfortunately, most of the studies reviewed by Lawler are subject to two major criticisms. First, they are mainly univariate studies looking only at pay satisfaction and one other variable. Lawler points out that, as a consequence, it is often '. . . impossible to tell whether the relationship found between a variable and pay satisfaction is due to the effect of the variable studied or another variable'.[8] For example, Andrews and Henry and Rosen and Weaver report that pay satisfaction is positively related to organization level.[9] However, when pay level is controlled, as was done by Lawler and Porter, the evidence suggests that pay satisfaction is negatively related to organization level.[10] Thus, the positive pay satisfaction-organization level link observed by Andrews and Henry and Rosen and Weaver may be a consequence of the fact that both are positively related to pay level.

There are several means available for disentangling the effects of various independent variables on pay satisfaction.[11] The most appropriate method is to control for multiple influences on pay satisfaction through multivariate statistical procedures. This alternative has the twin advantages of utilizing the entire sample and of simultaneously identifying the impact of each independent variable on pay satisfaction when all other independent variables are controlled. Lawler and Porter have reported the results of such a study among a sample of managers.[12] They found that only actual pay level was appreciably associated with pay satisfaction when measured with Porter's need satisfaction questionnaire. The other variables examined in their study were line/staff position, time in position and with company, organization size and level, age, and education. To our knowledge, no analogous study has been performed on nonexempt employees.

A second major problem with previous studies conducted on pay satisfaction concerns the measures of pay employed. These studies frequently used a few questionnaire items about satisfaction with pay that were tailor-made for the research in question. The nonstandardized nature of the measures makes it difficult to determine to what degree differences in the empirical findings are a function of differences in the measures used.

METHOD AND HYPOTHESES
The present study was designed to ameliorate the two major limitations in the evidence reviewed by Lawler.[13] Partial and multiple correlation analyses were employed to examine the joint influence of two organizational and four personal characteristics upon pay satisfaction: (1) organization level, (2) method of wage payment, (3) the individual's wage level, (4) age, (5) sex, and (6) tenure with the company. Partial correlation analysis enabled us to examine the relationship between any of the six independent variables and pay satisfaction while controlling for the linear effects of the other independent variables. Multiple correlation analysis allowed us to examine the joint impact of all independent variables on pay satisfaction. (Details of the analytical model are presented in Appendix B.)

Along with Lawler, we hypothesized that pay satisfaction would be positively related to pay level and negatively related to organization level, age, and tenure, and that males would be less satisfied with their pay than females.

Our review of the literature, however, led us to disagree with Lawler's prediction that employees paid according to the amount they produce will be more satisfied than those paid by the amount of time worked. Lawler cited only one unpublished study in support of this hypothesis,[14] and there is some limited additional evidence supporting the notion that a positive relation exists between satisfaction and perceptions about the strength of the linkage between performance and rewards (i.e. the stronger the perceived linkage, the higher the satisfaction).[15] However, three recent empirical studies suggest that performance-based pay systems may not result in higher pay satisfaction than time-based pay systems. In experimental studies Cherrington, Reitz, and Scott found no relationship between satisfaction and type of reinforcement system.[16] Pritchard, Dunnette, and Jorgensen found that persons paid by time actually had higher satisfaction than those paid on incentive.[17] A study of professional employees concluded that the pay of the more satisfied employees was based primarily on time in rank and educational level, while the pay of dissatisfied employees depended more on supervisory assessments of performance.[18] Therefore, contrary to Lawler, we predicted that employees would find incentive-based pay systems less satisfying than time-based systems.

SAMPLE AND MEASURES
The organization studied is a large manufacturer of durable consumer goods employing approximately 2,000 nonexempt male and female employees. About half of the work force is paid on an hourly basis while

the other half is paid under either a piece rate or group incentive plan. Individuals are assigned to pay systems primarily on the basis of organizational need rather than the interests or desires of the employees. Hence, there is no reason to suspect any systematic self-selection into various pay systems.

A random sample of 350 employees stratified by type of pay system was drawn from the total population of workers. Respondents included 273 (78 per cent) of the survey population. Of this group, 61 were hourly paid, 84 were under a group incentive plan and 128 worked under a piece rate system. Mean employee age was 35.6 years, mean tenure with the firm was 6.4 years, and average hourly earnings was $2.68. Sixty-five per cent of the sample were females and 66 per cent were married.

Data on three of the independent variables — age, sex, and tenure with the firm — were obtained from questionnaire responses. The type of pay system, wage level, and organizational level were obtained from the company's personnel records.

In order to alleviate the measurement problems identified earlier, pay satisfaction was measured by the Minnesota Satisfaction Questionnaire (MSQ) and the Cornell Job Description Index (JDI).[19] The MSQ asks each respondent to specify how satisfied he is with 100 aspects of his job and to respond by checking one of five categories on a rating scale ranging from very dissatisfied (1) to very satisfied (5). Five items constitute the compensation scale: (1) 'The amount of pay for the work I do', (2) 'The chance to make as much money as my friends', (3) 'How my pay compares with that for similar jobs in other companies', (4) 'My pay and the amount of work I do', and (5) 'How my pay compares with that of other workers'. Ratings are summed across the five items to derive a total pay satisfaction score.

The JDI asks each person to describe five aspects of his job by responding to an adjective check list. In the case of pay, nine adjectives or phrases are used: (1) 'income adequate for normal expenses', (2) 'satisfactory profit sharing', (3) 'barely live on income', (4) 'bad', (5) 'income provides luxuries', (6) 'insecure', (7) 'less than I deserve', (8) 'highly paid', and (9) 'underpaid'. A yes response to a positive item or a no response to a negative item is scored 3, a question mark to any item is scored 1, and a yes to a negative item or a no to a positive item is scored 0. Total pay satisfaction is obtained by summing across the nine items.

RESULTS
Intercorrelations between independent variables
The zero-order correlations between the independent variables are shown in Table 1. Intercorrelations are quite substantial between wage level and organization level, piece rate and group rate, and age and tenure.[20] The degree of these intercorrelations demonstrates the need to control for the joint effects of these independent variables on pay satisfaction (the degree of

Table 1   Intercorrelation between the independent variables

	Organization level	Wage level	Piece rate	Group rate	Age	Tenure	Sex
Organization level		.64	−.33	.09	.23	.17	.47
Wage level			−.13	.25	.22	.17	.38
Piece rate				−.62	.06	−.04	−.32
Group rate					−.21	−.15	.25
Age						.67	−.11
Tenure							.13
Sex							

multicollinearity does not appear high enough, however, to require deletion of any of the independent variables from the analyses). Even in the case of the three highest zero-order correlations, the maximum common variance (r^2) is still less than 50 per cent. The median intercorrelation among all independent variables (ignoring sign) is .21, indicating a median common variance of only 4 per cent.

Correlates of pay satisfaction
Correlations between each of the independent variables and the two measures of satisfaction with pay are presented in Table 2. The zero-order correlations between organization level and the two pay satisfaction measures are not significant. When the linear effects of other variables (including wage level) are partialled out, however, the relationships become statistically significant in a negative direction. That is, when wage

Table 2   Zero-order and partial correlations between the independent variables and pay satisfaction

Variable	MSQ		JDI	
	Zero-order	Partial	Zero-order	Partial
Organization level	.04	−.12[c]	−.05	−.16[d]
Wage level	.24[d]	.36[d]	.13[c]	.29[d]
Piece rate[a]	.07	−.12[c]	.00	−.14[c]
Group rate[a]	−.10	−.18[d]	.00	−.14[c]
Age	.11	−.02	−.08	−.03
Tenure	.03	−.01	−.16[d]	−.13[c]
Sex[b]	−.18[d]	−.24[d]	−.12[c]	−.12[c]
R		(.42)[d]		(.34)[d]

[a]Dummy coded, piece rate (group rate) = 1; other 0.
[b]Dummy coded, female = 0; male = 1.
[c]$p < .05$.
[d]$p < .01$.

level is held constant, persons higher in the organizational hierarchy are less satisfied with their pay. This finding supports Lawler's hypothesis.[21] His hypothesis with respect to the relationship between wage level and pay satisfaction is also supported: on both pay satisfaction measures, the zero-order and partial correlations are positive and significant, indicating that higher pay is associated with higher satisfaction.

Examination of the zero-order correlations between type of pay system and the two pay satisfaction measures yields no evidence that wage-payment method is related to pay satisfaction. However, when the influence of other variables is controlled, the relationships between piece rate payment and pay satisfaction and between group incentive payment and pay satisfaction are negative. Thus, as hypothesized, workers paid under piece rate and group incentive systems were less satisfied with their pay than were those who were paid under an hourly system. The data indicate no appreciable difference in the degree of pay dissatisfaction between piece rate and group rate members.

Our hypotheses are not supported in the case of age and only partially supported in the case of tenure. When the effects of other variables are held constant, age has no significant influence on pay satisfaction. Only in the case of the JDI pay measure does tenure appear to have a negative influence. Finally, our hypothesis concerning sex appears to be supported: females are significantly more satisfied with their pay than males on both scales. This is true in both the zero-order and partial correlation analyses.

DISCUSSION

Our results lend support to several of Lawler's hypotheses. Both measures of pay satisfaction were most highly related to pay level. Organization level and sex were also significantly related in the direction hypothesized. Age and tenure did not appear to have independent influences on pay satisfaction. These results are similar to those obtained by Lawler and Porter in a comparable study of managers.[22] They also found that pay level had the highest correlation with pay satisfaction. In addition, they found organization level to be negatively related with pay satisfaction but found a slight positive relation between satisfaction and tenure.

The most pronounced departure from Lawler's hypotheses was our finding that hourly paid employees were more satisfied with their pay than those paid under individual or group incentives. In other words, those who were paid by performance were actually less satisfied with their pay than those paid by time. These data lend support to Whyte's contention that incentive systems are likely to disrupt the social system and thus lead to feelings of inequity and dissatisfaction.[23] Generalization of these results, however, to other groups of employees (e.g. professional or managerial) and other types of pay systems (e.g. merit plans) must obviously await additional empirical investigations.

This study clearly shows the need to employ partial correlation analysis in addition to conventional zero-order analysis in studies of this sort. The need is demonstrated most dramatically in the cases of organization level and type of pay system. In both, nonsignificant zero-order correlations with pay satisfaction became significant negative partial correlations when the effects of the other independent variables were controlled. Results similar to these should generally be expected since characteristics of individuals and organizations such as age and tenure, organization level, wage level, and wage payment system are likely to be intercorrelated.[24]

It is also interesting to note that the observed relationships between each of the independent variables and pay satisfaction were strikingly similar using either the MSQ or the JDI as measures of satisfaction with pay. Only in the case of tenure was a significant partial correlation observed with one measure and not the other. Since the correlation between the pay satisfaction items of the two measures was only .56, the overall similarity in results using these measures was not statistically inevitable. We recommend that other investigators employ both measures to determine whether they yield approximately the same results and to use additional independent variables such as education level, socio-economic status, race or ethnic background, and job performance.

Finally, while our results are positive in several respects, they indicate that we are far from a complete understanding of the correlates of pay satisfaction. Reference to the multiple correlation coefficients for the MSQ (.42) and the JDI (.34) shows that organization and wage level, type of pay system, age, tenure, and sex together account for 18 per cent of the variance in pay satisfaction measured by the MSQ and only 12 per cent of the variance in pay satisfaction measured by the JDI. These results constitute an improvement over those obtained by Lawler and Porter, most likely because we included sex and type of pay system as independent variables.[25] Nevertheless, the results to date appear to have only limited practical significance. We need to learn a great deal more about the determination of pay satisfaction before management can be sure of influencing this job outcome through personnel policies and procedures.

APPENDIX A

Partial literature review and explanatory model

Lawler proposed that pay satisfaction be viewed as a function of the perceived discrepancy between: (1) the amount of money a person feels he should receive on his job, and (2) the amount of money he actually receives.[26] Equity theory enters the model by specifying the first perception. The standard against which a person compares his pay is a judgment of what he thinks the job *should* pay (i.e. what he perceives to be equitable). This judgment, according to Lawler, is not influenced by what a person would like to receive, but rather primarily by a number of equity factors: perceived personal job inputs, perceived inputs and

Table 3   Hypothesized influence of personal and job factors upon pay satisfaction

Factor	Hypothesized direction of relationship with pay satisfaction	Empirical evidence[b]
1. Education	−	Andrews & Henry; Cantril; Klein & Maher; Penzer
2. Skill	−	Equity research (see Goodman & Friedman; Pritchard; Milkovich & Campbell)
3. Job performance	−	Porter & Lawler; Penner
4. Age[a] and seniority[a]	−	Morse; Lawler & Porter (1966); Hulin and Smith
5. Sex (0 = female, 1 = male)[a]	−	Hulin & Smith; Morse; Stockford & Kunze
6. Organization level[a]	−	Lawler & Porter (1963, 1966); Andrews & Henry; Rosen & Weaver; Porter
7. Time span	−	Jacques; Richardson
8. Nonmonetary outcomes	+	Penner
9. Amount of pay[a]	+	Lawler & Porter (1963); Porter & Lawler; Locke; Morse; Centers & Cantril
10. Anticipated future earnings	?	Andrews & Henry; Klein & Maher
11. Wage payment method[a] (hourly = 0, incentive = 1)		Penner; Lawler; Wofford; Mitchell & Albright; Graen; Yukl, Wexley, & Seymore; Taylor; Roethlisberger & Dickson; Dalton; Whyte; Cherrington, Reitz & Scott; Finn & Lee; Pritchard, Dunnette, & Jorgensen

[a]Included in the present study.
[b]See References, pp. 124−6.

outcomes of referent others, perceived job characteristics, perceived nonmonetary outcomes, and wage history. The second perception, amount of pay received, is hypothesized to be influenced by the individual's pay history, perceived pay of referent others, and the individual's actual pay rate.

Lawler's model also specifies elements of perceived personal job inputs (skill, experience, training, effort, age, seniority, education, company loyalty, past performance, and present performance), elements of perceived job characteristics (level of difficulty, timespan of discretion, amount of responsibility), and elements of perceived nonmonetary outcomes (status and security).[27]

From his review of the literature on pay satisfaction, Lawler found 11 personal and organizational factors that bear on the model. These variables and their hypothesized relationships with pay satisfaction are shown in Table 3.[28] For example, the negative sign adjacent to the first variable means that education and pay satisfaction are hypothesized to be negatively related. This hypothesis is based partially on the model since education represents an input, and, other things being equal, the higher the input, the lower the satisfaction. The hypothesis is also partially based on the empirical evidence found by Lawler (although it should not be assumed that all the evidence reported for all the hypothesized relationships was in the directions posited in Table 3). Studies bearing on the relationships between pay satisfaction and each of the 11 independent variables are shown on the right side of Table 3. Some of these references are reported by Lawler and some were found during the review conducted for this study.

APPENDIX B
Analytical model
Multiple linear regression functions were fitted to the data to derive partial correlational coefficients between each of the independent variables and the two measures of pay satisfaction. The population model can be represented as:

$$S = a + b_1 x_1 + b_2 x_2 + b_3 x_3 + b_4 x_4 + b_5 x_5 + b_6 x_6 + b_7 x_7 + e$$

where

S = satisfaction
x_1 = organization level
x_2 = wage level
x_3 = piece rate = 1; group and hourly rate = 0
x_4 = group rate = 1; piece and hourly rate = 0
x_5 = age
x_6 = sex, male = 1; female = 0
x_7 = tenure
e = residual
a = constant
b = partial regression weights

Organization level, wage level, age, and tenure entered the functions as continuous variables. Sex was coded as a dummy variable. The three wage payment methods were entered into the functions as two dummy variables $(x_3 + x_4)$ in a manner described by Cohen.[29] The coding scheme was as follows:

	x_3	x_4
Piece rate	1	0
Group rate	0	1
Hourly rate	0	0

REFERENCES

Adams, J. Stacey, 'Injustice in Social Exchange', in *Advances in Experimental Social Psychology*, vol. 2, ed. L. Berkowitz (New York: Academic Press, 1965).

Andrews, I. R. and Henry, M. M., 'Management Attitudes toward Pay', *Industrial Relations*, III (1963) 29–39.

Argyris, C., 'Some Unintended Consequences of Rigorous Research', *Psychological Bulletin*, LXX (1968) 185–97.

Campbell, D. T. and Stanley, J. C., *Experimental and Quasi-Experimental Designs for Research* (Chicago: Rand McNally, 1963).

Cantril, H., 'Identification with Social and Economic Class', *Journal of Abnormal and Social Psychology*, XXXVIII (1943) 171–246.

Centers, R. and Cantril, H., 'Income Satisfaction and Income Aspiration', *Journal of Abnormal and Social Psychology*, XLI (1946) 64–9.

Cherrington, D. J., Reitz, H. J. and Scott, Jr, W. E., 'Effects of Contingent and Noncontingent Reward on the Relationship between Satisfaction and Task Performance', *Journal of Applied Psychology*, LV (1971) 531–6.

Cohen, J., 'Multiple Regression as a General Data-Analytic System', *Psychological Bulletin*, LXX (1968).

Dalton, M., 'The Industrial "Rate-Buster": a Characterization', *Applied Anthropology*, VII (1948) 5–18.

Dunnette, M. D., Campbell, J. P. and Hakel, M. D., 'Factors Contributing to Job Satisfaction and Job Dissatisfaction in Six Occupational Groups', *Organizational Behavior and Human Performance*, II (1967) 143–74.

Finn, R. H. and Lee, S. M., 'Salary Equity: its Determination, Analysis and Correlates', *Journal of Applied Psychology*, LVI (1972) 283–92.

Goodman, P.S. and Friedman, A., 'An Examination of Adams' Theory of Inequity', *Administrative Science Quarterly*, XVI (1971) 271–88.

Graen, G., 'Instrumentality Theory of Work Motivation: Some Experimental Results and Suggested Modifications', *Journal of Applied Psychology Monograph*, LIII (1969) 1–25.

Herzberg, F., *Work and the Nature of Man* (Cleveland: World Publishing, 1966).

House, R. J. and Wigdor, L. A., 'Herzberg's Dual-Factor Theory of Job Satisfaction and Motivation: a Review of the Evidence and a Criticism', *Personnel Psychology*, XX (1967) 369–89.

Hulin, C. L. and Smith, P. A., 'Sex Differences in Job Satisfaction', *Journal of Applied Psychology*, XLVIII (1964) 88–92.

Hulin, C. L. and Smith, P. A., 'A Linear Model of Job Satisfaction', *Journal of Applied Psychology*, LI (1967) 396–402.

Jacques, E., *Equitable Payment* (New York: Wiley, 1961).

King, N., 'Clarification and Evaluation of the Two-Factor Theory of Job Satisfaction', *Psychological Bulletin*, LXXIV (1970) 18–31.

Klein, S. M. and Maher, J. R., 'Education Level and Satisfaction with Pay', *Personnel Psychology*, XIX (1966) 195–208.

Lawler III, E. E., 'Managers' Attitudes toward How Their Pay Is and Should Be Determined', *Journal of Applied Psychology*, L (1966) 273–9.

Lawler III, E. E., *Pay and Organizational Effectiveness: A Psychological View* (New York: McGraw-Hill, 1971).

Lawler III, E. E. and Porter, L. W., 'Perceptions Regarding Management Compensation', *Industrial Relations*, III (1963) 41–9.

Lawler III, E. E. and Porter, L. W., 'Predicting Managers' Pay and Their Satisfaction with Their Pay', *Personnel Psychology*, XIX (1966) 363–73.

Locke, E. A., 'What is Job Satisfaction?', *Organizational Behavior and Human Performance*, IV (1969) 309–36.

Milkovich, G. T. and Campbell, K., 'A Study of Jacques' Norms of Equitable Payment', *Industrial Relations*, XI (1972) 267–71.

Mitchell, T. R. and Albright, D. W., 'Expectancy Theory Predictions of the Satisfaction, Effort, Performance, and Retention of Naval Aviation Officers', *Organizational Behavior and Human Performance*, VIII (1972) 1–20.

Morse, N. C., *Satisfactions in the White-Collar Job* (Ann Arbor: University of Michigan, Survey Research Center, 1953).

Patchen, M., *The Choice of Wage Comparisons* (Englewood Cliffs, N.J.: Prentice-Hall, 1961).

Penner, D. D., cited in Lawler, 1971, pp. 223–9.

Penzer, W. N., 'Education Level and Satisfaction with Pay: An Attempted Replication', *Personnel Psychology*, XXII (1969) 185–99.

Porter, L. W., 'A Study of Perceived Need Satisfactions in Bottom and Middle Management Jobs', *Journal of Applied Psychology*, XLV (1961) 1–10.

Porter, L. W. and Lawler, E. E., *Managerial Attitudes and Performance* (Homewood, Ill.: Irwin-Dorsey, 1968).

Pritchard, R. D., 'Equity Theory: a Review and Critique', *Organizational Behavior and Human Performance*, IV (1969) 176–211.

Pritchard, R. D., Dunnette, M. D. and Jorgensen, D. O., 'Effects of Perceptions of Equity and Inequity on Worker Performance and Satisfaction', *Journal of Applied Psychology Monograph*, LVI (1972) 75–94.

Richardson, R., *Fair Pay and Work* (Carbondale, Ill.: Southern Illinois University Press, 1971).

Roethlisberger, F. J. and Dickson, W. J., *Management and the Worker* (Cambridge, Mass.: Harvard University Press, 1939).

Rosen, H. and Weaver, C. G., 'Motivation in Management: a Study of Four Management Levels', *Journal of Applied Psychology,* XLIV (1960) 386–92.

Schwab, D. P. and Heneman III, H. G., 'Aggregate and Individual Predictability of the Two-Factor Theory of Job Satisfaction', *Personnel Psychology,* XXIII (1970) 55–66.

Smith, P. C., Kendall, L. M. and Hulin, C. L., *The Measurement of Satisfaction in Work and Retirement* (Chicago: Rand McNally, 1969).

Stockford, L. O. and Kunze, K. R., 'Psychology and the Pay Check', *Personnel,* XXVII (1950) 129–43.

Taylor, F. W., *The Principles of Scientific Management* (New York: Harper, 1911).

Vroom, V. H., *Work and Motivation* (New York: Wiley, 1964).

Weiss, D. J., Dawis, R. V., England, G. W. and Lofquist, L. H., *Manual for the Minnesota Satisfaction Questionnaires* (Minneapolis: University of Minnesota, Industrial Relations Center, 1967) Bulletin 45.

Whyte, W. F., *Money and Motivation* (New York: Harper and Brothers, 1955).

Wofford, J. C., 'The Motivational Bases of Job Satisfaction and Job Performance', *Personnel Psychology,* XXIV (1971) 501–18.

Yukl, G., Wexley, K. N. and Seymore, J. D., 'Effectiveness of Pay Incentives under Variable Ratio and Continuous Reinforcement Schedules', *Journal of Applied Psychology,* LVI (1972) 19–23.

NOTES

1. This study was supported in part by a grant to the senior author from the American Society for Personnel Administration Foundation and the Graduate School of the University of Wisconsin-Madison, and was completed while he was a Visiting Professor at the University of Kentucky. Both authors thank Bernard Gillet for research assistance.
2. Herzberg, 1966, pp. 71–90.
3. Lawler, 1971, p. 216; Vroom, 1964, p. 150.
4. Dunnette, Campbell and Hakel, 1967; House and Wigdor, 1967; King, 1970; Schwab and Heneman, 1970.
5. Locke, 1969; Porter, 1961.
6. Adams, 1965, pp. 267–99; Patchen, 1961; Jacques, 1961, pp. 151–72. For reviews of equity theory, see Goodman and Friedman, 1971; Milkovich and Campbell, 1972, pp. 267–71; Pritchard, 1969.
7. Lawler, 1971, pp. 205–30.
8. Ibid., p. 221.
9. Andrews and Henry, 1963; Rosen and Weaver, 1960.

10. Lawler and Porter, 1963. The same data are reported in Lawler and Porter, 1966.

11. One could orthogonalize the explanatory variables through an experimental design so that the independent impact of each on pay satisfaction could be observed. Experimental designs allow for high degrees of internal validity, but often have unintended consequences and hence create problems of external validity in studying organizational behavior. See Campbell and Stanley, 1963, pp. 5–6, for a discussion of internal and external validity; and Argyris, 1968, for a discussion of unintended consequences of experiments in organizational research. Lawler, 1971, p. 221, suggested that the impact of extraneous variables be controlled through sampling procedures. For example, the impact of pay level could be controlled by examining only subjects who receive approximately the same pay. This approach presents problems, however, because it is impossible to specify the impact of the controlled variables on the dependent variable, and the utilization of very many control variables quickly depletes the sample size.

12. Lawler and Porter, 1966.

13. Lawler, 1971, p. 221.

14. Ibid., p. 229.

15. Graen, 1969, pp. 12–15; Mitchell and Albright, 1972, p. 12; Wofford, 1971, p. 512. It should be noted that in the Graen study, the positive relationship was observed only when the objective link between performance and rewards was high.

16. Cherrington, Reitz and Scott, 1971, p. 534.

17. Pritchard, Dunnette and Jorgensen, 1972, pp. 88–9.

18. Finn and Lee, 1972.

19. Weiss, Dawis et al., 1967; Smith, Kendall and Hulin, 1969.

20. The highest correlations (wage level with organizational level and age with tenure) are to be expected because of personnel policies and the nature of organizational membership. The high correlation between the piece rate $v.$ group incentive rate or hourly rate (x_3 in Appendix B) and the group incentive rate $v.$ piece rate or hourly rate, on the other hand, is a matter of statistical definition. We dummy coded a three-place nominal variable by creating two 0,1 variables (x_3, x_4 in Appendix B). Membership in one type of pay system automatically precludes membership in either of the other two pay systems. Thus, we would expect a high negative zero-order correlation between x_3 and x_4. Cohen shows that the expected intercorrelation can be calculated knowing only the sample size in each nominal group. See Cohen, 1968, p. 429.

21. Lawler, 1971, p. 225.

22. Lawler and Porter, 1966.

23. Whyte, 1955, pp. 222–3.

24. Personnel policies and decisions, for example, often result in males being primarily assigned to piece rate jobs; or higher level jobs being paid more money; or males because of higher job levels and/or longer tenure being paid more than females; or males predominating in higher level jobs.
25. Lawler and Porter, 1966.
26. Lawler, 1971, p. 215.
27. Ibid.
28. Ibid., pp. 221–30. We have omitted a twelfth item included in Lawler's discussion, 'social comparison', because it reflects a psychological process and, as such, is not a factor. In determining pay satisfaction, social comparisons involve the 11 factors listed in Table 1.
29. Cohen, 1968.

10 Alienation, Environmental Characteristics, and Worker Responses[*]

MILTON R. BLOOD
College of Industrial Management, Georgia Institute of Technology
CHARLES L. HULIN
University of Illinois, Urbana

Data gathered from 1,900 male workers located in 21 plants in the eastern United States are presented. These data are analyzed to determine the influence of environmental characteristics presumed to index feelings of alienation from middle-class norms. Predictions were made that workers in communities which should foster integration with middle-class norms would structure their jobs differently and would respond differently than alienated workers. Workers in communities fostering integration with middle-class norms should report higher satisfaction on highly skilled jobs. They should value retirement and should plan for it while working. Alienated workers should report lower satisfaction on highly skilled jobs. Pay should have a stronger effect on the satisfaction of alienated workers, and these workers would be more likely to look for other work after retirement. The predictions were regarded as confirmed for blue-collar workers. The implications of these findings for striving need-theoretic models of human motivation are discussed.

Some recent industrial field studies have pointed up the importance of community variables as determiners of workers' responses. Katzell, Barrett, and Parker (1961) and Cureton and Katzell (1962) found job satisfaction and performance inversely related to the degree of urbanization of the community. They attribute this relationship to differences in needs and expectancies of the workers in the various environments. With increased urbanization, needs and expectancies rise and there is less satisfaction from any specific return. Hulin (1966), using the worker's

Journal of Applied Psychology, LI [3] (1967) 284–90. Copyright 1967, by the American Psychological Association. Reprinted by permission.

frame of reference as an intervening variable, predicted and empirically verified that job satisfaction is higher in communities with substantial slum areas. The assumption of his discussion is that the worker assesses his present status by referring to the alternative positions which are available to him. Since attractive alternatives are not readily apparent in slum conditions, the worker's present job will be seen as relatively more satisfactory. Turner and Lawrence (1965), in a study of workers' responses to the technological aspects of the work situation, found that rural and small town workers were more satisfied when their jobs were more autonomous, required more skill, were more varied, and contained more social interaction and responsibility. In essence, the most satisfying jobs demanded greater personal involvement. This was, of course, the 'expected' result. In contrast to this, city workers were more likely to be satisfied when their jobs were less personally involving. One of the possible explanations offered by Turner and Lawrence for this unexpected response from city workers is the notion of anomie, a state of societal normlessness brought about by industrialization, which has been frequently investigated in recent sociological researches.

In addition to these studies there are a growing number of studies of 'job enlargement' which present conflicting results. In general, results in line with predictions are obtained if the studies are done on workers with rural backgrounds, but contrary results are obtained if the workers are from urban backgrounds (see Friedlander, 1965; Kennedy and O'Neill, 1958; Kilbridge, 1960).

From these studies and from sociological studies of anomie and alienation a construct can be formulated which can be used in structuring and predicting workers' responses. This construct might most efficiently be conceived as a continuum running from 'integration with middle-class norms' to 'alienation from middle-class norms'. However, it should be pointed out that this is a complex phenomenon described as unidimensional only for ease of conceptualization. At the integrated end of the construct are found workers who have personal involvement with their jobs and aspirations within their occupations. Their goals are the type of upward mobility, social climbing goals generally associated with the American middle class. At the opposite pole of the construct, workers can be described as involved in their jobs only instrumentally; that is, the job is only a provider of means for pursuing extraoccupational goals.The concern of these workers is not for increased responsibility, higher status, or more autonomy. They want money, and they want it in return for a minimal amount of personal involvement. This difference between integrated and alienated workers is similar to Dalton's (1947) discrimination between overproducers who are likely to hold middle-class aspirations and underproducers who do not identify with middle-class ideals. The construct of alienation being proposed in this study stands in obvious relation to the Protestant ethic proposed and discussed by Weber (1958).

It is likely that conditions fostering integration with middle-class norms will also foster adherence to the Protestant ethic since the latter is an aspect of the former.

What environmental conditions should lead to alienation from middle-class norms? Data have suggested that anomie is associated with lower-class highly industrialized situations, Bell, 1957; Dean, 1961; Killian and Grigg, 1962; Mayo, 1933; McClosky and Schaar, 1965; Ruitenbeck, 1964; Simpson and Miller, 1963; Turner and Lawrence 1965). Though anomie is different conceptually from the construct being defined here, the measurement of anomie has been such that it might just as easily be interpreted as alienation from the middle class. It is postulated that 'alienation from middle-class norms' results from lack of socialization to middle-class norms. That is, where a segment of society exists which holds non-middle-class norms and which is large enough to sustain its own norms, the members of that subculture will become socialized to the norms of that subculture. A handful of industrial workers in a small community could not be expected to sustain a separate set of norms, but persons separated from middle-class identification by low educational attainment or low occupational status and living in ghettos, slums, and highly industrialized communities could develop and sustain a distinct norm system. Alienation from middle-class norms, then, is fostered by industrialized, socially heterogeneous, metropolitan conditions. This conceptualization of the background of the alienated worker coincides with the characterizations by Whyte (1955) of restrictors and rate busters. The social and family background of restrictors was urban working class, whereas rate busters were from farms or lower-middle-class families. Worthy (1950) has also pointed out the possible effects of living in urban areas on the motivation and especially the morale of industrial workers.

METHOD

Before describing the methods of this investigation, two cautions must be invoked. First, though the data to be presented are not such that they could support the contention of causality, a causal discussion is used here. A causal theory in this sense serves only as a working hypothesis to be altered as the data demand. This does not detract, however, from the usefulness of the construct as a guide to research and application. Second, no value judgment is intended by the use of the word 'alienated'. It would be as logical to consider such workers integrated to their norms from which middle-class persons are alienated (and whether or not it would be better for the workers or for society for them to be integrated to middle-class norms is a social question beyond the proper boundaries of this paper). Orientation to middle-class norms has been adopted as the point of reference here because middle-class norms predominate in our culture and among social scientists.

Data for this study were provided from a study carried out at Cornell

University (Smith, Kendall and Hulin, in press). Subjects (Ss) were 1,390 male blue-collar workers and 511 male white-collar workers representing 21 different plants located throughout the eastern half of the United States. These data were gathered in 1961 and 1962 as part of a large-scale study of retirement satisfaction sponsored by the Ford Foundation.[1]

Stimulus variables

To predict from the alienation construct it was necessary to have stimulus variables which indexed the environmental conditions which foster alienation and another set of variables which indicated the responses of workers to their jobs. The variates used to index community characteristics which should foster alienation among the workers were chosen from a principal component analysis of an intercorrelation matrix of per capita census variables originally provided by Kendall (1963). While the original solution was simply a set of statistical variates which could be used to describe communities, several of these dimensions appear to be useful as indexes of alienation. These variates consisted of the weighted sum of variables where the weights were proportional to the loadings of the variables on the component. The complex variates were used since it was felt that the variates would provide more reliable and meaningful indexes than would individual variables. See Kendall (1963) for a complete description of this solution.

The variates used in this research were descriptively named Slum Conditions indexed mainly by the weighted sum of the standard scores of percentage of native white (reversed scoring), percentage of non-white, and percentage of owner-occupied housing (reversed scoring); Urbanization, indexed mainly by the sum of percentage of rural nonfarm (reversed scoring), percentage of urban population, total population, and per capita motor vehicle deaths (reversed scoring); Urban Growth, indexed mainly by percentage of immigration, percentage of dwellings vacant (reversed scoring), and percentage of new homes; Prosperity and Cost of Living, indexed by the sum of percentage of sound housing, medium income, percentage of workers in wholesale, per capita retail sales, and percentage with income over $10,000; and Productive Farming, indexed by the sum of percentage of workers in wholesale (reversed scoring), average farm income, percentage of workers in agriculture, and percentage of change in farm level of living. A sixth variable, Population Density (population per square mile), was chosen as a final index of alienating conditions.

There were no data indicating that these variates behave in the manner predicted. Thus, confirmation of the predictions of this report would serve also to enlarge existing knowledge of the community conditions fostering alienation. It was possible that one or more of the variates would prove to be a poor index for the present purpose, and it was almost certain that these six indexes would differ in the strength with which they gauge the postulated conditions. For this reason, all of them were used in the position of the independent variable. Even if some of them did not show the anticipated relationship or showed it only weakly, the consideration of all six of them together provided more understanding of the construct (cf. Webb, Campbell, Schwartz and Sechrest, 1966).

Response variables

Fourteen variables were chosen which were expected to show differences between integrated and alienated workers. Four of them concerned retirement. Workers were asked to rate the importance of planning for retirement, whether or not they had made plans yet for retirement, and whether they would look for other work after they retired. Also a Preparation for Retirement Index was established for each worker indicating the extent of preparation the worker had made for his retirement years. On the three planning-and-preparation-for-retirement variables it was predicted that the integrated workers would score higher since it was felt that the desire for a leisurely retirement has become imbued with a great deal of prestige or status significance in the middle class. For the same reason, integrated workers were expected to be less likely to say that they would look for other work after retirement.

Workers were asked to rank their job as well as their family life, hobbies, etc., as a provider of personal satisfaction. Integrated workers were expected to be more likely to rank their job first or second as a provider of personal satisfaction.

It was predicted that the correlation of the work satisfaction of the Job Description Index (JDI) with a rating of job level would be lower for alienated workers than for integrated workers since alienated workers are more satisfied when their jobs are *less demanding*. The same prediction was made for the correlation of the JDI work satisfaction scale and ratings of job-skill requirements.

As the job was expected to play a more central role in the lives of the integrated workers, the correlation between satisfaction with the job in general (JIG) and satisfaction with life in general (LIG) was predicted to be higher for them. JIG and LIG were measured by General Motors Faces Scales (Kunin, 1955). Using JDI scales, satisfaction with work and satisfaction with promotional opportunities should be more highly correlated with JIG and LIG in the integrated sample. On the other hand, pay satisfaction should be more highly correlated with JIG and LIG in the alienated sample because these are the persons who view their job as primarily an activity which is instrumental to the achievement of other goals. A summary of these predictions can be seen in Table 1 where the response variables are listed and an 'x' is placed under the heading of the situation in which the level of the variable was predicted to be higher.

It was possible to assign each of the 21 plant locations a score on each of the indexes of alienating conditions and on each of the indexes of workers' responses. The analysis was carried out by correlating these two

Table 1   Worker response variables and the condition under which the variable is predicted to be higher

Variable	Alienated	Integrated
1. Importance of planning for retirement		x
2. Made plans yet for retirement		x
3. Preparation for retirement index		x
4. Look for other work after retirement	x	
5. Personal satisfaction from the job		x
6. JDI work satisfaction — Skill correlation		x
7. JDI work satisfaction — Job-level correlation		x
8. JDI work satisfaction — JIG correlation		x
9. JDI pay satisfaction — JIG correlation	x	
10. JDI promotion satisfaction — JIG correlation		x
11. JDI work satisfaction — LIG correlation		x
12. JDI pay satisfaction — LIG correlation	x	
13. JDI promotion satisfaction — LIG correlation		x
14. JIG — LIG correlation		x

sets of variables,— the alienation indexes and the response variables. It should be noted that the *n* for each of these correlations was 21 and not 1,900. This of course means that this study, in spite of the large number of subjects, was a very small study considering the type of analysis which was being carried out. Further, 54 of the predictions are predictions about the relative size of a *correlation*. Differences were being predicted in the relationship between two response variables as determined by differences in the stimulus condition. For these two reasons a prediction will be simply regarded as being supported if the finding was in the expected direction and the results will be discussed as a whole and not as specific findings.

RESULTS
Using all of the workers of the sample, the correlations were computed and the results can be seen in Table 2. The first column gives the predicted direction of the correlations for each row. Of the 84 predictions represented in this table, 45 are in the predicted direction. This, of course, does not support the construct.

It scarcely seemed appropriate to abandon the construct after such limited analysis, and a further step was proposed. It was assumed that middle-class ideals were much more likely to be found among white-collar workers than among blue-collar workers, regardless of community environment. If that assumption is correct the results might have been masked by the inclusion of white-collar workers in the sample. Accordingly, the 511 white-collar workers were dropped, and the analyses were redone. Again showing the direction of predictions in the first column, the results using only blue-collar workers are shown in Table 3. Here 61 of 84 predictions

Table 2 Prediction tests using all workers: correlations (Pearson r's) between stimulus and response variables

Response variables	Predicted direction	Slum conditions	Urbaniza-tion	Urban growth	Cost of living	Productive farming (reversed)	Population density
				Stimulus variables			
Importance of planning for retirement	−	**−.05**	**−.46**	+.31	**−.42**	**−.16**	**−.51**
Made plans yet for retirement	−	**−.18**	**−.60**	+.24	**−.57**	**−.20**	**−.61**
Preparation for retirement index	−	**−.37**	**−.33**	+.15	**−.28**	**−.01**	**−.41**
Look for other work after retirement	+	**+.35**	**+.11**	**+.21**	**+.18**	−.36	**+.25**
Personal Satisfaction from the job	−	+.50	+.16	+.43	+.19	**−.15**	00
Correlations between:							
Work satisfaction-Skill level	−	00	**−.03**	**−.07**	**−.05**	+.07	+.06
Work satisfaction-Job level	−	**−.25**	**−.23**	**−.14**	**−.19**	**−.24**	**−.13**
Work satisfaction-Job-in-general satisfaction	−	+.26	+.31	**−.04**	+.33	+.32	+.38
Pay satisfaction-Job-in-general satisfaction	+	−.19	−.02	−.06	**+.04**	**+.19**	**+.09**
Promotion satisfaction-Job-in-general satisfaction	−	**−.31**	**−.15**	**−.38**	**−.19**	+.18	**−.04**
Work satisfaction-Life-in-general satisfaction	−	+.39	+.32	+.08	+.30	+.27	+.34
Pay satisfaction-Life-in-general satisfaction	+	−.28	00	−.21	−.01	**+.28**	**+.28**
Promotion satisfaction-Life-in-general satisfaction	−	00	**−.05**	**−.20**	**−.13**	+.28	+.04
Job-in-general satisfaction-Life-in-general satisfaction	−	+.16	+.14	**−.11**	+.07	+.19	+.02

Note: N = 21 companies. Numbers in bold are in the direction of the prediction.

Table 3 Prediction tests using blue-collar workers: correlations (Pearson r's) between stimulus and response variables

		Stimulus variables					
Response variables	Predicted direction	Slum conditions	Urbaniza-tion	Urban growth	Cost of living	Productive farming (reversed)	Population density
Importance of planning for retirement	−	+.23	−.22	+.42	−.18	−.09	−.35
Made plans yet for retirement	−	−.25	−.55	+.09	−.57	−.05	−.65
Preparation for retirement index	−	−.46	−.19	−.11	−.20	+.20	−.28
Look for other work after retirement	+	+.32	+.11	+.02	+.16	−.22	+.23
Personal satisfaction from the job	−	+.52	+.16	+.46	+.20	−.21	+.01
Correlations between:							
Work satisfaction—Skill level	−	−.03	−.07	−.10	−.09	−.02	+.07
Work satisfaction—Job level	−	−.65	−.18	−.47	−.20	+.17	−.14
Work satisfaction—Job-in-general satisfaction	−	−.12	+.20	−.34	+.17	+.37	+.25
Pay satisfaction—Job-in-general satisfaction	+	+.13	+.02	+.18	+.11	+.09	+.12
Promotion satisfaction—Job-in-general satisfaction	−	−.31	−.23	−.30	−.23	−.02	−.17
Work satisfaction—Life-in-general satisfaction	−	−.31	+.15	−.48	+.05	+.47	+.13
Pay satisfaction—Life-in-general satisfaction	+	+.05	+.13	+.09	+.10	+.37	+.28
Promotion satisfaction—Life-in-general satisfaction	−	−.48	−.10	−.47	−.18	+.26	−.06
Job-in-general satisfaction—Life-in-general satisfaction	−	−.30	+.03	−.22	−.01	00	−.21

Note: N = 21 companies. Numbers in bold are in the direction of the prediction.

are in the proper direction. Using the normal approximation to the binomial distribution, the probability of finding this many confirmations out of 84 predictions by chance is less than .001. Though extreme caution must be used in attempting to interpret the results of any specific variable, three of the response variables warrant mention. Those are the three which did *not* confirm the construct. JDI work-JIG correlation, and JDI work-LIG correlation do not present any clear pattern. The equivocal results with these two correlations are not easily explained. Perhaps the relationship between work satisfaction and global satisfaction is too strong to allow modification by the social environmental differences which are being measured here. The other nonconfirming variable, 'Personal satisfaction from the job', is in the direction opposite the prediction in five of the six opportunities. The present analysis is not so powerful that this response can be concluded to act in this direction in all cases. This particular response and related areas should certainly enjoy increased interest in any continuation of this line of research.

The Slum Conditions, Cost of Living, and Urban Growth variates work best as predictors of alienated responses having 12, 11, and 11 correct predictions, respectively. Urbanization and Population Density each had 10 correct predictions, while Productive Farming had only 7. Thus, empirically as well as logically, the Slum Conditions variate is the one most closely aligned with the alienation construct. The Productive Farming variate does not seem useful.

DISCUSSION
In general it appears that the construct of alienation has been demonstrated to be useful for structuring workers' responses. It has been shown that workers living in communities which should foster alienation from middle-class norms structure their jobs and their lives predictably differently from workers in communities where adherence to middle-class norms would be expected. Further, these differences were predicted from a theoretical framework consistent with the construct of alienation. Since this study should be regarded as a pilot study, this discussion will emphasize the problems and future research direction rather than the implications of the findings.

It is true that in this study as in the previous research, 'alienation from middle-class norms' is not the only tenable hypothesis. Katzell et al. (1961) invoked an explanation based on differing 'needs' being generated by urban and rural environments. Hulin (1966) and Kendall (1963) used the concepts of 'frame of reference' and the 'alternatives available to the workers' in economically depressed and slum-ridden communities. Turner and Lawrence (1965) used the concept of 'anomie' to explain their results. Even in the present study it is possible that an economic-frame-of-reference hypothesis would be useful in understanding the results.

The cost of living variate made 11 out of 14 correct predictions suggesting that frames of reference of the workers in the community play a significant role in structuring workers' jobs. On the other hand, communities with a high cost of living would be expected to be less than optimal as places for workers to live. Alienation from the norms of the dominant social group might be a reasonable response of the economically disadvantaged workers who might well see the 'middle class' as the cause of their unenviable position. Thus, both of these constructs may be similar. Also, since 'productive farming' proved useful in predicting *level* of pay satisfaction consistent with a frame-of-reference explanation (Hulin, 1966; Kendall, 1963) but not alienated responses regarding job structure, the economic-frame-of-reference explanation in the present study is a bit tenuous. It also could be argued that anomie remains a tenable explanation for these findings and all that has been found is that 'integrated' workers are more predictable than 'alienated' workers who are truly normless (anomic). Table 1 indicates that in the majority of the cases prediction has been made for stronger relationships between response variables for the integrated sample. However, of the 18 cases where higher relationships were predicted for the alienated workers, 17 were in the expected direction. Thus, it does not appear that anomie is a tenable explanation. The alienated workers are not normless. They have norms but they are different from those of the middle classes. It would appear that 'alienation from middle-class norms' is the only construct so far invoked which is capable of structuring all of these diverse findings.

The construct was not confirmed above the level of skilled blue-collar workers. The fact that it was not found in a sample of white-collar workers is in line with the definition of the construct. The possibility that different occupations may generate different susceptibility to alienation is similar to Blauner's (1964) reasoning and certainly has not been ruled out. While the upper boundary of blue-collar workers was arbitrarily set at the level of skilled workers in this study, future research may show that some other level will be optimal in applications of the construct.

The present data delineate attitude changes which accompany alienation. An area of at least equal and probably greater importance will be to see if there are related behavioral changes. Related to job-performance differences is the question of what job-design criteria will be most effective in maximizing satisfaction and performance among alienated workers. As the Turner and Lawrence (1965) findings suggest, the best job design in alienating conditions may be contrary to the models usually proposed by human-relations-oriented investigators. Although integrated workers desire greater responsibility and autonomy, alienated workers may be happiest when given a job which demands little personal involvement either in terms of task skills or identification with the goals of management.

It should be reiterated that this represents a pilot study and although predictions regarding all of the relationships were made a priori there is still only a rudimentary knowledge of the effects of the independent variable. Eventually, with increasing knowledge and sophistication one may know enough about alienation to attempt direct psychological assessment rather than indexing it by means of environmental variables. To the deplorers of 'actuarial research' (such as has been conducted here) this would represent a significant step forward. However, if this direct assessment is carried out, researchers will be back in the domain of verbal response-verbal response correlations with all of the attendant problems of response sets, halo, acquiescence, and unreliability. Even with the 'slippage' that occurs between an index and a construct, it seems preferable to use a stimulus-response paradigm as was employed in this study.

This study does seem to have strong implications for theorists who would like to talk about 'basic human needs'. Both the currently popular need hierarchy approach and the human relations theorists talk about needs for self-actualization, needs for autonomy, needs for a demanding job, etc., which are supposedly basic needs of all people. These data indicate that at the very least these systems need to be revised to take cultural differences into account.

REFERENCES

Bell, W., 'Anomie, Social Isolation, and the Class Structure', *Sociometry*, XX (1957) 105—16.

Blauner, R., *Alienation and Freedom: The Factory Worker and His Industry* (Chicago: University of Chicago Press, 1964).

Cureton, E. E. and Katzell, R. A., 'A Further Analysis of the Relations among Job Performance and Situational Variables', *Journal of Applied Psychology*, XLVI (1962) 230.

Dalton, M., 'Worker Response and Social Background', *Journal of Political Economy*, LV (1947) 323—32.

Dean, D. G., 'Alienation: Its Meaning and Measurement', *American Sociological Review*, XXVI (1961) 753—8.

Friedlander, F., 'Comparative Work Value Systems', *Personal Psychology*, XVIII (1965) 1—20.

Hulin, C. L., 'Effects of Community Characteristics on Measures of Job Satisfaction', *Journal of Applied Psychology*, L (1966) 185—92.

Katzell, R. A., Barrett, R. S. and Parker, T. C., 'Job Satisfaction, Job Performance, and Situational Characteristics', *Journal of Applied Psychology*, XLV (1961) 65—72.

Kendall, L. M., 'Canonical Analysis of Job Satisfaction and Behavioral, Personal Background, and Situational Data'. Unpublished doctoral dissertation, Cornell University, 1963.

Kennedy, J. E. and O'Neill, H. E., 'Job Content and Workers' Opinions', *Journal of Applied Psychology*, XLII (1958) 372—5.

Kilbridge, M. D., 'Do Workers Prefer Larger Jobs?', *Personnel,* XXXVII [5] (1960) 45–8.

Killian, L. M. and Grigg, C. M., 'Urbanism, Race and Anomia', *American Journal of Sociology,* LXVII (1962) 661–5.

Kunin, T., 'The Construction of a New Type of Attitude Measure', *Personal Psychology,* VIII (1955) 65–77.

Mayo, E., *The Human Problems of an Industrial Civilization* (New York: Macmillan, 1933).

McClosky, H. and Schaar, J. H., 'Psychological Dimensions of Anomy', *American Sociological Review,* XXX (1965) 14–40.

Ruitenbeck, H. M., *The Individual and the Crowd* (New York: Nelson, 1964).

Simpson, R. L. and Miller, H. M., 'Social Status and Anomia', *Social Problems,* X (1963) 256–64.

Smith, P. C., Kendall, L. M. and Hulin, C. L., *Measurement of Satisfaction in Work and Retirement* (New York: Rand McNally, 1969).

Turner, A. N. and Lawrence, P. R., *Industrial Jobs and the Worker: An Investigation of Response to Task Attributes* (Boston: Harvard University Press, 1965).

Webb, B. J., Campbell, D. T., Schwartz, R. D. and Sechrest, L., *Unobtrusive Measures: Nonreactive Research in the Social Sciences* (Chicago: Rand McNally, 1966).

Weber, M., *The Protestant Ethic and the Spirit of Capitalism,* tr. Talcott Parsons (New York: Scribner, 1958).

Whyte, W. F., *Money and Motivation: An Analysis of Incentives* (New York: Harper, 1955).

Worthy, J. C., 'Organizational Structure and Employee Morale', *American Sociological Review,* XV (1950) 169–79.

NOTE

1. The authors would like to thank Patricia Cain Smith of Bowling Green University who very generously made these data available for this analysis.

11 The Occupational Reference Group — a Neglected Concept in Employee Attitude Studies[*]

GEORGE W. ENGLAND and CARROLL I. STEIN
University of Minnesota

The research literature concerning employee attitudes and job satisfaction clearly shows a general relationship between satisfaction and occupational level. For example, Super (1939) shows a significant but not linear relationship between occupational level and job satisfaction. He also demonstrates a tendency for the direction of occupational change to affect satisfaction.

Herzberg et al. (1957) point out that lower occupational groups have lower satisfaction. Their findings indicate that office workers consider intrinsic aspects of the job to be most important whereas factory workers consider security and wages to be most important.

Darley and Hagenah (1936) conclude that work below a certain level is primarily a means for survival and that the tasks of these jobs are not intrinsically interesting. Above some point, however, the job may be satisfying, challenging, and interesting.

This paper stems from our belief that, despite the available evidence, both researchers and users of employee attitude surveys do not focus enough attention on the occupational variable. Its purpose is to investigate occupational differences between certain attitudinal areas in the employment setting and secondly to consider implications of such differences for both research and application.

PROCEDURE

The study utilized responses to the Triple Audit Employee Attitude questionnaire (1954) which had been collected from 3207 nonsupervisor employees in 26 companies. This employee attitude scale consists of 54 items (scored on a Likert 5-point scale) concerning various aspects of the

Personnel Psychology, XIV (1961) 299–304. Reprinted by permission.

Table 1   Occupation breakdown
of sample

Occupation	Number of employees
Professional	270
Craftsmen	528
Sales	345
Clerical	1005
Semi-skilled	782
Service	66
Laborer	211
Total	3207

employment situation. The 54 items are grouped into seven subscales which reflect employee attitudes towards such areas as working conditions, hours and pay, type of work, and supervision. Table 1 shows the occupational composition of the sample.

Each of seven occupational groups was compared with every other occupational group to determine the extent of occupational differences. Items rather than subscales were used in comparing occupational groups for two reasons. First, it was found that two occupational groups could have similar distributions on a subscale but show extreme response distribution differences on specific items within the subscale.

Secondly, the subscales were originally constructed on a combined sample of all occupations and might not represent the best possible subscale grouping for any specific occupation.

The prospect of doing chi-square tests for all combinations of occupational groups for each of the 54 items appeared so unwieldy that an alternate method was used. Zubin's nomographs (1939) were employed since they were constructed for just such a case and are not restricted to 2 x 2 tables. In 2 x N tables, each response position (in this case, Likert 5-point scales) can be contrasted with all remaining response positions by means of the nomographs and the significance of each comparison determined. Occupations would be considered significantly different on a particular item if they differed on any of the response positions. All occupational levels were first compared on the highest-scored response position of each item.

RESULTS AND DISCUSSION
Table 2 shows the number of items on which pairs of occupations differed significantly (.05 level) when compared on the highest-scored response position.

The number of significant item differences shown in Table 2 is undoubtedly on the conservative side since only one response position was

Table 2 Number of significant item differences found among occupational groups

	Sales	Semi-skilled	Craft	Service	Laborer	Professional
Clerical	34	47	45	15	41	23
Sales		50	49	20	43	30
Semi-skilled			18	7	12	34
Craft				11	11	38
Service					6	18
Laborer						33

Note: Total number of items = 54.

used in the comparisons. It is quite likely that more differences would occur on other response positions. The number of differences disclosed in Table 2 made it unnecessary to check other response positions since it was obvious from the first check that large occupational differences in attitudes existed. On the average, pairs of occupations differed significantly on approximately 50 per cent of the items. This conservative estimate of occupational item differences clearly indicates the extent of occupational differences in attitudes.

A second way of looking at occupational differences in attitudes is in terms of different areas of the working environment. Table 3 shows the percentage of responses to the 'Strongly Agree' category for each occupational group on twelve content categories (areas of the working environment) describing the subject matter of the items. Here again, this is a conservative estimate of the magnitude of occupational differences because only one response position was used.

While it is difficult to evaluate the data in Table 3 in a rigorous fashion, it can be seen that not all occupations differ from each other on any one

Table 3 Percentage answering 'Strongly Agree'

Content of items	Professional	Sales	Clerical	Craft	Semi-skilled	Labor	Service
Working Conditions	19	20	16	9	10	11	15
Company	12	24	16	12	12	12	19
Pay	21	17	15	13	12	10	7
Hours	17	28	21	16	17	14	15
Co-workers	36	37	33	24	23	26	21
Type of work	26	35	26	18	14	14	18
Supervision	22	30	25	14	18	14	17
Promotions	11	20	14	9	9	7	8
Communications	14	29	17	10	11	13	17
Recognition	17	21	16	9	10	9	13
Security	15	21	22	14	12	10	17

content area. Semi-skilled, craft, and labor occupational groups tend to be quite similar. However, a number of large differences are found across occupational groups. These results suggest that it may be necessary to specify the particular attitudinal area when asking which occupation has the most or least favorable attitude.

The data presented in Tables 2 and 3 point out that there are significant occupational differences among attitude item responses in the employment setting and suggest the possibility of identifying differentially important areas for various occupational groups. The implications which stem from these findings seem of major importance.

IMPLICATIONS FOR RESEARCH

The possibility that specific attitudinal areas may be crucial for some occupational groups and not for others implies that the use of scores on the same attitude scale for all groups may hide more than it reveals. Strong's statement (1958), 'A way must be found to consider only those who are really satisfied or dissatisfied with each factor and to disregard those who don't really care about the factor', seems most appropriate. Perhaps attitude scales (which emphasize particular areas of concern) should be developed for each occupation.

The large occupational differences found on the Triple Audit Employee Attitude Scale imply that attitude data should be stratified occupationally before being related to other variables. It is possible that some of the confusion and conflict in morale-productivity relationships, as summarized by Brayfield and Crockett (1955), could be traced to inadequate control of the occupational variable.

It would seem, then, that each occupational group has a different attitudinal reference point. It becomes necessary, therefore, to develop occupational norms when using a single attitude scale for all groups. Such norms should facilitate a more meaningful measurement of changes for a given group and of differences among groups as reckoned against their appropriate reference points. The relevant reference point is overlooked or confused all too often in attitude research.

IMPLICATIONS FOR USE OF ATTITUDE SURVEYS

The use of occupational norms should aid in interpreting the meaning of attitude scores for a given organization. Without such norms it is difficult to determine whether a company has high morale because of its work environment or whether it simply differs from some comparison group because of its occupational make-up. A method of combining standard scores based on deviations from occupational norms should give a more accurate picture of a company's over-all attitude complex.

Departmental differences in attitudes within a single company are often the most useful comparisons which can be made in attempting to pinpoint actual trouble spots. The use of occupational norms would again seem valuable in controlling for differences in occupational composition between departments and in identifying 'sore spots' which actually reflect the work environment.

Organizations which measure attitudes periodically may be acting on changes which reflect only change in occupational composition of the company or of a department between two time periods. If, for example, a firm changes its proportion of common labor from 30 per cent of all employees to 10 per cent between two administrations of an attitude scale, an increase in over-all scores could be expected. This would not mean, however, that company practices and policies had improved. Again, occupational norms would seem to provide a useful base against which to measure change.

The value of differential norms has long been recognized in the use of psychological tests. It would appear that attitude measurement could also benefit from greater use of differential norms, particularly through the use of occupational norms.

SUMMARY
Analysis of responses of 3207 employees in 26 firms to an employee attitude scale clearly shows that there are large occupational differences in terms of item responses. Such differences highlight the importance of the occupational variable in attitude research and emphasize the need for occupational norms. The possibility of identifying important areas of the work setting for specific occupations as related to attitudes was explored and found to be feasible. Major implications from the study are: (a) It may be useful to develop special attitude scales for different occupational groups; (b) The occupational variable should be controlled before attitudes are related to other variables such as productivity, turnover, and absenteeism; and (c) The use of occupational norms would provide a more accurate picture of an organization's total attitude complex and permit change and deviation from an appropriate standard to be evaluated meaningfully.

REFERENCES
Brayfield, A. H. and Crockett, W. H., 'Employee Attitudes and Employee Performance'. *Psychological Bulletin*, LII (1955) 396–424.
Darley, J. G. and Hagenah, Theda, *Vocational Interest Measurement* (Minneapolis: University of Minnesota Press, 1936).
Herzberg, F., Mausner, B., Petersen, R. O. and Capwell, Dora, *Job Attitudes: Review of Research and Opinions* (Pittsburgh: Psychological Services of Pittsburgh, 1957).
Strong, E. K., 'Satisfaction and Interests', *American Psychologist*, XIII (1958) 449–56.
Super, D. E., 'Occupational Level and Job Satisfaction', *Journal of Applied Psychology*, XXIII (1939) 547–64.

Yoder, D., Heneman, H. G., Jr. and Fox, H., *Auditing Your Manpower Management*, Bulletin 13, Industrial Relations Centre (Minneapolis: University of Minnesota Press, 1954).

Zubin, J., 'Nomographs for Determining the Significance of the Difference Between the Frequencies of Events in Two Contrasted Series or Groups', *Journal of the American Statistical Association*, XXXIV (1939) 539–44.

12 The Effects of 'Tall' versus 'Flat' Organization Structures on Managerial Job Satisfaction*

LYMAN W. PORTER and EDWARD E. LAWLER III
University of California, Berkeley

Ever since 1950, when Worthy published his widely-cited article on 'Organizational Structure and Employee Morale', considerable attention has been focused on the merits of 'flat' organization structures in comparison with 'tall' structures. (See, for example, Gardner and Moore, 1955; Strauss and Sayles, 1960; Viteles, 1953; Whyte, 1961.) Worthy's basic conclusion was: 'Flatter, less complex structures, with a maximum of administrative decentralization, tend to create a potential for improved attitudes, more effective supervision, and greater individual responsibility and initiative among employees. Moreover, arrangements of this type encourage the development of individual self-expression and creativity which are so necessary to the personal satisfaction of employees and which are an essential ingredient of the democratic way of life' (Worthy, 1950, p. 179). Despite the fact that Worthy presented no empirical evidence to back up his statements, and despite the fact that his observations were based on the situation in a single company, his views have been frequently quoted by other authors to support their view that flat organizations produce higher morale than tall ones.

It is also interesting to note that, since the appearance of Worthy's article, not a single article (to the writers' knowledge) has appeared until 1962 that offered any evidence in support or denial of Worthy's conclusions. In 1962 Meltzer and Salter published a study that reported on the job satisfactions of 704 physiologists (in non-university organizations) in relation to the type of organization structure in which they worked. Meltzer and Salter categorized their questionnaire respondents by size of company (fewer than 20 professional employees, 21—50, and 51 or more),

Personnel Psychology, XVII (1964) 135—48. Reprinted by permission.

and by number of levels of administration within the organization (1–3 levels, 4–5, and 6 or more). They found that, when size was not held constant, the number of levels of administration related negatively to over-all job satisfaction. However, when size was controlled so that they had ratios of number of supervisory levels to size, they found generally insignificant relationships between 'tallness' or 'flatness' and job satisfaction. Thus, their results did not provide confirmation of Worthy's theories about flat structure producing better job attitudes, if flatness is measured by the number of supervisory levels relative to organization size. It should be pointed out that they studied organizations of extremely small size, and hence their findings should be evaluated in that context.

The present study is an investigation of the relation of tall *v.* flat types of organization structure to managerial job satisfactions. The sample of managers, over 1,900, was a nationwide sample representing all levels of management in all sizes and types of companies, both manufacturing and nonmanufacturing.[1] Data were collected which enabled respondents to be classified on the basis of the ratio of number of levels of supervision in their organization to the total size of their organization. This ratio formed the independent variable of type of organization structure. The dependent attitude variables constituted thirteen need satisfaction questions used in previous studies (e.g. Porter, 1962). These items were based on a Maslow-type classification of needs according to their prepotency (Maslow, 1954). The specific aim of the present study was to determine if perceived need satisfactions of managers were greater in flat or in tall organizations.

METHOD

Questionnaire

The data for this study were collected by means of a questionnaire described in detail in previous articles (Porter, 1961; Porter, 1962) and were based on answers to parts of thirteen items contained in the questionnaire. All thirteen items relate to a Maslow-type need hierarchy system. A sample item, as it appeared in the questionnaire, was as follows:

The *opportunity for independent thought and action* in my management position:

(a) How much is there now?   (min) 1 2 3 4 5 6 7 (max)
(b) How much should there be?   (min) 1 2 3 4 5 6 7 (max)
(c) How important is this to me?   (min) 1 2 3 4 5 6 7 (max)

As will be explained in the Results section, only the answers to parts (a) and (b) of each item were used to assess the degree of need satisfaction.

Categories of needs and specific items

Listed below are the categories of needs studied in this investigation along with the specific items used to elicit information on each category. The items were randomly presented in the questionnaire, but are here listed systematically according to their respective need categories. The rationale behind the categorization system has been presented in a previous article (Porter, 1961). Essentially, it is based on Maslow's system of classifying different needs according to their prepotency of elicitation (Maslow, 1954). The categories and their specific items follow:

I. Security needs
   1. The *feeling of security* in my management position.
II. Social needs
   1. The *opportunity*, in my management position, *to give help to other people*.
   2. The *opportunity to develop close friendships* in my management position.
III. Esteem needs
   1. The *feeling of self-esteem* a person gets from being in my management position.
   2. The *prestige* of my management position *inside* the company (that is, the regard received from others *in* the company).
   3. The *prestige* of my management position *outside* the company (that is, the regard received from others *not* in the company).
IV. Autonomy needs
   1. The *authority* connected with my management position.
   2. The *opportunity for independent thought and action* in my management position.
   3. The *opportunity*, in my management position, *for participation in the setting of goals*.
   4. The *opportunity*, in my management position, *for participation in the determination of methods and procedures*.
V. Self-actualization needs
   1. The *opportunity for personal growth and development* in my management position.
   2. The *feeling of self-fulfillment* a person gets from being in my management position (that is, the feeling of being able to use one's own unique capabilities, realizing one's potentialities).
   3. The *feeling of worthwhile accomplishment* in my management position.

Procedure and sample
The questionnaire was distributed nationwide to approximately 6,000 managers. It was sent to a random sample of 3,000 members of the American Management Association and to another random sample of some 3,000 managers whose names were on mailing lists available to the Association. The distribution of the questionnaire was accomplished by

mail. Responses were received from 1,958 managers with the number of usable questionnaires being 1,913.

From the personal data questions asked on the last page of the questionnaire, it was possible to classify respondents on a number of independent variables. The two relevant variables for this study were type of organization structure and (as a control variable) company size. Respondents were classified as being employed in organizations with either Tall, Intermediate, or Flat structures. The categories for type of structure were based upon a ratio of the number of levels of management to the total size of company.

Answers to the following question were used to determine the number of management levels in each respondent's company:

How many levels of supervision are there in your company (from first-level supervisor to president)? (Give number.)

The size of the companies in which the respondents were employed was determined by their answers to the following question:

Approximately how many employees (management and nonmanagement) are there in your company?

The following classifications of company size were used in analyzing the data:

1–99	5,000–9,999
100–499	10,000–29,999
500–999	30,000–99,999
1,000–4,999	100,000–or over

Within each size classification, respondents were classified as being employed in either Flat, Intermediate, or Tall organizations on the following basis:

Flat   Managers employed by companies having the fewest levels relative to their size were classified as being employed in flat organizations. Approximately one-quarter of the managers employed by companies of a given size were assigned this classification.

Intermediate   Managers employed by companies having a middle number of levels relative to their size were classified as being employed by intermediate organizations. Approximately one-half of the managers employed by companies of a given size were assigned to this classification.

Tall   Managers employed by companies having greatest number of levels relative to their size were classified as being employed in tall organizations. Approximately one-quarter of the managers employed by companies of a given size were assigned to this classification.

Table 1   Distribution of N of total sample by three types of organization structure and eight size groups

Organization structure	1–99	100–499	500–999	1,000–4,999	5,000–9,999	10,000–29,999	30,000–99,999	100,000 or over	Total N for structure type
Flat	25	54	55	68	49	110	38	20	419
Intermediate	71	178	130	309	96	116	69	41	1,010
Tall	15	63	42	168	69	60	49	18	484
Total N for size	111	295	227	545	214	286	156	79	1,913

(Column group header: Size groups)

An important advantage of tabulating responses by company size as well as by type of organization structure was that, by having eight size groups and three different types of organization structure, the effect of organization structure could be studied in eight independent samples. Thus it was possible to assess the effect of organization structure on companies of different sizes.

Table 1 presents the number of respondents coming from companies with each type of organization structure within each company size group. This table can be referred to in determining the N's for the subgroups of subjects in Table 2.

Three other relevant distributions of the sample (not shown in Table 1) are those for line v. staff type of position, management level (see Porter, 1962, for details of classification system), and type of company. About 31 per cent of the sample were line managers, 28 per cent were combined line/staff managers and 41 per cent were staff managers. Approximately six per cent of the respondents were Presidents, 32 per cent were Vice-Presidents, 34 per cent were Upper-Middle managers, 23 per cent were Lower-Middle managers, and 5 per cent were Lower managers. About 66 per cent of the respondents came from manufacturing companies, 7 per cent from transportation and public utilities, 7 per cent from finance and insurance, 5 per cent from wholesale and retail trade, and the remaining 15 per cent from among other types of companies. When the total sample was divided according to type of organization structure and company size, each of the subsamples showed distributions similar to that of the total sample for line/staff type of position and management level. However, there was a somewhat smaller percentage of respondents from wholesale and retail trade companies in tall than in flat organizations. It should also be pointed out that due to the method of distribution of the questionnaire, a nationwide sample was obtained; furthermore, except by chance, any particular company would not be represented more than a few times in the total sample.

Table 2 Mean need fullfillment deficiencies for each category and item: three types of organization structure by eight size groups[a]

Need category	Item	Organization structure	1–99	100–499	500–999	1,000–4,999	5,000–9,999	10,000–29,999	30,000–99,999	100,000 or over
Security	I-1	Flat	.48	.48	.55	.32	.55	.48	.79	.87
		Intermed.	.82	.41	.38	.40	.52	.24	.09	.56
		Tall	—	.63	.50	.39	.34	.36	-.06	—
Social	II-1	Flat	.64	.32	.51	.39	.49	.57	.63	.52
		Intermed.	.47	.46	.41	.38	.34	.40	.32	.24
		Tall	—	.47	.43	.39	.38	.44	.41	—
	II-2	Flat	.92	.01	.07	.09	.39	.15	.42	.47
		Intermed.	.32	.30	.10	.26	.37	.22	.23	.24
		Tall	—	.31	-.07	.22	.34	.01	.24	—
Esteem	III-1	Flat	.64	.73	.56	.62	.77	.71	1.00	1.20
		Intermed.	.75	.82	.61	.81	.56	.93	.65	1.00
		Tall	—	1.00	1.03	.87	.77	1.12	.73	—
	III-2	Flat	.36	.71	.65	.67	.82	.68	.89	1.26
		Intermed.	.54	.62	.50	.72	.54	.69	.65	.71
		Tall	—	.64	.45	.61	.58	.93	.55	—
	III-3	Flat	.52	.22	.46	.38	.43	.30	.63	1.60
		Intermed.	.33	.36	.59	.39	.26	.34	.36	.39
		Tall	—	.30	.55	.34	.22	.42	.23	—

Autonomy	IV-1	Flat	.16	.07	.96	.81	.92	.95	1.53	1.07
		Intermed.	.76	.62	.75	.80	.66	.91	1.03	1.10
		Tall	—	1.03	.45	.77	.87	.94	.90	—
	IV-2	Flat	.32	.53	.90	.57	.67	.79	.90	.80
		Intermed.	.79	.69	.68	.63	.68	.62	.76	.86
		Tall	—	.59	.57	.72	.82	.78	.80	—
	IV-3	Flat	.76	1.11	.18	1.06	1.24	.99	1.34	1.27
		Intermed.	.79	.84	.74	1.07	1.00	1.11	1.15	.91
		Tall	—	.94	.66	1.06	.90	1.15	1.13	—
	IV-4	Flat	.14	.78	.69	.59	.77	.69	.53	1.00
		Intermed.	.55	.36	.53	.62	.62	.56	.76	.51
		Tall	—	.70	.47	.77	.45	.77	.35	—
Self-actualization	V-1	Flat	.76	1.09	.98	.73	1.41	1.04	1.34	1.07
		Intermed.	.98	1.12	.95	1.08	.95	.97	.64	.98
		Tall	—	1.07	1.05	1.07	.99	1.18	.82	—
	V-2	Flat	.64	.94	.84	.88	.98	1.00	1.52	1.40
		Intermed.	1.18	1.01	.96	.94	.99	1.03	1.00	1.49
		Tall	—	1.18	.98	1.01	1.11	1.47	1.00	—
	V-3	Flat	.68	1.12	1.09	.93	1.16	1.04	1.21	1.27
		Intermed.	1.18	1.09	.99	1.08	1.20	1.21	.82	1.42
		Tall	—	1.30	.86	1.20	1.19	1.45	1.00	—

[a]It should be noted that no inferences about the effects of company size on managerial job satisfactions can be made from this table since management level has not been held constant for the various size-of-company groups. (Average management level is, however, constant across the three shapes with a given size category.)

RESULTS

The degree of perceived deficiency in need fulfillment for each respondent on each questionnaire item was obtained by subtracting the answer to part (*a*) of an item ('How much of the characteristic *is there now* connected with your position?') from part (*b*) of the item ('How much of the characteristic do you think *should be* connected with your position?'). An *a priori* assumption was made that the smaller the difference − (*a*) subtracted from (*b*) − the smaller the degree of dissatisfaction or the larger the degree of satisfaction. This method of measuring perceived need satisfaction is an indirect measure derived from two direct answers by the respondent for each item, and it is thus a more conservative measure than would be a single question concerning simple obtained fulfillment. In effect, this method asks the respondent, 'How satisfied are you in terms of what you expected from this particular management position?'

Table 2 presents the mean need fulfillment deficiencies for each of the thirteen items in the questionnaire and for each subgroup of respondents. The values for each entry in Table 2 were obtained by subtracting each respondent's answer to part (*a*) of each item from his answer to part (*b*) of each item, and then calculating the arithmetic mean of these values for each subgroup of respondents. No entries are given where the *N* for a cell is less than 20 because of the lack of stability in values based on such small numbers of respondents.

Examination of Table 2 yields three points that will be considered further in succeeding tables. First, there is no tendency for mean need deficiencies for most items to be smaller in flat than in tall organizations when all sizes of company are considered. Secondly, when companies with less than 5,000 employees are viewed, the need deficiencies for most items reported by respondents from tall organizations appear to be *greater* than those reported by respondents from flat organizations. Thirdly, when companies with more than 5,000 employees are viewed, the need deficiencies reported by respondents from tall organizations are *less* than those reported by respondents from flat organizations for most questions.

Tables 3, 4, and 5 are concerned with the results of sign-rank tests performed on the mean deficiencies presented in Table 2. In order to carry out the sign-rank tests, the differences between the mean deficiencies in flat and intermediate organizations and those between intermediate and tall organizations were obtained within each size group for each item. If a mean deficiency were greater for a 'taller' structure the difference in the deficiencies was considered positive, whereas if the deficiency were smaller in a taller structure the difference was considered negative. The differences across size-of-company groups for a given item or category of items were then ranked for size of difference, and the sums of the positive and of the negative ranks were obtained. Where the sum of the positive ranks (of the differences in mean deficiencies) exceeded the sum of the negative ranks,

Table 3   Results of sign-rank tests on mean deficiencies for flat, intermediate, and tall organizations in eight size groups (larger sum of positive ranks indicates greater satisfaction in flat organizations)

Need category	Item[a]	Sum of positive ranks	Sum of negative ranks	Number of comparisons	p value for items[b]	p value for categories[b]
Security	I-1	38.0	67.0	14	NS	NS
Social	II-1	35.0	70.0	14	NS	
	II-2	36.0	69.0	14	NS	
	Total	137.5	268.5	28		.20
Esteem	III-1	72.5	32.5	14	NS	
	III-2	32.0	73.0	14	NS	
	III-3	29.5	75.5	14	NS	
	Total	406.5	496.5	42		NS
Autonomy	IV-1	51.5	53.5	14	NS	
	IV-2	58.5	46.5	14	NS	
	IV-3	41.0	64.0	14	NS	
	IV-4	53.5	51.5	14	NS	
	Total	763.5	823.5	56		NS
Self-actuali-zation	V-1	56.5	48.5	14	NS	
	V-2	92.0	13.0	14	.05	
	V-3	79.0	26.0	14	.20	
	Total	638.0	265.0	42		.01
Total all items		8,904.5	7,748.5	182	NS	

[a]For complete wording of items refer to text in Methods section.
[b]For method of computing p values, refer to text in Results section.

it represented a trend for respondents in flat organizations to be better satisfied than those in tall organizations. Where the sum of the negative ranks exceeded the sum of the positive ranks, it indicated that respondents from tall organizations were more satisfied than those from flatter organizations. Sign-rank tests were performed on individual items, on all items in a need category considered together, and on all thirteen items considered together.

Table 3 presents the results of the sign-rank test performed on the need deficiencies shown in Table 2 for companies of all sizes. From Table 3 it is apparent that flat organizations produced smaller need deficiencies for one item in the esteem need area (III-1) and for two items (V-2 and V-3) and the category total for the self-actualization need area, compared with tall organizations. On the other hand, respondents from tall organizations indicated smaller need fulfillment deficiencies for the security need category (item I-1), for the two social need items (II-1 and II-2) and the social category, and for two of the three esteem need area items (III-2 and

Table 4   Results of sign-rank tests on mean deficiencies for flat, intermediate, and tall organizations in four small size groups: sizes 1—4,999 (larger sum of positive ranks indicates greater satisfaction in flat organizations)

Need category	Item[a]	Sum of positive ranks	Sum of negative ranks	Number of comparisons	p value for items[b]	p value for categories[b]
Security	I-1	20.0	8.0	7	NS	NS
Social	II-1	14.0	14.0	7	NS	
	II-2	13.5	14.5	7	NS	
	Total	51.5	53.5	14		NS
Esteem	III-1	28.0	0.0	7	.05	
	III-2	10.5	17.5	7	NS	
	III-3	12.0	16.0	7	NS	
	Total	150.0	81.0	21		NS
Autonomy	IV-1	18.0	10.0	7	NS	
	IV-2	15.0	13.0	7	NS	
	IV-3	16.5	11.5	7	NS	
	IV-4	12.0	16.0	7	NS	
	Total	228.5	177.5	28		NS
Self-actualization	V-1	20.5	7.5	7	NS	
	V-2	28.0	0.0	7	.05	
	V-3	21.0	7.0	7	NS	
	Total	191.5	39.5	21		.01
Total all items		2,728.0	1,458.0	91	.05	

[a]For complete wording of items refer to text in Method section.
[b]For method of computing p values, refer to text in Results section.

III-3), compared with respondents from flat organizations. When the results were computed across all thirteen items, the sign-rank test showed no difference between tall and flat organizations in terms of perceived need deficiencies.

Table 4 presents the results of sign-rank test performed on the need deficiencies reported in Table 2 for companies with *less* than 5,000 employees. Two questions, one in the esteem need area (III-1) and one in the self-actualization need area (V-2), gave significant trends toward greater need satisfaction (smaller need deficiencies) in flat than in tall organizations. Also, the self-actualization need category showed a similar significant trend. Further, when all questions were considered together, respondents from flat organizations reported significantly greater satisfaction than did those from tall organizations ($p = .05$).

Table 5 presents the results of the sign-rank tests for companies employing *more* than 5,000 individuals. This table shows that the security, social and esteem need categories all produced trends towards more

Table 5   Results of sign-rank tests on mean deficiencies for flat, intermediate, and tall organizations in four large groups: sizes 5,000 or above (larger sum of positive ranks indicates greater satisfaction in flat organizations)

Need category	Item[a]	Sum of positive ranks	Sum of negative ranks	Number of com-parisons	p value for items[b]	p value for cate-gories[b]
Security	I-1	2.0	26.0	7	.05	.05
Social	II-1	6.0	22.0	7	NS	
	II-2	5.0	23.0	7	.20	
	Total	23.0	82.0	14		.10
Esteem	III-1	13.5	14.5	7	NS	
	III-2	7.5	20.5	7	NS	
	III-3	4.5	23.5	7	NS	
	Total	70.0	161.0	21		.20
Autonomy	IV-1	8.0	20.0	7	NS	
	IV-2	16.5	11.5	7	NS	
	IV-3	6.0	22.0	7	NS	
	IV-4	9.0	19.0	7	NS	
	Total	157.5	248.5	28		NS
Self-actualiza-tion	V-1	10.0	18.0	7	NS	
	V-2	21.0	7.0	7	NS	
	V-3	20.0	8.0	7	NS	
	Total	136.0	95.0	21		NS
Total all items		1,414.0	2,772.0	91	.01	

[a]For complete wording of items refer to text in Method section.
[b]For method of computing p values, refer to text in Results section.

satisfaction in tall than in flat organizations. For all thirteen items considered together, the trend towards greater satisfaction in tall organizations was significant at the .01 level of confidence by the sign-rank test.

DISCUSSION AND CONCLUSIONS
It is clear that our findings show no over-all superiority of flat over tall organizations in producing greater need satisfaction for managers. However, two qualifications to this general finding should be pointed out. First, organization size seemed to have some effect on the relative effectiveness of flat versus tall structures. In companies employing fewer than 5,000 people, managerial satisfactions did seem somewhat greater in flat rather than in tall organizations. For companies of more than 5,000 employees the picture was reversed with a tall type of structure producing perceptions of greater need satisfaction. The reasons for this seeming interaction of size and degree of tallness or flatness in affecting job satisfactions are not clear from the present data. However, in this

connection it is interesting to refer to the comments that Haire (1955) has made concerning the importance of size-shape interactions. Haire, using the analogy of living organisms, points out that large and small social organizations may require somewhat different shapes of structure in order to function effectively. Our results point to one possible change in structure that might be crucial in affecting job satisfaction attitudes as organizations grow in total size.

The second qualification that should be mentioned in connection with the over-all finding of no difference between tall and flat structures is the fact that the effects of organization structure on satisfactions appear to vary with the type of psychological need being considered. As was evident from the results presented in the preceding section, a tall type of structure seems especially advantageous in producing security and social need satisfactions, whereas a flat structure has superiority in influencing self-actualization satisfactions. For the esteem and autonomy areas, the type of structure seemed to have relatively little effect. The results thus point to the fact that future research may have to consider which types of needs are being investigated, if the effects of tall v. flat structures on satisfactions are to be validated.

From our results, we would draw two conclusions: (1) The effects of a tall or a flat organization structure do not appear to be as simple and unequivocal (in favor of a flat structure) as Worthy seems to imply. Our findings point to organization size as one of the factors affecting the relative advantages of one or the other type of structure. Future research will also undoubtedly show that the type of company – e.g. retail trade firms versus manufacturing companies – will have an important bearing on which type of structure is most advantageous in terms of morale and efficiency. Another factor that may turn out to be important is the level at which the employee works in the organization. Worthy's conclusions were based primarily on nonmanagement employees, while ours were based solely on managers. (2) A flat organization structure does seem to have some of the advantages claimed for it in the self-actualization need area, that is, in such opportunities as those for self-development and for the realization of an individual's unique capabilities. However, no superiority for a flat type of structure was found to extend to the autonomy need area involving opportunities for participation and for independent thought and action.

REFERENCES

Gardner, B. B. and Moore, D. G., *Human Relations in Industry*, 3rd ed. (Homewood, Ill.: Richard D. Irwin, 1955).

Haire, M., 'Size, Shape and Function in Industrial Organizations', *Human Organization*, XIV (1955) 17–21.

Meltzer, L. and Salter, J., 'Organization Structure and the Performance and Job Satisfaction of Physiologists', *American Sociological Review,* XXVII (1962) 351–62.

Porter, L. W., 'A Study of Perceived Need Satisfactions in Bottom and Middle Management Jobs', *Journal of Applied Psychology,* XLV (1961) 1–10.

Porter, L. W., 'Job Attitudes in Management: I. Perceived Deficiencies in Need Fulfillment as a Function of Job Level', *Journal of Applied Psychology,* XLVI (1962) 375–84.

Strauss, G. and Sayles, L. R., *Personnel: The Human Problems of Management* (Englewood Cliffs, N.J.: Prentice-Hall, 1960).

Viteles, M. S., *Motivation and Morale in Industry* (New York: W. W. Norton and Company, 1953).

Whyte, W. F., *Men at Work* (Homewood, Ill.: Richard D. Irwin, 1961).

Worthy, J. C., 'Organizational Structure and Employee Morale', *American Sociological Review,* XV (1950) 169–79.

NOTE

1. The assistance of the American Management Association in obtaining the sample of respondents is gratefully acknowledged.

13 Validation of a Sociometric Regrouping Procedure*

RAYMOND H. VAN ZELST
Psychometric Affiliates

In spite of the assumed importance of job satisfaction and interpersonal relations of workers a survey of the relevant literature (Bellows, 1949; Hoppock and Spiegler, 1938; Hull and Kolstad, 1942; Kornhauser and Sharp, 1932; Maier, 1946; Mayo and Lombard, 1944; Speroff and Kerr, 1951) shows a definite lack of systematic evaluation of these important determiners of employee attitudes and output. In a previous study (1951) the author explored the relationships existing between interpersonal desirability of workers (as determined by co-worker ratings), job satisfaction, and ten other more specific attributes of job satisfaction. Results of this study showed interpersonal desirability to bear a very definite relationship to job satisfaction (r of .82). Further analysis of the data also showed the interpersonally desirable worker (1) to have a greater feeling of job security, (2) to believe he has good working conditions, (3) to consider his co-workers very friendly, (4) to believe the company is interested in his welfare, (5) to believe he possesses opportunity of communication with management, and (6) to possess confidence in the good intentions of and good sense of management.

In the belief that sociometric regrouping of the work teams would produce an increase in the amount of production and quality of work as well as a reduction in turnover the author — working in conjunction with the supervisor and foreman of the work groups, and a top member of management — set about validating the sociometric regrouping.

SUBJECTS
Subjects used in this study are identical with those used in the previous study (1951). They comprised four total work groups — a carpenter group of twenty members, another carpenter group of eighteen members and two separate groups of bricklayers, each having sixteen members. All workers were well acquainted with each other's personality and skill. None

*Journal of Abnormal and Social Psychology, XLVII (1952) 299–301. Copyright 1952 by the American Psychological Association. Reprinted by permission.

of the workers was in any way related to each other and few, if any, had known other members of his group previous to their present job.

THE CRITERIA

Effectiveness of the sociometric regrouping was ascertained by means of four criteria — job satisfaction, turnover rate, an index of labor cost, and an index of materials cost.

Job satisfaction was measured by the *Tear Ballot for Industry* (Kerr, 1948, 1951) previous to the experimental period and upon completion of the three-month experimental period. Turnover records for the groups were taken from company kept, monthly compiled personnel records. Actual labor and materials costs were made available from cost account records kept on a 'row-of-units' basis. Labor and material costs are unaffected here by size of work force. Because of the company's desire for anonymity of identity and of cost figures no actual monetary results will be reported here. Instead the indices of labor cost and materials cost were arrived at by taking actual expenses in dollars and dividing through by a constant to arrive at the particular index used. Fluctuations in output criteria are displayed graphically in Figures 1 and 2.

EXPERIMENTAL PROCEDURE

The construction job upon which these groups were working was a large housing project on the outskirts of Chicago. The project was separated into two parts by a highway running through its center. All workers had previously been split up into two separate and comparatively remote

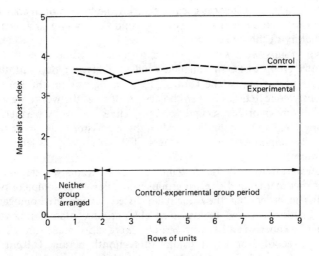

Fig. 1 Comparative fluctuations between experimental and control groups on materials cost for entire three-month experimental period

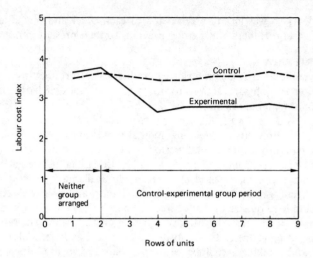

Fig. 2   Comparative fluctuations between experimental and control
groups on labor costs for entire three-month experimental period

groups — each working on a different side of the highway under different
foremen and having little or no contact with the other group.

Houses were constructed in rows of eight — beginning on the highway
and moving away. Each row was identical with every other row, but
houses within rows varied. Each group, then, performed identical jobs,
thus controlling the job content factor.

No disrupting incidences occurred during the three-month course of the
experiment and similarity of working conditions was guaranteed by the
propinquity of the two groups.

Two groups were set up. The experimental group consisted of the
carpenter group of twenty members and a bricklayer group with the other
two groups serving as the control. Regrouping was on the basis of the
previously collected co-worker choices. In all cases the worker received his
first (30 times) or his second (6 times) choice of work partner. Actual
rearrangement was accomplished when the supervisor in assigning the day's
work also announced work partners. This in no way violated previous
procedures.

However, before the rearrangement of work teams was put into effect
both experimental and control groups were allowed to complete two rows
of units in order that they might be tested for present homogeneity in
work performance and to insure an absence of contaminating variables.
Further comparisons between groups were also made on all criteria
utilizing records for the previous three-month period. Output criteria
(labor and materials costs) when analyzed for this time span yielded
critical ratios of −.32 and −.58 respectively. A previous measurement of

job satisfaction (prior to the experimental period) showed no significant difference — critical ratio of —.78 — while turnover records of the previous three-month period also indicated a similarity, the critical ratio being —.10. It can be assumed, therefore, that the two groups are adequately matched.

All statistical comparisons were made between experimental and control groups during the same three-month period because of the effect of adverse weather conditions upon out-of-doors jobs and other contaminating influences due to the nature of the occupations studied (e.g. lack of other job opportunities for the worker during the winter months, etc.).

RESULTS AND DISCUSSION
As shown in Table 1 the experimental group varied significantly from the control group — the former being markedly superior on all four criteria. Job satisfaction scores show a mean increase of 5.5 points with a critical ratio of 3.52. Turnover in the sociometric group is virtually nonexistent with a mean of .33 per month, the critical ratio between groups being 14.65. The marked decrease in turnover rate is of especially great significance since the building trades, at least in the Chicago area, are currently experiencing a critical skilled labour shortage and are characterized by an unusually high turnover rate even for a 'transient-employer' industry always noted for its high turnover. Labor costs and materials savings also show definite drops having critical ratios of 5.45 and 3.10 respectively.

Definite financial savings which cannot be presented here led the company's chief construction engineer to state in his report to management,

Table 1   Critical ratios computed between experimental and control groups for three-month period preceding and for three-month period of the experiment (labor and materials costs are based on a 'row-of-units' basis of 8 houses)

Variable	Control mean SD		Experimental mean SD		Critical ratio
Job satisfaction					
Before experimental period	39.7	6.20	38.5	6.72	—.78
During experimental period	39.3	6.88	44.8	6.08	3.52
Turnover rate					
Before experimental period	2.3	1.25	2.7	2.06	—.10
During experimental period	3.7	1.25	.33	.47	14.65
Index of labor cost					
Before experimental period	3.59	.65	3.66	.74	—.32
During experimental period	3.49	.51	2.87	.45	5.45
Index of materials cost					
Before experimental period	3.30	.28	3.34	.30	—.58
During experimental period	3.32	.25	3.14	.23	3.10

savings due to this psychological procedure have exceeded those of any previous work saving device or any combination of five previous work saving methods. Financial benefits are such that we are now constructing every 29th building entirely free from labor and materials costs. Even greater financial gains would occur were it possible to evaluate monetarily savings due to the great reduction in turnover.

It must be noted, however, that the building trades with their 'buddy-work-teams' are especially suited for a sociometric regrouping. The main drawback to a universal adoption of sociometric procedures is the shifting of workers into different teams while avoiding any change in job duties which would have a negative effect on job performance, necessitate retraining the worker, etc., and so cancel any benefits accruing from the sociometric regrouping. Among these building trade workers such a limitation was not a hindrance, for these workers do not operate according to assembly line procedures and so must be more or less equally adept at all phases of construction. The necessity of working together in a rather mutually co-operating series of tasks may also be viewed as conducive to stress upon interworker relations.

Further suppositions which must be met lie on management's side of the ledger. It is necessary that management have a democratic approach to the government of workers as well as recognizing the importance of group relations and manifesting an interest in worker preferences. Any adequate handling of such procedures as used here should be based on objective study and a recognition of social stimuli impinging upon the worker, his attitudes and expectations.

Looking back upon the results of both this study and its predecessor it would seem that a careful employment of 'human relations' procedures increases the worker's sense of belongingness, and molds worker and management together in a mutually satisfied group solidarity. Sociometric procedure as here used has resulted in increased satisfaction on the part of the worker and greater financial returns on the part of management.

REFERENCES

Bellows, R. M., *Psychology of Personnel in Business and Industry* (New York: Prentice-Hall, 1949).

Hoppock, R. and Spiegler, S., 'Job Satisfaction, Research of 1935–7', *Occupations*, No. 16, 1938, 636–9.

Hull, R. and Kolstad, A., 'Morale on the Job', in *Civilian Morale*, ed. G. Watson (Boston: Houghton Mifflin, 1942).

Kerr, W. A., 'On the Validity and Reliability of the Job Satisfaction Tear Ballot', *Journal of Applied Psychology*, XXXII (1948) 275–81.

Kerr, W. A., *Industrial Morale Diagnosis*, Chicago 90: Box 1625, Psychometric Affiliates, 1951..

Kornhauser, A. and Sharp, A., 'Employee Attitudes: Suggestions from a Study in a Factory', *Personnel Journal*, X (1932) 393–401.

Maier, N., *Psychology in Industry* (Boston: Houghton Mifflin, 1946).

Mayo, E. and Lombard, G., *Teamwork and Labor Turnover* (Harvard Business School: Business Research Series, 1944).

Speroff, B. J. and Kerr, W. A., 'Interpersonal Desirability and Steel Mill "Hot-Strip" Accidents'. Paper read at Midwestern Psychological Association, Chicago, 1951.

Van Zelst, R. H., 'Job Satisfaction and the Interpersonally Desirable Worker', *Personnel Psychology*, IV (1951) 405–12.

PART IV
Job Satisfaction and Individual Differences

A number of biographical factors affect job satisfaction and these are considered in Part IV. The relationship between age and job satisfaction has been reported by Herzberg et al. (1957) as being a U-shaped curve — that morale starts off high, declines until the late twenties and starts to rise again for the remainder of the worker's life. The paper presented by Saleh and Otis shows that this curve is not universally true. For managers, job satisfaction increased up to sixty years and then declined with approaching retirement.

The paper by Hulin and Smith once again emphasises that no overall generalisation can be made about job satisfaction. Their study indicated significant differences between males and females for job satisfaction, with females less satisfied with their job. Kuhlen, too, found males and females to require different satisfactions from their job. Of course, sex co-varies with a great many other factors such as pay level, type of job, promotion opportunities and so on. What is clear from the study of Hulin and Smith is that women are not necessarily 'contented cows' and that the disadvantages that women suffer on the job may well be reflected in lower job satisfaction. It should be noted however that there are exceptions to the finding that women are less satisfied than men.

In considering education and job satisfaction, Klein and Maher make the point in their paper that job satisfaction depends to some extent on the social reference group of the individual. Those who compare themselves with groups more favoured financially are likely to be more dissatisfied with pay than those who compare themselves with others earning similar salaries. Klein and Maher found college educated managers to be less satisfied with pay compared to a non-college educated group, presumably because of the different reference groups each was relating back to. The results of this study cannot of course be generalized to non-managerial groups, where the study of England and Stein, considered earlier, showed higher occupational level, and therefore presumably higher educational level, to be related positively to job satisfaction. The study of Klein and Maher highlights the complexity of such variables as educational level.

The final study in this part, by Wild and Dawson, examines the effect

167

of age, marital status and length of service on the relative importance of factors making for job satisfaction. Their finding was that age and marital status did affect the perceived importance of various aspects of their job. The importance of pay, for example, appears to increase with length of service, although self-actualization decreases.

REFERENCE

Herzberg, F., Mausner, B., Peterson, R. O. and Capwell, D. F. *Job Attitudes: A Review of Research and Opinion* (Psychological Services of Pittsburgh, 1957).

14 Age and Level of Job Satisfaction*

SHOUKRY D. SALEH
Ontario Department of Civil Service

JAY L. OTIS
Western Reserve University

BACKGROUND

A number of studies have indicated differences between various age groups with respect to job satisfaction. The results of these studies generally show an increase in the level of job satisfaction with age (Benge and Capwell, 1947; Hoppock, 1960; Super, 1939). In fact, this trend was noted as early as 1935 in one of the earliest studies of job satisfaction among teachers (Hoppock, 1935). These studies indicated essentially a continuous increase in job satisfaction as a function of age, and one would be led to predict that the greatest period of job satisfaction is in the pre-retirement period.

On the other hand, there have been studies indicating generally unfavorable attitudes toward old age and retirement, and these attitudes may be expected to affect the level of job satisfaction in pre-retirement. For example, Turner's study (1955) showed that workers begin to feel hopeless as they contemplate growing older in a job which holds little interest for them and which may, in addition, begin to demand a pace too fast for their advancing years. He mentions that their morale decreases and they begin dreaming of ways to leave the company, although they can not afford to do so. Johnson's study (1958) indicated that symptoms of a depressive type are often evoked as an expression of the emotional meaning of retirement. In view of such studies, it is not feasible to infer that the level of job satisfaction in the pre-retirement period will be higher than other age periods. In the present study, it is hypothesized that the level of stated job satisfaction will increase with age to the pre-retirement period and, within that period, will show a decline.

RESEARCH METHOD

Subjects were 80 male employees at the managerial level between the ages of 60 and 65 (Group A) and 38 comparable managers between the ages of

Personnel Psychology, XVII (1964) 425–30. Reprinted by permission.

50 and 55 (Group B). They were all employed in organizations having a compulsory retirement age of 65. These organizations included a company manufacturing electrical appliances and several companies engaged in the production of chemicals, oil, and steel. Also included were three major utilities and a bank.

All subjects were given a questionnaire in which work experience was divided into five age periods. They were asked:

> In the light of *your past work experience* and *your anticipation for the remaining working years,* indicate the age period in which you have been most satisfied in your work, and the age period in which you have been least satisfied. Write the number 1 in front of the period of least satisfaction and the number 5 in front of the period of most satisfaction. After doing this, try to arrange the other three periods in rank order according to job satisfaction, by using the numbers 2, 3 and 4.

Age periods	*Ranking numbers*
a. Up to 29	( )
b. 30–39	( )
c. 40–49	( )
d. 50–59	( )
e. 60 and over	( )

RESULTS

The results show that the level of job satisfaction increased for both groups from age periods A to B, B to C, and C to D, but that it declined in E, the terminal period. Thus the results confirm the hypothesis that the level of job satisfaction increases with age until the pre-retirement period, when it declines.

Table 1   Sums and means of ranks of periods of job satisfaction

Period	Group A (60–65)		Group B (50–55)	
	Sums of ranks	Means of ranks	Sums of ranks	Means of ranks
Up to 29	177	2.2	76	2.0
30–39	206	2.6	125	3.3
40–49	267	3.3	142	3.7
50–59	299	3.7	144	3.8
60–65	250	3.1	83	2.2
N	80		38	
χr^2	47		42.5	
df	4		4	
P	$<.001$		$<.001$	

Table 2   Number and percentages of subjects indicating most and least satisfaction in each age period

| | Group A (60–65) ($N = 80$) | | | | Group B (50–55) ($N = 38$) | | | |
| | Most satisfaction | | Least satisfaction | | Most satisfaction | | Least satisfaction | |
Period	No.	%	No.	%	No.	%	No.	%
Up to 29	10	12.5	35	43.8	0	0.0	19	50.0
30–39	10	12.5	19	23.8	10	26.3	3	7.8
40–49	22	27.5	9	11.2	13	34.2	5	13.2
50–59	26	32.5	5	6.2	15	39.5	2	5.3
60–65	12	15.0	12	15.0	0	0.0	9	23.7
χ^2	14.0		34.6		26.3		25.2	
df	4		4		4		4	
P	<.01		<.001		<.001		<.001	

Table 1 shows that the sums of the ranks increase in the first four periods (A to B to C to D) and then drop in the pre-retirement period (E). It is of interest to note that this drop is more drastic for the younger group, who have not yet reached the pre-retirement period, than for the older group, who are actually in their pre-retirement years. The Friedman two-way analysis of variance for the sums of ranks (Siegel, 1956) yields a value of 47 for Group A (ages 60–65) and 42.5 for Group B (ages 50–55). Both are significant well beyond the .001 level.

When the percentages of subjects indicating most and least satisfaction in each age period were considered, the same trend was found. Table 2 shows a continuous increase in the percentages for the most satisfaction through the first four periods, and then a drop in the terminal period. For the case of least satisfaction, the trend is reversed. The differences between these percentages are statistically significant in all cases.

For both groups the period 50–59 had the highest mean rank and had the highest percentage of first-ranked responses. The lowest level of satisfaction is found in the starting age period, up to 29. Figure 1 shows the levels of job satisfaction through the various periods of work experience. For each group, the highest sum of ranks was considered as one hundred and the other sums of ranks were equated proportionally.

DISCUSSION

Up to a point, these results support previous studies which indicated the increase of job satisfaction with age. This study has shown, however, that the increase in stated job satisfaction does not continue until retirement, but rather that it decreases in the terminal period, i.e. the five years before mandatory retirement. Tuckman and Lorge (1954) reported similar results

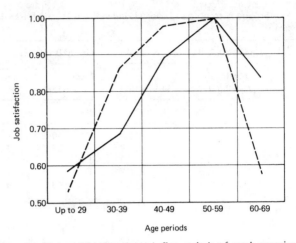

Fig. 1. Levels of job satisfaction through five periods of work experience for two age groups
Note: Job satisfaction is expressed as a ratio of each mean rank to the largest mean rank of the group.

concerning the period after age 60. None of their subjects (average age, 74) selected this period as the most favorable for job satisfaction. Super (1939), testing a wide range of occupations, reported that there was a slight decrease in job satisfaction between the ages of 45 and 54. When his data were analyzed by occupational level, however, he found that the decline was evident only in the 'commercial' group. Super stated 'the increase in the relatively dissatisfied commercial group at ages 45—54 might explain the relative decline in job satisfaction at that period'. Super explained that because of the large proportion of the commercial group the decline may have been due to a sampling error.

The general trend towards increased job satisfaction with increased age has been explained by the upward trend in adjustment and satisfaction with life (Herzberg et al., 1957). The hypothesis which states that satisfied workers tend to transfer from jobs where morale is low to other jobs is also plausible.

If results for Group A were considered alone, the decline in level of satisfaction in the pre-retirement period might be a function of a 'present versus the past' comparative evaluation, as opposed to '60—65 versus other ages' evaluation. That interpretation is countered by the results obtained with Group B, showing a similar decline in job satisfaction anticipated for the terminal work period.

It is most probable that the decline is due to the actual blocking, or anticipated blocking, of the channels for self-actualization and psychological growth. The factors which are related to actualization and growth, such as achievement, recognition, advancement, responsibility and growth in skill, have been indicated (Herzberg et al., 1959; Saleh, 1964) as the sources of true satisfaction. Pre-retirees do not have ready access to such sources of satisfaction and, in their advancing years, the level of their job satisfaction declines. For instance, they may have, or at least feel that they have, little chance for advancement and growth in skill. Because their time is limited until retirement, companies do not usually give them an opportunity for promotion or for holding a new position, while younger workers with less experience have these opportunities. This treatment tends to make pre-retirees feel that they are not as useful or even wanted as much as they once were and, consequently, their job satisfaction declines.

Another explanation for this decline may be related to the decline in physical health. Pre-retirees, because of the perceived feeling of slowing down as a consequence of older age, may feel the pressure of their jobs more than they did in middle age. The responsibilities once handled with ease now become a source of pressure which leads to dissatisfaction. Pre-retirees may prefer, therefore, to retire or leave their present jobs for other kinds of activities for which they feel better suited and in which they can control the pace.

SUMMARY AND CONCLUSIONS

Pre-retirees ranking the five periods of their working experience according to their relative feelings of job satisfaction indicated that the level of job satisfaction increases in the first four periods (up to age 60) and then declines in the terminal period (age 60 to 65).

The increases in the first four periods were explained by the general adjustment to life which comes with increased age. The decline in the pre-retirement period was explained by the blockage of the channels for self-actualization and psychological growth and was related to the decline in physical health.

REFERENCES

Benge, E. J. and Capwell, D. F., 'Employee Morale Survey', *Modern Management*, VII (1947) 19–22.

Herzberg, F., Mausner, B., Peterson, R. O. and Capwell, D. F., *Job Attitudes: Review of Research and Opinion* (Pittsburgh: Psychological Service of Pittsburgh, 1957).

Herzberg, F., Mausner, B. and Snyderman, B. B., *The Motivation to Work* (New York: Wiley, 1959).

Hoppock, R., 'Comparisons of Satisfied and Dissatisfied Teachers', *Psychological Bulletin*, XII (1935) 661.

Hoppock, R., 'A 27-Year Follow-up on Job Satisfaction of Employed Adults', *Personnel Guidance Journal*, XXXVIII (1960) 489–92.

Johnson, D. E., 'A Depressive Retirement Syndrome', *Geriatrics*, XII (1958) 314–19.

Saleh, S. D., 'A Study of Attitude Change in the Pre-retirement Period', *Journal of Applied Psychology*, X L V I I I (1964) 310–12.

Siegel, S., *Nonparametric Statistics for the Behavioral Sciences* (New York: McGraw-Hill, 1956).

Super, D. E., 'Occupational Level of Job Satisfaction', *Journal of Applied Psychology*, X X I I I (1939) 547–64.

Tuckman, J. and Lorge, I., 'Old People's Appraisal of Adjustment Over the Life Span', *Journal of Personality*, X X I I (1954) 417–22.

Turner, A. N., 'The Older Worker: New Light on Employment and Retirement Problems', *Personnel*, X X X I I (1955) 246–57.

15 Sex Differences in Job Satisfaction*

CHARLES L. HULIN
University of Illinois

PATRICIA CAIN SMITH[1]
Cornell University

Measures of 5 separate aspects of job satisfaction gathered from 295 male workers and 163 female workers drawn from 4 different plants were analyzed with respect to the mean job satisfaction for the male and female workers. T^2 analyses indicated that in 3 plants the female workers were significantly less satisfied than their male counterparts (p < .05) while in the 4th plant there was no significant difference. A test of concordance on the relative size of the differences indicated that the ordering of the differences in satisfaction level was somewhat consistent across the 4 samples (p < .01).

What are the antecedent conditions which lead to high or low job satisfaction? Various writers have investigated the contribution of job level to satisfaction (Ash, 1954; Centers, 1948; Hulin, 1963; Katz, 1949), the contribution of wage level (Hulin, 1963; Inlow, 1951; Miller, 1940, 1941; Survey Research Center, 1950), the effects of type of leadership or leadership climate (Fleishman, 1955; Kahn and Katz, 1953; Pelz, 1952; Vroom and Mann, 1960), the age of the worker as it affects job satisfaction (Bernberg, 1954; Cain, 1942; Hinrichs, 1962; Hulin, 1963; Mann, 1953; Smith, 1955), and even the effects of the personality of the workers on their job satisfaction (Cain, 1942; Peterson and Stone, 1942; Smith, 1936; Smith, 1955; Weitz, 1952).

The net result of these studies seems to be that higher job levels and higher wages generally contribute to higher job satisfaction; the type of leadership has certain effects on job satisfaction, but these effects are modified greatly by situational factors; age and tenure seem to be positively related to job satisfaction (for a dissenting opinion on this latter conclusion see Herzberg, Mausner, Peterson and Capwell, 1957); and job

Journal of Applied Psychology, XLVIII [2] (1964) 88–92. Copyright 1964 by the American Psychological Association. Reprinted by permission.

satisfaction seems to be related to a general life adjustment—maladjustment factor.

The relation of the sex of the worker to job satisfaction is an additional topic which has received a great deal of attention. The findings of the investigations on sex differences in job satisfaction, however, are somewhat contradictory and permit no neat cogent statement of the relationship between sex and job satisfaction.

For example, Benge (1944) and Stockford and Kunze (1950) concluded that women are *more* satisfied than men, while Cole (1940) reported women to be *less* satisfied than men, and Blood, Harwood, and Vernon (1942), in a study of the psychological problems of adjusting to the rather severe wartime working conditions which existed in Great Britain during World War II, reported that women exhibited more serious psychological maladjustment than did their male counterparts.

In the area of satisfaction with teaching, Chase (1951) reported women teachers to be more satisfied than men, while Peck (1936) concluded that women were more poorly adjusted than men teachers.

Not only do these results contradict each other to a considerable extent, but also some of them contradict the findings, reported above, concerning wages and job level and their effects on job satisfaction. Based on these findings, women should be less satisfied than men, since they are usually placed on lower level jobs, which have a lower pay rate, and which usually offer few promotional opportunities. Thus, barring the possible effects of adaptation level, women should be less satisfied on their jobs.

In addition to the factors of wages and job level, there is the issue of societal norms concerning appropriate roles for men and women. When males are employed in industry they are filling the role that society has come to expect of them. Women in industry (in spite of their increasing numbers) are in a relatively alien role. In addition, if they are married and working full time they may be faced with a certain amount of role conflict, which also may affect their job satisfaction. (See Mead, 1949, for a discussion of some of these problems of dual roles which female workers must face when they hold a full-time job.)

It should be noted that there may be some methodological problems connected with many of the studies of sex differences. In general the questionnaires which have been used to measure job satisfaction seem to have been designed for, and 'validated' on, male workers. With the known differences in the motivation of male and female workers (Jurgensen, 1949) this practice may introduce a bias of unknown but substantial magnitude. An additional problem is the fact that these investigations all used different and not necessarily equivalent measures of job satisfaction (see Smith and Kendall, 1963). Thus, we do not know if the apparently contradictory results are due to differences in the measures used or to true differences in satisfaction levels between men and women.

The present investigation reports an analysis of data of workers drawn from four different plants representing three different companies. The same questionnaire was administered to all of these workers. Thus, one source of the apparent contradiction may be eliminated. Secondly, the measures of job satisfaction used were validated and item analyzed using both male and female subjects. (This questionnaire will be described in more detail below.)

METHOD
Sample
The workers included in this analysis were given a guarantee of complete anonymity in all cases. It was stressed that their results would never be made known to the company officials.

They were drawn by means of a systematic sample from the employment rolls of the companies involved. (*a*) Company I, a large electronics firm located in a large metropolitan area in New England. Two units of the company, Plants A and B, were studied with each plant employing between 1,000 and 1,500 workers. Sampling was stratified by age, with no further restrictions. (*b*) Company II, a manufacturer of cardboard products, a medium-sized (300 to 400 employees) family-owned plant located in a small city in New England. Sampling was alphabetical. (*c*) Company III, a brass foundry, a medium-sized company (300 to 400 employees) located in a large city in the Midwest. Sampling was by clock number.

The sampling procedure used yielded a sample of 99 men and 35 women from Plant A, Company I; and 86 men and 40 women from Plant B, Company I. Company II gave a sample of 50 men and 43 women. Company III gave a sample of 60 men and 25 women. The analysis to be presented in this paper is based on a total sample of 295 male workers and 163 female workers.

Measures of job satisfaction
The device used to measure satisfaction in this study had been developed as part of a nationwide survey of retirement satisfaction. It had been subjected to an intensive validation program. The results of these validation studies were presented by Smith (1961, 1963), Hulin (1961), Hulin, Smith, Kendall, and Locke (1963), Macaulay (1961), Macaulay, Smith, Locke, Kendall, and Hulin (1963), Kendall (1961), Kendall, Smith, Hulin, and Locke (1963). Locke (1961), and Locke, Smith, and Hulin (1963). The brief discussion presented here will not attempt to present the complete details of these studies but will give only a short summary of these papers.

Basically, the Job Descriptive Index (JDI) is an adjective check list on which each worker is asked to describe several aspects of his job by means of a 'yes' '?' or 'no' response to each of the adjectives. The aspects of the job which the workers describe are their work, their pay, their opportunities for promotion, their supervision, and the people with whom they work. These areas or aspects of the job were chosen so as to be consistent with the findings of the factor analytic studies which have been done on the dimensions of job satisfaction (Ash, 1954; Austin, 1958; Baehr, 1954, 1956; Baehr and Renck, 1958; Gordon, 1955; Harrison, 1960, 1961; Twery, Schmid, and Wrigley, 1958; Wherry, 1954, 1958).

Each response to each adjective in the final form of the JDI has been item analyzed against total scale score to determine the proper scoring direction. Items were retained which discriminated significantly for *both* male and female workers separately.

Before this final scoring key was developed, however, the investigators developed and used several other methods of scoring the JDI. In the early studies, each worker's JDI was scored in four different ways. Each of the four different resulting scores was correlated with several different job satisfaction ratings made by both interviewers and the workers themselves. Different scoring methods were systematically eliminated from consideration on the basis of these 'validity' estimates. The final method of scoring and selection of items were those which yielded the highest estimates of convergent and discriminant validity (Campbell and Fiske, 1959) across several different samples for both male and female subjects.

In addition to the validity estimates, which averaged .50 to .70 across several samples, the JDI also has several other desirable characteristics.

1. The scores on it are unaffected by acquiescence or yes-saying and no-saying tendencies.

2. The resulting five scales, while not completely orthogonal, have the virtue of relatively low intercorrelations (.30 to .50) with each other.

3. Factor analyses of the data from several samples indicate that the workers are indeed capable of thinking along the lines of five separate aspects of job satisfaction. The factors extracted do seem to correspond to the five dimensions chosen by the investigators.

4. The five scales, while being quite short and easily administered, have adequate split-half reliabilities (.80 to .88 corrected by the Spearman-Brown formula).

RESULTS

Due to the multivariate nature of the measures of job satisfaction which were used in this study, the sex differences in job satisfaction could not be analyzed by the usual univariate test of significance. Instead Hotelling's T^2 analysis was used. This test is simply the multivariate analogue of the t test. The T^2 analysis, instead of using a single difference between means $(\bar{x}_i - \bar{x}_j)$ and a variance estimate $(s_{x_i}^2 + s_{x_j}^2)$, is based on a vector of mean differences $(\bar{x}_1 - \bar{x}_2, \bar{y}_1 - \bar{y}_2, \ldots)$ and the inverse of the variance-covariance matrix. This procedure has the advantage of providing an overall test of the significance of a vector of mean differences and of

Table 1   Vectors of mean differences

Company	Work	Pay	Area of job satisfaction			
			Promotions	Supervision	People	*p*
I, Plant A	.88	1.28	8.64	5.08	5.10	<.05
I, Plant B	−1.88	−3.28	2.92	.14	−1.18	ns
II	2.80	−.48	4.91	1.10	6.37	<.05
III	.00	−2.00	6.72	2.37	1.86	<.05

taking into account both the variance and the covariance of the variables as well as the magnitude of the difference. It thus avoids many of the problems connected with multiple comparisons. It has the disadvantage, however, of testing for the significance of the vector as a whole and providing no estimate of the contribution of the individual elements which make up the vector. For a complete discussion of this statistical test see Hotelling (1931) or Anderson (1958, pp. 101–3).

Table 1 gives the vectors of differences which were obtained from the four plants studied. A positive element in the vectors indicates that the male workers were more satisfied with that aspect of their work than were the females.

It can be seen from this table that in three of the four plants the female workers were significantly less satisfied than the male workers. These findings would seem to support, to a limited extent, our hypothesis that female workers should be less satisfied than male workers. This finding is not completely general in our sample of plants since one plant indicated no differences between male and female workers.

It also should be noted that a test of concordance done on these data indicates that not only are the *levels* of satisfaction different between the two sexes, but the *relative ordering* of these differences remains reasonably constant across the four different samples (*w* = .78, *p* < .01). In three of the four plants the females were more dissatisfied (relative to the males) with their promotional opportunities than with any other factor of their jobs. This is about what one would expect considering their opportunities for promotions. In three of the four plants females were slightly more satisfied with their pay than males. It is also an objective fact that women get *less* pay than men. When their pay is considered relative to their job level, type of work, and economic needs, however, it may not be out of line with the men's pay.

DISCUSSION

The data we have presented, based on a sample of 295 male workers and 163 female workers, seem to indicate that the female workers tend to be somewhat less satisfied with their jobs than their male counterparts. Further, the relative magnitude of the obtained differences was somewhat consistent across samples and was not out of line with what one might reasonably expect to obtain. There are two points, however, which merit further discussion. Firstly, we do not maintain that sex per se is the crucial factor which leads to either high or low satisfaction. It is, rather, the entire constellation of variables which consistently covary with sex; for example, pay, job level, promotion opportunities, societal norms, etc., that is likely causing the differences in job satisfaction. It is also likely that if these variables were held constant or if their effects were partialled out, the differences in job satisfaction would have disappeared. This study was intended primarily to establish the actual facts of the situation and not to offer an explanation. In the industrial setting these factors are *not* controlled or held constant and they do covary with sex. In each of the four samples the women were receiving less pay and were working on lower level jobs than the men, and in three of the samples the women were less satisfied than the men. The fact is that a large (and increasing) percentage of our work force is working under the handicap of relative dissatisfaction.

A second important point is that the difference in satisfaction did not hold up across all four samples, even though (as mentioned above) in all four samples the women were working on lower level jobs and were receiving less pay. This failure could perhaps be attributed to sampling fluctuations. On the other hand it is more likely that situational factors play a very important role, not only in the level of satisfaction of the workers, but also in the relative satisfaction of the male and the female workers. Thus, even though we can conclude now that women are generally less satisfied than men, additional precision concerning this conclusion could likely be gained by considering situational factors.

REFERENCES

Anderson, T. W., *Introduction to Multivariate Statistical Analysis* (New York: Wiley, 1958).

Ash, P., 'The SRA Employee Inventory: A Statistical Analysis', *Personnel Psychology,* VII (1954) 337–64.

Astin, A. W., 'Dimensions of Work Satisfaction in the Occupational Choices of College Freshmen', *Journal of Applied Psychology,* XLII (1958) 187–90.

Baehr, Melany E., 'A Factorial Study of the SRA Employee Inventory', *Personnel Psychology,* VII (1954) 319–36.

Baehr, Melany E., 'A Reply to R. J. Wherry Concerning "An orthogonal re-rotation of the Baehr and Ash studies of the SRA employee inventory" ', *Personnel Psychology,* IX (1956) 81–92.

Baehr, Melany E. and Renck, R., 'The Definition and Measurement of Employee Morale', *Administrative Science Quarterly,* III (1958) 157–84.

Benge, E. J., 'How to Learn what Workers Think of Job and Boss', *Factory Management and Maintenance*, CII [5] (1944) 101–4.

Bernberg, R. E., 'Socio-Psychological Factors in Industrial Morale: III. Relation of Age to Morale', *Personnel Psychology*, VII (1954) 395–9.

Blood, W., Harwood, J. and Vernon, H. M., 'Discussion on Effects of War-Time Industrial Conditions on Mental Health', *Proceedings of the Royal Society of Medicine*, XXXV (1942) 693–8.

Cain, Patricia A., 'Individual Differences in Susceptibility to Monotony'. Unpublished doctoral dissertation, Cornell University, 1942.

Campbell, D. T. and Fiske, D. W., 'Convergent and Discriminant Validation by the Multitrait-Multimethod Matrix', *Psychological Bulletin*, LVI (1959) 81–105.

Centers, R., 'Motivational Aspects of Occupation Stratification', *Journal of Social Psychology*, XXVIII (1948) 287–317.

Chase, F. S., 'Factors for Satisfaction in Teaching', *Phi Delta Kappan*, XXXIII (1951) 127–32.

Cole, R. J., 'A Survey of Employee Attitudes', *Public Opinion Quarterly*, IV (1940) 497–506.

Fleishman, E. A., 'Leadership Climate, Human Relations Training, and Supervisory Behavior', *Personnel Psychology*, VI (1955) 205–22.

Gordon, O. J., 'A Factor Analysis of Human Needs and Industrial Morale', *Personnel Psychology*, VIII (1955) 1–18.

Harrison, R., Sources of Variation in Managers' Job Attitudes', *Personnel Psychology*, XIII (1960) 425–34.

Harrison, R., 'Cumulative Communality Cluster Analysis of Workers' Job Attitudes', *Journal of Applied Psychology*, XLV (1961) 123–5.

Herzberg, F., Mausner, B., Peterson, R. O. and Capwell, Dora F., *Job Attitudes: Review of Research and Opinion* (Pittsburgh, Pa.: Psychological Service of Pittsburgh, 1957).

Hinrichs, J. R., 'The Impact of Industrial Organization on the Attitudes of Research Chemists'. Unpublished doctoral dissertation, Cornell University, 1962.

Hotelling, H., 'The Generalization of Student's Ratio', *Annals of Mathematical Statistics*, II (1931) 360–78.

Hulin, C. L., 'Cornell Studies in Methods of Measuring Job Satisfaction: I – A Systematic Approach to the Measurement of Job Satisfaction'. Paper read at American Psychological Association, New York, 1961.

Hulin, C. L., 'A Linear Model of Job Satisfaction'. Unpublished doctoral dissertation, Cornell University, 1963.

Hulin, C. L., Smith, Patricia C., Kendall, L. M. and Locke, E. A., 'Cornell Studies of Job Satisfaction: II. Model and Method of Measuring Job Satisfaction' (Ithaca: Cornell University, 1963). (Mimeo)

Inlow, G. M., 'Job Satisfaction of Liberal Arts Graduates', *Journal of Applied Psychology*, XXXV (1951) 175–81.

Jurgensen, C. E., 'What Job Applicants Look for in a Company', *Personnel,* XXV (1949) 352–5.

Kahn, R. and Katz, D., 'Leadership Practices in Relation to Productivity and Morale', in *Group Dynamics,* ed. D. Cartwright and A. Zander (Evanston, Ill.: Row, 1953).

Katz, D., 'Morale and Motivation in Industry', in *Current Trends in Industrial Psychology,* ed. W. Dennis (Pittsburgh: Univer. Pittsburgh Press, 1949).

Kendall, L. M., 'Cornell Studies in Methods of Measuring Job Satisfaction: III. The Relative Validity of Different Methods of Measurement for Predicting Criteria of Satisfaction'. Paper read at American Psychological Association, New York, 1961.

Kendall, L. M., Smith, Patricia C., Hulin, C. L. and Locke, E. A., 'Cornell Studies of Job Satisfaction: IV. The Relative Validity of the Job Descriptive Index and Other Methods of Measurement of Job Satisfaction' (Ithaca: Cornell University, 1963). (Mimeo)

Locke, E. A., 'Cornell Studies in Methods of Measuring Job Satisfaction: II. Importance and Satisfaction in Several Job Areas'. Paper read at American Psychological Association, New York, 1961.

Locke, E. A., Smith, Patricia C. and Hulin, C. L., 'Cornell Studies of Job Satisfaction: V. Scale Characteristics of the Job Descriptive Index' (Ithaca: Cornell University, 1963). (Mimeo)

Macaulay, D. Anne., 'Cornell Studies in Methods of Measuring Job Satisfaction: Development of Criteria of Job Satisfaction'. Paper read at American Psychological Association, New York, 1961.

Macaulay, D. Anne, Smith, Patricia C., Locke, E. A., Kendall, L. M. and Hulin, C. L., 'Cornell Studies in Job Satisfaction' III. Convergent and Discriminant Validity for Measures of Job Satisfaction by Rating Scales' (Ithaca: Cornell University, 1963). (Mimeo)

Mann, F. C., 'A Study of Work Satisfaction as a Function of the Discrepancy between Inferred Aspirations and Achievement', *Dissertation Abstracts,* XIII (1953) 902.

Mead, Margaret, *Male and Female* (New York: Morrow, 1949).

Miller, D. C., 'Morale of College-Trained Adults', *American Sociological Review,* V (1940) 880–9.

Miller, D. C., 'Economic Factors in the Morale of College-Trained Adults', *American Journal of Sociology,* XLVII (1941) 139–56.

Peck, L., 'A Study of the Adjustment Difficulties of a Group of Women Teachers', *Journal of Educational Psychology,* XXVII (1936) 401–16.

Pelz, D. C., 'Influence: A Key to Effective Leadership in the First-Line Supervisor', *Personnel,* XXIX (1952) 209–17.

Peterson, D. G. and Stone, C. H., 'Dissatisfaction with Life Work among Adult Workers', *Occupations,* XXI (1942) 219–21.

Smith, May, 'The Temperamental Factor in Industry', *Human Factors* (London), X (1936) 301–14.

Smith, Patricia C., 'The Prediction of Individual Differences in Susceptibility to Industrial Monotony', *Journal of Applied Psychology*, X X X IX (1955) 322–9.

✗ Smith, Patricia C., 'Cornell Studies in Methods of Measuring Job Satisfaction: Introduction and Scope'. Paper read at American Psychological Association, New York, 1961.

Smith, Patricia C., 'Cornell Studies of Job Satisfaction: I. Strategy for the Development of a General Theory of Job Satisfaction' (Ithaca: Cornell University, 1963). (Mimeo)

Smith, Patricia C. and Kendall, L. M., 'Cornell Studies of Job Satisfaction: VI. Implications for the Future' (Ithaca: Cornell University, 1963). (Mimeo)

Stockford, L. O. and Kunze, K. R., 'Psychology and the Pay Check', *Personnel*, X X V II (1950) 129–43.

Survey Research Center, 'Effective Morale. Part 3', *Fortune*, XL II [8] (1950) 46–50.

Twery, R., Schmid, J., Jr. and Wrigley, C., 'Some Factors in Job Satisfaction: A Comparison of Three-Methods of Analysis', *Educational and Psychological Measurement*, X V III (1958) 189–202.

Vroom, V. and Mann, F. C., 'Leader Authoritarianism and Employee Attitudes', *Personnel Psychology*, X III (1960) 125–40.

Weitz, J., 'A Neglected Concept in the Study of Job Satisfaction', *Personnel Psychology*, V (1952) 201–5.

Wherry, R. J., 'An Orthogonal Re-rotation of the Baehr and Ash Studies of the SRA Employee Inventory', *Personnel Psychology*, V II (1954) 365–80.

Wherry, R. J., 'Factor Analysis of Morale Data: Reliability and Validity', *Personnel Psychology*, X I (1958) 78–89.

NOTE

1. This study is part of the Cornell University Studies of Retirement Policies financed by a grant from the Ford Foundation and is based on a doctoral dissertation by the senior author submitted to the graduate school of Cornell University in partial fulfillment of the requirements for the degree of Doctor of Philosophy. The dissertation was directed by the second author. Both authors participated in collection of the data.   We wish to express our gratitude to the cooperating companies who made their records available and contributed the time of their personnel to make these studies possible, and to the interviewers who contributed their time to the validation studies.

16 Education Level and Satisfaction with Pay*

S. M. KLEIN
International Business Machines

J. R. MAHER
Columbia University

BACKGROUND OF THE STUDY

As our society becomes increasingly complex and technical, more and more people with higher education will be brought into the work force. This trend has been evident over the past two decades in that there has been an increasing percentage of the total work force that can be classified as white collar. These jobs ordinarily require more educational training than the typical blue collar job. Moreover, the content of a large portion of the white collar job pool requires a high degree of technical training and competence. For example, companies in the electronics and data processing fields expect substantial increases in the percentage of the total work force that will be comprised of engineers, accountants, and lower and middle levels of administrative personnel.

As a consequence, it would be useful to understand in both an empirical and theoretical sense the attitudes of the college-educated group and their relation to those of their less educated peers. There are a number of attitudinal areas that can be investigated, such as attitudes about job and job content, supervision, administrative policies, the company, and salary. The study of these attitudes can be placed in the context of the overall relationship between the college-educated people and their work, thus providing insight into a group that may become a dominant work force in American society. As a beginning, we have chosen to examine the relationship between education and satisfaction with salary.

Few contemporary studies have been done which directly involve satisfaction with salary as it relates to education. Herzberg et al. (1957) have summarized findings to that time, but as a group the studies are sufficiently contradictory to prevent the drawing of a definite conclusion

Personnel Psychology, XIX (1966) 195–208. Reprinted by permission.

at first glance. According to the authors, 'Of the 13 studies relating education to job attitudes, 5 show no differences in job attitudes among workers differing in education; 3 studies show an increase in morale with increased education; another 5 show that the higher these workers' education level, the lower their morale'.

However, close scrutiny of the studies reporting a positive relationship between education and worker attitudes reveals that these findings are open to question regarding their generality. One study, for example, used only college graduates, with the independent variable being the amount of graduate training (AVA, 1948). Another focused on a population of trainees under Public Law 16 who were not applying the skills with which they had been trained at the time of the study (Kessler, 1954). In discussing these and other studies, Herzberg et al. (1957) say, 'these studies . . . were carried out either with groups having a restricted range of education, or with groups in unusual circumstances'. In any event, it is clear that these studies do not provide enough evidence to conclude that education is positively related to satisfaction with salary.

There is, however, a fair amount of evidence that suggests that workers who have attended college are less satisfied with their pay than those who have not attended college. Centers and Cantril (1946), for example, find such a relationship and discuss it in terms of aspiration level. They feel that a better-than-average income is associated with social contact with still more affluent individuals, causing an increase in aspiration level and a concomitant dissatisfaction brought about by an increased discrepancy between reality and aspiration. In addition, Cantril (1943) maintains that the higher a person's social class identification, the more he is likely to feel that his income is less than his social class.

Thomsen (1943), using a college population, found that the incomes which students reported they would be receiving in their chosen careers at some point in the future were often ridiculously high and completely out of line with the national norms. Suspecting that these subjects were joking, Thomsen interviewed them and had them write essays. He reports 'None of them . . . was familiar with the average incomes of people in their chosen fields, and most were incredulous when figures were shown'. An additional conclusion was that 'students expect a great deal higher income than most people feel would be satisfactory'. As Ganguli (1957) indicates, both expectations and aspirations may be largely a function of education.

Generalizing somewhat from these results, it seems that a key variable in determining salary satisfaction is the important groups to which the individual compares himself. This point has been amply demonstrated in past studies. For example, Patchen (1961) found that refinery workers who chose to compare themselves to others thought to be making more money than themselves were more dissatisfied with their salaries than the workers who compared themselves to others making the same or less money. Theoretically this ties in with the concept of reference groups as developed by Newcomb (1950), Sherif (1953) and others. This concept has been used to explain such surprising findings as the lower satisfaction with promotion rate in the Army Air Force than in the Military Police during World War II, despite the fact that promotions came much faster in the former (Stouffer et al., 1949). In fact, Form and Geschwender (1962) and Hadley and Levy (1962) find that satisfactions of *any* kind in industry depend to some extent on the reference groups of the individual.

A related aspect involves a comparison of present wage levels and the subjective determination of where one ought to be. This partly determined by reference groups and partly by a host of other variables such as self-concept, level of aspiration, and information regarding salary levels of similar jobs. Thus, if one is led to expect certain salary attainments and his present level is well below this, one would expect dissatisfaction.

This kind of result was obtained by Andrews and Henry (1963), who found that people who expect higher monetary rewards in the future are less satisfied with their present pay. In addition, Lawler and Porter (1963) found that satisfaction with pay seems to be more a function of where an individual currently slots himself on pay, relative to where he feels he should be, than of his absolute pay level.

HYPOTHESES

While the identification of antecedent variables is difficult, our conceptual scheme includes the following train of events. College education or lack thereof constitutes a key input in the individual's self-evaluation. This self-evaluation in turn leads to expectations regarding salary opportunities which in turn affect satisfactions with present salary conditions. As a consequence, we would expect that having attended college would negatively affect satisfaction with pay since, for any given pay level, the college-trained person will be further away from the set of expectations he holds for himself. Further, if these expectations are held constant, then the difference between the college educated and the non-college educated should disappear because this would also partially control for reference groups, self-concept, and aspiration level. More formally, we predict:

1. Those people who have attended college will exhibit less satisfaction with their salary than those who have not.

2. Satisfaction with pay is largely a function of expectation, both external and internal to the company, of what salary the individual feels he can get.

   (a) The better he feels his chances of getting comparable positions elsewhere, the less favorable he will rate his current pay.

   (b) The better he feels his chances of getting more money internally on the same job, the less favorable he will rate his current pay.

3. Those who have attended college will perceive both internal and external possibilities for pay as greater than those who have not attended college.

4. When we control for internal and external perceptions of pay possibilities (expectations), the differences in satisfaction with pay between the college and the non-college groups will disappear.

PRESENT STUDY

In order to test the above predictions, a study was conducted using questionnaire survey data from a population of first-level managers in an electronics manufacturing population. This population is made up of both college and non-college people and is homogeneous in that they all are part of a manufacturing operation, though some supervise direct labor and others supervise support labor. Thus we are talking about college and non-college people performing roughly the same level work. A clear distinction must be made between this population and such other groups as engineers or college-trained salesmen.

The study focuses on the relationship between education and satisfaction with salary, using subjective estimates of (*a*) the probability of getting a comparable paying job elsewhere and (*b*) making more money on the present job as operational measurements of the general concept of personal expectations.

The data were collected through the use of an attitude questionnaire administered on company time. These managers correspond to foremen or first-level supervisors in companies that do not designate first-level supervision as a managerial group. The questionnaires were anonymous, were composed of 426 items primarily of the Likert type, and required the better part of two hours to fill out. The subjects were 727 managers, representing a 50 per cent random sample.

Variables

The variables, together with the questionnaire items used to measure them, include the following:

1. Satisfaction with pay
   Questions:
   (*a*) How would you rate your salary considering your duties and responsibilities? and
   (*b*) How would you rate your salary considering what you could get from other companies?
   Both items had five response categories ranging from 'very good' to 'very poor'.

2. Education
   Question: How much education have you had?
   There were six categories ranging from grade school to master's or doctoral degree. Individuals were grouped according to whether they had attended (not necessarily graduated from) college or not.

3. *Perceived probability of getting a comparable job elsewhere* (hereafter
   referred to as *external expectations*)
   Question: Suppose you quit your job. Do you think you would be able
   to get another job in your line of work at about the same salary?
   There were four categories ranging from 'Yes, definitely' to 'No,
   definitely not'. Individuals were grouped according to whether they fell
   above or below the mean score on this item.

4. *Perceived probability of earning more money on present job* (hereafter
   referred to as *internal expectations*)
   Question: How would you rate your opportunity to earn more money
   on your present job?
   There were five categories ranging from 'very good' to 'very poor'.
   Individuals were grouped according to whether they fell above or below
   the mean score on this item.

5. *Age and skill level*
   These two variables served as control variables, both for their intrinsic
   importance and because they related to both education and salary level.
   Thus each partially controls for the effects of actual salary. Age was
   measured by the item, 'How old are you?' — with the categories ranging
   from 'Under 25' to '60 or older'. Skill level was measured by an item
   asking the code level of the departments supervised.
       Those 40 or over were considered 'older' and those under 40 were
   considered 'younger'. Individuals were assigned to 'higher' or 'lower'
   skill levels according to job classification level.
       In testing for the differences between any of our groupings, we used *t*
   tests or chi square depending upon the suitability of the data. When *t* tests
   were used, it was always a two-tailed test because the hypotheses were not
   postulated prior to data collection. Analysis of variance was not used
   because of the non-orthogonality of the data.

RESULTS
Table 1 illustrates that education was found to be negatively related to
satisfaction. The college educated group is significantly less satisfied than
the non-college educated group on both of the pay items. In both
instances the level of significance is well beyond the .001 level. Moreover,
this relationship is maintained even when controls are instituted for salary
level. Controlling for skill level and for age, both of which are highly
related to salary level and thus approximate a control for salary, we find
that the basic relationship between education and satisfaction with salary
remains (Tables 2 and 3).
    The first prediction, that the college educated are less satisfied with their
pay than the non-college educated, is thus supported.
    The second prediction is also supported but in an unexpected way

Table 1   Overall comparison of college educated and non-college educated managers with respect to pay satisfaction

	Internal pay rating				
	N	$\bar{X}$	σ_X	t	p
College educated	323	2.64	0.94	4.32	<.001
Non-college educated	291	2.32	0.91		

	External pay rating				
	N	$\bar{X}$	σ_X	t	p
College educated	317	2.37	0.88	7.71	<.001
Non-college educated	288	1.83	0.85		

Note: The lower the mean score the higher the satisfaction. This will be true for all mean scores reported in this study.

Table 2   Comparison of college educated and non-college educated managers with respect to pay satisfaction, controlling for skill level

Internal pay rating								
	College educated			Non-college educated				
	N	$\bar{X}$	σ_X	N	$\bar{X}$	σ_X	t	p
Low skill level	138	2.60	0.90	215	2.34	0.92	2.63	<.01
	College educated			Non-college educated				
	N	$\bar{X}$	σ_X	N	$\bar{X}$	σ_X	t	p
High skill level	185	2.67	0.95	76	2.25	0.88	3.41	<.001

External pay rating								
	College educated			Non-college educated				
	N	$\bar{X}$	σ_X	N	$\bar{X}$	σ_X	t	p
Low skill level	135	2.24	0.85	213	1.81	0.85	4.57	<.001
	College educated			Non-college educated				
	N	$\bar{X}$	σ_X	N	$\bar{X}$	σ_X	t	p
High skill level	182	2.46	0.90	75	1.87	0.84	5.00	<.01

Table 3   Comparison of college educated and non-college educated managers with respect to pay satisfaction, controlling for age

	Internal pay rating							
	College educated			Non-college educated				
	N	$\bar{X}$	σ_X	N	$\bar{X}$	σ_X	t	p
Under 40	202	2.64	0.91	103	2.43	0.95	1.84	<.075
	College educated			Non-college educated				
	N	$\bar{X}$	σ_X	N	$\bar{X}$	σ_X	t	p
40 or older	137	2.66	0.93	202	2.26	0.89	3.96	<.001
	External pay rating							
	College educated			Non-college educated				
	N	$\bar{X}$	σ_X	N	$\bar{X}$	σ_X	t	p
Under 40	198	2.40	0.86	102	1.99	0.89	3.83	<.001
	College educated			Non-college educated				
	N	$\bar{X}$	σ_X	N	$\bar{X}$	σ_X	t	p
40 or older	135	2.33	0.91	200	1.73	0.82	6.12	<.001

(Table 4). Both internal and external optimism about pay possibilities are significantly related to satisfactions with pay but, contrary to prediction 2*b*, the better the individual feels his chances of getting more money on the same job, the *higher* his satisfaction with pay. Moreover, prediction 3 receives only partial support. The college educated are more optimistic about getting a similar paying job elsewhere ($p < .001$), but they are *less* optimistic about getting more money on the present job ($p < .05$) (Table 5).

In any event it seems that certain perceptions held to a higher degree by the college-educated are also associated with relative pay dissatisfaction, and this may be a major factor in the negative relationship between education and pay satisfaction that we find. This brings us to a test of prediction 4, i.e. if we control for internal and external optimism, the difference in satisfaction with pay between the college and non-college groups will disappear. The results appear in Table 6.

We see that the differences between the high and low education groups decline approximately a third in both of the groups when we control for both perceived internal and external expressions of optimism regarding

Table 4   Relationship between perceived opportunity for pay inside and outside the company and pay satisfaction

	Low internal pay rating	High internal pay rating		Low internal pay rating	High internal pay rating
High internal optimism	29% ($N = 78$)	71% ($N = 193$)	High internal optimism	26% ($N = 69$)	74% ($N = 198$)
Low internal optimism	67% ($N = 254$)	33% ($N = 125$)	Low internal optimism	58% ($N = 217$)	42% ($N = 157$)
		$x^2 = 92.46$			$x^2 = 65.27$
		$p < .001$			$p < .001$
High external optimism	64% ($N = 224$)	36% ($N = 125$)	High external optimism	59% ($N = 205$)	41% ($N = 141$)
Low external optimism	36% ($N = 108$)	64% ($N = 193$)	Low external optimism	27% ($N = 81$)	73% ($N = 214$)
		$x^2 = 51.80$			$x^2 = 65.13$
		$p < .001$			$p < .001$

Table 5   Comparison of college educated and non-college educated managers with respect to perceived opportunity for pay inside and outside the company

	Low internal optimism	High internal optimism		Low external optimism	High external optimism
College educated	46% ($N = 154$)	51% ($N = 180$)	College educated	30% ($N = 90$)	70% ($N = 211$)
Non-college educated	38% ($N = 115$)	62% ($N = 187$)	Non-college educated	59% ($N = 202$)	41% ($N = 134$)
		$x^2 = 4.17$			$x^2 = 58.29$
		$p < .05$			$p < .001$

Table 6   Comparison of college educated and non-college educated managers with respect to pay satisfaction, controlling for perceived opportunity for pay inside and out outside the company

| | Internal pay rating | | | | | | | |
| | College educated | | | Non-college educated | | | | |
	N	$\bar{X}$	σ_X	N	$\bar{X}$	σ_X	t	p
High internal optimism, High external optimism	104	2.54	0.80	50	2.36	0.91	1.19	N.S.
High internal optimism, Low external optimism	85	2.11	0.86	140	1.89	0.71	1.98	<.05
Low internal optimism, High external optimism	103	3.12	0.83	44	3.09	0.83	0.20	N.S.
Low internal optimism, Low external optimism	50	2.76	0.82	74	2.62	0.82	0.93	N.S.

| | External pay rating | | | | | | | |
| | College educated | | | Non-college educated | | | | |
	N	$\bar{X}$	σ_X	N	$\bar{X}$	σ_X	t	p
High internal optimism, High external optimism	102	2.44	0.77	49	2.06	0.85	2.66	<.01
High internal optimism, Low external optimism	83	1.78	0.81	140	1.41	0.56	3.70	<.001
Low internal optimism, High external optimism	101	2.88	0.77	43	2.90	0.68	0.44	N.S.
Low internal optimism, Low external optimism	50	2.18	0.75	73	1.82	0.78	2.57	<.02

pay possibilities. However, despite the fact that the controls we use decrease the relationship between education and satisfaction with pay, the differences between the college and the non-college educated groups remain significant in three of the four cases concerning the ratings of present salary considering what is available at other companies. This is not the case for the comparisons between the two educational groups on rating present pay considering their *duties* and *responsibilities*, where three of the four comparisons are statistically insignificant. It is noteworthy that the exception in the former set of comparisons occurs where there is pessimism with regard to making more money on their present job and optimism with regard to getting a similar job at the same pay rate elsewhere – both conditions which are associated with low pay ratings.

Apparently under this condition, the comparisons that people make regarding their present pay position are so pessimistic that it does not matter whether or not they have been exposed to higher education. Thus, prediction 4 receives partial support, but there is nevertheless a residual effect of education regarding satisfaction with external pay comparisons.

DISCUSSION

It is clear that higher education in our sample is associated with relative dissatisfaction with pay. The first-level managers in the study who have had higher education are less satisfied with their pay, both considering their duties and responsibilities and considering what they feel they can get in other companies. We also find that these differences in satisfaction are not due to differences in actual level of salary. When we control for age and skill level as approximations of salary level, we find that the differences still remain.

The major predictors for satisfaction with pay appear to be the expectations of what salary an individual feels he will get internally or could get externally. We find that, contrary to the findings of Andrews and Henry (1963), the former is a positive predictor of pay satisfaction and, surprisingly, the college-educated manager feels less optimistic about his internal pay chances than the non-college educated manager. The expectation of external pay opportunities is a negative predictor to salary satisfaction and, as predicted, the college-educated manager feels more optimistic about his external opportunities than his non-college counterpart.

When we control for these salary expectations, the differences between the college and the non-college group wash out when the two groups are compared on satisfaction with *internal* wage comparisons. When they are compared on satisfaction with *external* wage comparisons, however, the differences diminish but remain statistically significant. Thus we were wrong in two instances: First, when we erroneously predicted that education, being an important input to self-evaluation, would cause the more highly educated manager to have more optimistic expectations, both externally and internally, about how well he could do with pay; and, second, when we predicted that controlling for these expectations would cause the differences in pay satisfaction between the college and non-college group to disappear.

Apparently our original conceptualization of expectation being a function of perceived self-worth, which in turn is based partly upon educational attainment, requires further scrutiny as being directly applicable to some of the issues that we are dealing with. In the first place, if the college-educated people in fact have a higher self-evaluation, it does not cause them to rate their internal opportunities as better than the non-college educated do. In fact, they rate them worse. However, the reasons for this may not be at odds with our original conceptual framework. What we may be dealing with is the paradox of a perception distorted negatively because of a higher self-evaluation. We say this because the college-educated manager has in fact somewhat better pay opportunities. Thus his less optimistic expectation is a perception contrary to reality but explainable in terms of the context within which he makes this judgment. This context includes a higher self-evaluation and set of expectations, that have developed partly as a consequence of his higher educational attainment. Thus equal or somewhat higher increments in pay would look smaller to him than to the non-college educated manager who has developed lower salary expectations within his somewhat different frame of reference.

In the second instance, when our initial conceptualization did not adequately handle our results (i.e. the residual effects of education on external satisfactions when controlled for expectations), we find an explanation more difficult. Perhaps it resides in the fact that college people tend to choose reference groups outside the company to a larger extent than non-college people, as Andrews and Henry (1963) and Patchen (1961) have shown. This may make them more susceptible to a 'grass is greener' perception than the non-college people. This same perception is not true when internal pay ratings are made because it becomes clear that people with the same 'duties and responsibilities' are making about the same money. When these expectations are controlled for, the differences between the college and the non-college groups disappear.

One other point that deserves consideration is that, somewhat contrary to inferences which can be drawn from other studies (e.g. Andrews and Henry, 1963), we find that those who perceive better opportunities to make more money in the future on their present job are also relatively satisfied with their present pay position both with internal comparisons (Pearson $r = .44$) and external comparisons (Pearson $r = .35$). It appears that, with our population, satisfaction with pay is partially determined by future prospects on the same job even though the pay satisfaction items are phrased to tap current satisfactions. Apparently our subjects used future anticipated salaries as a potentially positive referent that generalizes to an evaluation of their current pay.

If a more general inference can be drawn from this study, it is that potentially the college-exposed industrial work force represents a comparatively less satisfied group than its non-college educated counterpart, performing roughly similar jobs. While satisfaction with salary by no means encompasses the entire spectrum of satisfactions, it nevertheless involves a critical aspect of one's working life. The dynamics involved in the relationship between education and salary satisfaction are probably at work in many other areas of satisfaction, as Ganguli (1957), Form and Geschwender (1962), and Hadley and Levy (1962) suggest. If it is likely that in the future more college-educated people will hold jobs similar to non-college people, then their higher self-evaluation and resulting higher set of expectations portend new relationships between organizations and their more highly educated work force.

REFERENCES

American Vocational Association, Committee on Research Publications, 'Factors Affecting the Satisfactions of Home Economics Teachers' (Washington, D.C.: AVA, 1948, Research Bulletin No. 3).

Andrews, I. R. and Henry, Mildred M., 'Management Attitudes Toward Pay', *Industrial Relations*, III (1963) 29–39.

Cantril H., 'Identification with Social and Economic Class', *Journal of Abnormal and Social Psychology*, XXXVIII (1943) 74–80.

Centers, R. and Cantril, H., 'Income Satisfaction and Income Aspiration', *Journal of Abnormal and Social Psychology*, XLI (1946) 64–9.

Form, W. H. and Geschwender, J. A., 'Social Reference Basis of Job Satisfaction: The Case of Manual Workers', *American Sociological Review*, XXVII (1962) 228–37.

Ganguli, H. C., 'Some Factors Influencing Income Aspiration', *Journal of Applied Psychology*, XLI (1957) 32–6.

Hadley, R. G. and Levy, W. V., 'Vocational Development and Reference Groups', *Journal of Counseling Psychology*, IX (1962) 110–14.

Herzberg, F., Mausner, B., Peterson, R. O. and Capwell, Dora F., *Job Attitudes: Review of Research and Opinion* (Pittsburgh, Pa.: Psychological Service of Pittsburgh, 1957).

Kessler, M. S., 'Job Satisfaction of Veterans Rehabilitated Under Public Law 16', *Personnel and Guidance Journal*, XXXIII (1954) 78–81.

Lawler, E. E. III and Porter, L. W., 'Perceptions Regarding Management Compensation', *Industrial Relations*, III (1963) 41–9.

Newcomb, T. M., *Social Psychology* (New York: Dryden Press, 1959).

Patchen, M., *The Choice of Wage Comparisons* (Englewood Cliffs, N.J.: Prentice Hall, 1961).

Sherif, M., 'The Concept of Reference Groups in Human Relations', in *Group Relations at the Crossroads*, ed. M. Sherif and M. O. Wilson (New York: Harper Brothers, 1953).

Stouffer, S. A., Suchman, E. A., Devinney, L. C., Star, S. A. and Williams, R. M., Jr., *The American Soldier: Adjustment During Army Life* (Princeton, N.J.: Princeton University Press, 1949, I).

Thomsen, A., 'Expectation in Relation to Achievement and Happiness', *Journal of Abnormal and Social Psychology*, XXXVIII (1943) 58–73.

17 The Relationship of Specific Job Attitudes with Overall Job Satisfaction and the Influence of Biographical Variables*

RAY WILD and J. A. DAWSON

Attitudinal research amongst manual workers has flourished during the past twenty years. Many researchers have studied the extent of overall or general job satisfaction, whilst attitudes to specific aspects of jobs such as work content, payment, supervision, etc., have not been neglected. In attempts to answer the question 'What does a worker want from his job?', many researchers have studied the relative importance attached by workers to certain aspects of jobs. A good deal of controversy rests on the influence of specific job factors on overall satisfaction, the relative merits of the 'two-factor'[1] and the 'bi-polar'[2] theories being a subject of continuing debate.

Some researchers, in attempts to refine theory in this area, have dealt with the relationships of both overall satisfaction and specific job attitudes to individual workers' characteristics, notably biographical variables. Wild,[3] for example, has demonstrated the relationship of age, marital status, and length of service with the overall job satisfaction of female manual workers. However, to our knowledge, comparatively few people have examined the influence of such variables on the relationships between specific job attitudes and overall job satisfaction. The influence of worker characteristics on the declared importance or ranking of job factors has of course been studied. But it can be argued that such information is less important to those concerned with job design and labour selection and placement than information concerning the effect of worker characteristics on the contribution of specific job attitudes to overall job satisfaction.

*_Journal of Management Studies_, IX (1972) 150–7. Reprinted by permission.

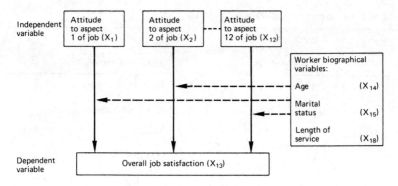

Fig. 1 Diagrammatic representation of relationships examined

The overall or general job satisfaction of workers is often taken as an important objective in both job design and in labour selection and placement. However, the design of jobs and effective labour selection and placement can only be achieved by considering *aspects of jobs* rather than jobs as a whole. In other words, management must of necessity be concerned with aspects of jobs such as the work, payment systems, supervision, etc., and with the 'matching' of such aspects with the characteristics of workers in such a way as to ensure not only favourable specific job attitudes but also the overall job satisfaction of workers. To pursue such an objective, a knowledge of the contribution or relationship of specific job attitudes to overall job satisfaction is important, and furthermore it is necessary to know whether such relationships are in any way affected by different worker characteristics.

The research reported in this paper was undertaken with the objective of investigating the influence of biographical variables on the relationship of specific job attitudes to overall job satisfaction. Figure 1 is a diagrammatic representation of some of the relationships studied.

METHOD [4]
The sample consisted of 2543 female manual workers engaged on similar unskilled repetitive work in ten plants in the electronics industry in the United Kingdom.

Attitudinal information was collected by means of a questionnaire, which was also used for collection of biographical data, i.e. age (divided into five classes), marital status (two classes), and length of service (six classes). Forty-six forced choice questions were used to explore workers' attitudes to eight features of their jobs: namely, the work itself, supervision, induction, training, wages, social relations, management, and physical working conditions. A further question was used, consisting of six statements relating to the job as a whole, ranging from 'I love it' to 'I hate

Table 1   Interpretation of Varimax factors

Varimax factor number	Percentage of total variance of original correlation matrix accounted for	Interpretation of factor*
1	5.23	Pay (+)
2	7.92	Self-actualization (−)
3	5.37	Induction (+)
4	5.25	Recognition (+)
5	3.54	Training (+)
6	3.16	Physical effort and conditions (+)
7	6.74	Supervision (−)
8	5.52	Working conditions (−)
9	3.29	Mental v. physical work (+) (−)
10	3.34	Control of work v. output required (+) (−)
11	2.82	Social peer relations (+)
12	2.47	Responsibility for quality (−)

*Signs indicate nature of factor loading on which interpretations are based.

it'. Respondents were asked to endorse one statement to indicate the extent of their overall satisfaction with their job.

The product-moment intercorrelations of responses to each of the forty-six attitudinal questions were calculated for the entire sample. A principal components analysis was performed using this matrix and twelve components each having roots greater than unity were extracted, together accounting for 54.63 per cent of total variance. In order to obtain a simpler structure the component axes were rotated orthogonally in accordance with the Varimax criterion.[5] The interpretation of the Varimax factors is given in Table 1. Using the Thomson[6] method, factor scores were calculated for each respondent for each of the twelve Varimax factors in order to provide a measure of each respondent's attitude to these twelve aspects of her job.

A product-moment intercorrelation of all factor scores, overall job satisfaction and the three biographical variables was calculated. In order to establish the influence of biographical variables on the relationship between specific job attitudes and overall job satisfaction, several multiple linear regression analyses were performed. In each regression analysis the measure of overall job satisfaction $(X_{13})^7$ was taken as the dependent variable, whilst the independent variables consisted of one of the twelve measures of specific job attitudes $(X_{1,2} \ldots_{12})$ and two of the three biographical variables $(X_{14,15,16})$. For example, in order to examine the influence of marital status (X_{15}) on the relationship of attitudes to pay (X_1) with overall job satisfaction (X_{13}), two multiple regression analyses were performed, i.e. in standard score form.

1. For married workers

$$z'_{13} = \beta_{13,1.14,16}z_1 + \beta_{13,14.1,16}z_{14} + \beta_{13,16.1,14}z_{16}$$

2. For single workers

$$z'_{13} = \beta_{13,1.14,16}z_1 + \beta_{13,14.1,16}z_{14} + \beta_{13,16.1,14}z_{16}$$

Thus the values obtained for the standard partial regression coefficients $\beta_{13,14.6}$, provide measures of the relationship of this job attitude with overall job satisfaction for single and for married workers, with the effects of the other biographical variables, 'partialled out'. The difference between these two β values is a measure of the influence of marital status on the relationship of this job attitude with overall satisfaction.

The significance of the β weights was established using the formula presented by Guilford.[8] Since no method was found for testing the significance of the difference of more than two β weights, the influence of each biographical variable on the relationship of specific job attitudes to overall job satisfaction was examined by reference to the amount of variance of the dependent variable (overall job satisfaction) accounted for by the independent variable (the job attitude). The significance of the differences of these variances for each specific job attitude for each of the three biographical variables was tested using Bartlett's test of homoscedascity.[9]

RESULTS

Tables 2, 3, and 4 give the β weights obtained between each job attitude and overall job satisfaction, for each biographical grouping with the other two biographical variables 'partialled out'. For example, the first colunm in Table 2 gives β weights which show the relationship between each job attitude and overall job satisfaction for persons under twenty-one years of age. The second column shows equivalent figures for people between twenty-one and twenty-five years, etc. The difference of the β weights in each *row* of Tables 2, 3, and 4 is a measure of the effect of the particular biographical variable on the relationship of each job attitude with overall job satisfaction.

Table 2 Standard partial regression coefficients between specific job attitudes and overall job satisfaction for various age groups (decimal points omitted)

Job attitude* (taken as independent variable together with marital status and length of service)	<21 (N = 844)	21–25 (N = 502)	Age (years) 26–30 (N = 245)	31–40 (N = 439)	>40 (N = 513)	
1. Pay	1742	2277	2353	1328	0890	‡
2. Self-actualization	6118	5286	5247	6133	4606	‡
3. Induction	1485	1977	1843	2021	2095	‡
4. Recognition	1673	1396	1703	1605	2022	‡
5. Training	0468†	0905	1241	1261	0446†	‡
6. Physical effort and conditions	−0358†	0239†	−0544†	0848†	0559†	‡
7. Supervision	1024	1506	1703	2020	1404	‡
8. Physical working conditions	2166	1721	1853	0713†	0560†	‡
9. Mental v. physical work	−1815	1934	2346	0827†	0192†	‡
10. Control of work v. output required	1098	1641	1398	1464	1275	‡
11. Social peer relations	0820	0918	0201†	1769	0717†	‡
12. Responsibility for quality	0150†	−0486†	−0208†	−0498†	0028†	‡

*Table 1 shows the interpretation of components used to measure job attitudes.
†β not significantly different from zero at $P < 0.05$.
‡Amount of variance of overall job satisfaction accounted for by attitude is significantly different amongst biographical groups ($P < 0.01$).

Table 3   Standard partial regression coefficients between job attitudes and overall job satisfaction for two marital status groups (decimal points omitted)

Job attitude* (taken as independent variable together with age and length of service)	Marital status		
	Single (N = 1422)	Married (N = 1121)	
1. Pay	1483	2036	‡
2. Self-actualization	5810	5413	‡
3. Induction	1659	1966	‡
4. Recognition	1550	1830	‡
5. Training	0746	0810	‡
6. Physical effort and conditions	−0109†	0176†	‡
7. Supervision	1261	1681	‡
8. Physical working conditions	1994	0825	‡
9. Mental *v.* physical work	−1713	−1179	‡
10. Control of work *v.* output required	1170	1571	‡
11. Social peer relations	1023	0704	‡
12. Responsibility for quality	−0011†	−0225†	‡

Notes as for Table 2.

DISCUSSION

The general importance of self-actualization attitudes to job satisfaction is evident from Tables 2, 3, and 4. For all but one of the thirteen groupings this attitude appears to account for over twice the criterion variance accounted for by any of the other job attitudes.

Considering the results from a labour selection and placement view-point both age (Table 2) and marital status (Table 3) have significant effects on the relationship of job attitudes to job satisfaction. In particular the relationships of the attitudes to pay, supervision, physical working conditions, mental *v.* physical work and social peer relations with job satisfaction appear to be influenced by these two biographical variables. Age appears to affect the extent to which the attitude to self-actualization is related to job satisfaction. To a lesser extent the relationship of attitudes to induction, recognition, training and the control of work, with job satisfaction are also affected by one or both of these two biographical variables.

In many cases the nature of the influence of biographical variables on the relationships is clear, e.g. in the case of marital status, but in others, the effect of the variable is less apparent. Attitudes to pay, physical working conditions and the balance of mental and physical work appear to be of greater importance in determining overall job satisfaction for younger persons, whilst attitudes to recognition, supervision and perhaps also induction appear to be more important as determinants of job satisfaction for older respondents.

The relationship of many of the job attitudes to overall job satisfaction is clearly affected by the third biographical variable — length of service. As

Table 4 Standard partial regression coefficients between specific job attitudes and overall job satisfaction for various length of service groups (decimal points omitted)

Job attitude* (taken as independent variable together with age and marital status)	Length of service (months)						
	<1 (N = 80)	1–3 (N = 271)	4–6 (N = 306)	7–12 (N = 385)	12–24 (N = 40)	>24 (N = 1096)	
1. Pay	0211†	0603	2706	1582	1734	1836	‡
2. Self-actualization	7007	6094	6150	5324	5546	5321	‡‡
3. Induction	4357	2093	2227	1893	1659	1460	‡
4. Recognition	3322	1171†	2677	1211	1842	1391	‡‡
5. Training	3021	1616	0949†	0591†	−0305†	0689†	‡‡
6. Physical effort and conditions	2266	0710†	−0230†	0210†	−0668†	−0157†	‡
7. Supervision	3457	1932	0740†	1684	0563†	1613	‡
8. Physical working conditions	2792	1053†	2109	1475	1567	1415	‡
9. Mental v. physical work	−0983†	−1484†	−2244	−1510	−1636	−1248	‡
10. Control of work v. output required	3068	0870†	0791†	1934	1182	−1251	‡
11. Social peer relations	1166†	1371†	1306	1031	1108	0571†	‡
12. Responsibility for quality	−0753†	−1064†	−0985†	0310†	0850	−0155†	‡

Notes as for Table 2.

would have been expected attitudes to induction are more closely associated with job satisfaction for newer employees. With increasing length of service the relationship of job satisfaction with attitudes to self-actualization, training, physical effort and conditions decreases whilst the relationship with attitudes to pay tends to increase. In other cases the differences in weights suggest a more complex relationship with the biographical variables. Comparing the columns of Table 4 there is a general trend of decreasing β weights for increasing length of service which would seem to indicate that the extent of job satisfaction is less readily accounted for in terms of these job attitudes for longer service employees.

It should be noted that the β weights in Tables 1, 2, 3, and 4 reflect the joint contribution of all the specific job attitudes to overall satisfaction. Notice, however, that job attitude scores were developed from orthogonally rotated factors, which should not therefore be intercorrelated. However, in order to further investigate this point a further series of regression analyses were performed in which each of the job attitudes were included in the sets of independent variables. The results as would be expected in view of the orthogonal nature of the factors were very similar to those shown in Tables 1 to 4.

The results of this exploratory investigation appear to have implications for both research and practice. The importance of the self-actualizing characteristics of the job as regards overall job satisfaction has been demonstrated previously for this type of worker,[10] and the results presented here reinforce the fact that this attitude is dominant in determining the nature of job satisfaction for all categories of workers considered. The relative and absolute importance of other specific attitudes appears to be less static, a result which may be seen to suggest weaknesses in both the 'two-factor' and the 'bi-polar' theories of job satisfaction. It is clear that the attitudinal basis of overall job satisfaction is not static as might have been inferred from previous theory, but is dependent (in this case) upon three individual worker characteristics. Whether the change in the importance of specific job attitudes is associated with the differing importance attached to features of jobs by different groups of workers cannot be established from this investigation. However, it is worth noting that in other respects the importance of different aspects of jobs suggested by this study does not support the findings of a similar study[11] in which operatives were asked to rank their work needs. Nor is it possible from this study to formulate principles to assist in job design or labour selection and placement. However, the results do suggest inadequacies in the global or general theories of job satisfaction and job design by indicating not only the need to consider the characteristics of workers in the design of jobs and in selection for these jobs, but also the possible need for regular redeployment of labour or redesign of jobs in order to maintain the job satisfaction of current employees.

NOTES
1. Herzberg, F., Mausner, B. and Snyderman, B. B., *The Motivation to Work* (New York: Wiley, 1959).
2. Ewen, R., Smith, P. C., Hulin, C. L. and Locke, E., 'An Empirical Test of the Herzberg Two-factor Theory', *Journal of Applied Psychology*, L [6] (1966) 544–50.
3. Wild, R., 'Job Needs, Job Satisfaction and Job Behaviour of Women Manual Workers', *Journal of Applied Psychology*, LIV (1970) 157–62
4. The sample, the questionnaire and part of the analysis derive from a previous study; see Wild, R., 'Influence of Community and Plant Characteristics on the Job Attitudes of Manual Workers', *Journal of Applied Psychology*, LVI (1972) 106–13.
5. Kaiser, H. F., 'Computer Program for Varimax Rotation in Factor Analysis', *Educational and Psychological Measurement*, XIX (1959) 413–20.
6. Thomson, G. H., *The Factorial Analysis of Human Ability*, 5th ed. (London: University of London Press, 1951).
7. Numbers in brackets refer to Figure 1.
8. Guilford, J. P., *Psychometric Methods* (New York: McGraw-Hill, 1954).
9. McNemar, Q., *Psychological Statistics*, *4th ed. (New York: Wiley, 1969)*.
10. *Wild, R., 1970*, op cit.
11. *Ibid.*

PART V

The Effects of Job Satisfaction and Dissatisfaction

In the *Psychological Bulletin* for 1955 A. H. Brayfield and W. H. Crockett undermined the notion that there is a high relationship between job satisfaction and high productivity. Indeed in their review they pointed to many studies which found no relationships between job satisfaction and productivity, although they did point out in fact that studies showed a relationship between absenteeism and turnover, and job satisfaction. Lawler and Porter return to the question of the relationship between job satisfaction and productivity. It is obviously a vitally important question because if there truly is no relationship between the two factors, some of the importance of the topic of job satisfaction for practical management may be reduced. In fact, as Lawler and Porter point out, the view spread by Brayfield and Crockett is just too pessimistic. There is indeed a positive relationship between job satisfaction and productivity, but the relationship is complex, and depends on those aspects of the job that are satisfying being intimately related to productivity. As Lawler and Porter point out, 'Individuals perform effectively . . . to the extent that effective performance leads to the attainment of what they desire'. When the variables relating job satisfaction and performance are adequately examined, there is every reason to believe that where rewards relate to productivity there will be a correlation between satisfaction and performance. It goes without saying, of course, that rewards need not be only financial. It is however a possibility, argue Lawler and Porter, that it is the rewards for performance that cause satisfaction, and not satisfaction per se which is causing improved performance. (See also the paper by Lawler in Part II.)

The paper by Hulin is an example of a study showing a well-established relationship in the study of job satisfaction, that between job satisfaction and turnover. Hulin is careful to point out, however, that factors other than dissatisfaction affect the decision to leave a job, for example the availability of suitable alternatives. The paper by Metzner and Mann examines the relationship between job satisfaction and absence, and finds that for different groups there are different relationships between job satisfaction and absence. There is a relationship for white-collar men workers and low levels of skill, but not for women white-collar workers at low levels of skill, or white-collar men at higher level jobs.

As far as the relationship between mental health and job satisfaction is concerned, Kornhauser (1965) has presented evidence that men in routine production jobs have on average less satisfactory mental health than those in more skilled occupations. Furthermore, the most job-satisfied workers in each occupation enjoyed better mental health than the least satisfied. The last paper by Orpen shows that even allowing for possible methodological defects in earlier studies of the relationship between job satisfaction and mental health, as measured by personal adjustment, there is still a correlation between mental health and job satisfaction. That the correlation is small is due principally to the large number of job dissatisfied individuals who are resilient enough not to have poor adjustment under the stress of an inadequate job. It does appear at least possible that job dissatisfaction can be associated with mental ill health, as many writers have suggested.

REFERENCES

Brayfield, A. and Crockett, W., 'Employee Attitudess and Employee Performance', *Psychological Bulletin*, L II (1955) 396–424.

Kornhauser, A., *Mental Health of the Industrial Worker: A Detroit Study* (New York: Wiley, 1965).

18 The Effect of Performance on Job Satisfaction[*]

EDWARD E. LAWLER III
Professor of Administrative Sciences and Psychology, Yale University

LYMAN W. PORTER
Professor of Administration and Psychology, University of California, Irvine

The human relations movement with its emphasis on good interpersonal relations, job satisfaction, and the importance of informal groups provided an important initial stimulant for the study of job attitudes and their relationship to human behavior in organizations. Through the thirties and forties, many studies were carried out to determine the correlates of high and low job satisfaction. Such studies related job satisfaction to seniority, age, sex, education, occupation, and income, to mention a few. Why this great interest in job satisfaction? Undoubtedly some of it stemmed from a simple desire on the part of scientists to learn more about job satisfaction, but much of the interest in job satisfaction seems to have come about because of its presumed relationship to job performance. As Brayfield and Crockett have pointed out, a common assumption that employee satisfaction directly affects performance permeates most of the writings about the topic that appeared during this period of two decades.[1] Statements such as the following characterized the literature: 'Morale is not an abstraction; rather it is concrete in the sense that it directly affects the quality and quantity of an individual's output', and 'Employee morale — reduces turnover — cuts down absenteeism and tardiness; lifts production.'[2]

It is not hard to see how the assumption that high job satisfaction leads to high performance came to be popularly accepted. Not only did it fit into the value system of the human relations movement but there also appeared to be some research data to support this point. In the Western Electric studies, the evidence from the Relay Assembly Test Room showed a dramatic tendency for increased employee productivity to be associated

Industrial Relations, VIII (1967) 20–8. Reprinted by permission.

with an increase in job satisfaction. Also, who could deny that in the Bank Wiring Room there was both production restriction and mediocre employee morale. With this background it is easy to see why both social scientists and managers believed that if job dissatisfaction could be reduced, the human brake on production could be removed and turned into a force that would increase performance.

PREVIOUS RESEARCH
But does the available evidence support the belief that high satisfaction will lead to high performance? Since an initial study, in 1932, by Kornhauser and Sharp, more than thirty studies have considered the relationship between these two variables.[3] Many of the earlier studies seemed to have assumed implicitly that a positive relationship existed and that it was important to demonstrate that it in fact did exist. Little attention was given to trying to understand *why* job satisfaction should lead to higher performance; instead, researchers contented themselves with routinely studying the relationship between satisfaction and performance in a number of industrial situations.

The typical reader of the literature in the early fifties was probably aware of the fact that some studies had failed to find a significant satisfaction-performance relationship. Indeed, the very first study of the problem obtained an insignificant relationship.[4] However, judging from the impact of the first review of the literature on the topic, by Brayfield and Crockett, many social scientists, let alone practicing managers, were unaware that the evidence indicated how little relationship exists between satisfaction and performance.[5] The key conclusion that emerged from the review was that 'there is little evidence in the available literature that employee attitudes bear any simple — or, for that matter, appreciable — relationship to performance on the job'. (The review, however, pointed out that job satisfaction did seem to be positively related, as expected, to two other kinds of employee behavior, absenteeism and turnover.)

The review had a major impact on the field of industrial psychology and helped shatter the kind of naive thinking that characterized the earlier years of the Human Relations movement. Perhaps it also discouraged additional research, since few post-1955 studies of the relationship between satisfaction and performance have been reported in scientific journals.

Another review, covering much of the same literature, was completed about the same time.[6] This review took a more optimistic view of the evidence: 'there is frequent evidence for the often suggested opinion that positive job attitudes are favorable to increased productivity. The relationship is not absolute, but there are enough data to justify attention to attitudes as a factor in improving the worker's output. However, the correlations obtained in many of the positive studies were low'.[7] This review also pointed out, as did Brayfield and Crockett, that there was a definite trend for attitudes to be related to absenteeism and turnover. Perhaps the chief reasons for the somewhat divergent conclusions reached by the two reviews were that they did not cover exactly the same literature and that Brayfield and Crockett were less influenced by suggestive findings that did reach statistical significance. In any event, the one conclusion that was obvious from both reviews was that there was not the *strong, pervasive* relationship between job satisfaction and productivity that had been suggested by many of the early proponents of the Human Relations movement and so casually accepted by personnel specialists.

A more recent review of the literature by Vroom has received less attention than did the two earlier reviews,[8] perhaps because it is now rather generally accepted that satisfaction is not related to performance. However, before we too glibly accept the view that satisfaction and performance are unrelated, let us look carefully at the data from studies reviewed by Vroom. These studies show a median correlation of +.14 between satisfaction and performance. Although this correlation is not large, the consistency of the direction of the correlation is quite impressive. Twenty of the 23 correlations cited by Vroom are positive. By a statistical test such consistency would occur by chance less than once in a hundred times.

In summary, the evidence indicates that a low but consistent relationship exists between satisfaction and performance, but it is not at all clear *why* this relationship exists. The questions that need to be answered at this time, therefore, concern the place of job satisfaction both in theories of employee motivation and in everyday organizational practice. For example, should an organization systematically measure the level of employee satisfaction? Is it important for an organization to try to improve employee job satisfaction? Is there theoretical reason for believing that job satisfaction should be related to job behavior and if so, can it explain why this relationship exists?

WHY STUDY JOB SATISFACTION?

There are really two bases upon which to argue that job satisfaction is important. Interestingly, both are different from the original reason for studying job satisfaction, that is, the assumed ability of satisfaction to influence performance. The first, and undoubtedly the most straightforward reason, rests on the fact that strong correlations between absenteeism and satisfaction, as well as between turnover and satisfaction, appear in the previous studies. Accordingly, job satisfaction would seem to be an important focus of organizations which wish to reduce absenteeism and turnover.

Perhaps the best explanation of the fact that satisfaction is related to absenteeism and turnover comes from the kind of path-goal theory of motivation that has been stated by Georgopoulos, Mahoney and Jones; Vroom; and Lawler and Porter.[9] According to this view, people are motivated to do things which they feel have a high probability of leading to rewards which they value. When a worker says he is satisfied with his job, he is in effect saying that his needs are satisfied as a result of having his job. Thus, path-goal theory would predict that high satisfaction will lead to low turnover and absenteeism because the satisfied individual is motivated to go to work where his important needs are satisfied.

A second reason for interest in job satisfaction stems from its low but consistent *association* with job performance. Let us speculate for a moment on why this association exists. One possibility is that, as assumed by many, the satisfaction *caused* the performance. However, there is little theoretical reason for believing that satisfaction can cause performance. Vroom, using a path-goal theory of motivation, has pointed out that job satisfaction and job performance are caused by quite different things: 'job satisfaction is closely affected by the amount of rewards that people derive from their jobs and . . . level of performance is closely affected by the basis of attainment of rewards. Individuals are satisfied with their jobs to the extent to which their jobs provide them with what they desire, and they perform effectively in them to the extent that effective performance leads to the attainment of what they desire.'[10]

RELATIONSHIP BETWEEN SATISFACTION AND PERFORMANCE
Vroom's statement contains a hint of why, despite the fact that satisfaction and performance are caused by different things, they do bear some relationship to each other. If we assume, as seems to be reasonable in terms of motivation theory, that rewards cause satisfaction, and that in some cases performance produces rewards, then it is possible that the relationship found between satisfaction and performance comes about through the action of a third variable — rewards. Briefly stated, good performance may lead to rewards, which in turn lead to satisfaction; this formulation then would say that satisfaction, rather than causing performance, as was previously assumed, is caused by it. Figure 1 presents this thinking in a diagrammatic form.

This model first shows that performance leads to rewards, and it distinguishes between two kinds of rewards and their connection to performance. A wavy line between performance and extrinsic rewards indicates that such rewards are likely to be imperfectly related to performance. By extrinsic rewards is meant such organizationally controlled rewards as pay, promotion, status, and security — rewards that are often referred to as satisfying mainly lower level needs.[11] The connection is relatively weak because of the difficulty of tying extrinsic rewards directly to performance. Even though an organization may have a policy of rewarding merit, performance is difficult to measure, and in dispensing rewards like pay, many other factors are frequently taken into consideration. Lawler, for example, found a low correlation between amount of

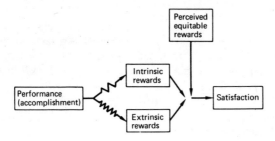

Fig. 1 The theoretical model

salary and superiors' evaluation for a number of middle and lower level managers.[12]

Quite the opposite is likely to be true for intrinsic rewards, however, since they are given to the individual by himself for good performance. Intrinsic or internally mediated rewards are subject to fewer disturbing influences and thus are likely to be more directly related to good performance. This connection is indicated in the model by a semiwavy line. Probably the best example of an intrinsic reward is the feeling of having accomplished something worthwhile. For that matter, any of the rewards that satisfy self-actualization needs or higher order growth needs are good examples of intrinsic rewards.

The model also shows that intrinsic and extrinsic rewards are not directly related to job satisfaction since the relationship is moderated by expected equitable rewards. This variable refers to the level or amount of rewards that an individual feels he *should* receive as the result of his job performance. Thus, an individual's satisfaction is a function both of the number and amount of the rewards he receives as well as what he considers to be a fair level of reward. An individual can be satisfied with a small amount of reward if he feels that it is a fair amount of reward for his job.[13]

This model would seem to predict that because of the imperfect relationship between performance and rewards and the importance of expected equitable rewards there would be a low but positive relationship between job satisfaction and job performance. The model also leads to a number of other predictions about the relationship between satisfaction and performance. If it turns out that, as this model predicts, satisfaction is dependent on performance, then it can be argued that satisfaction is an important variable from both a theoretical and a practical point of view despite its low relationship to performance. However, when satisfaction is viewed in this way, the reasons for considering it to be important are quite different from those that are proposed when satisfaction is considered to cause performance. But first, let us look at some of the predictions that are derivable from the model and at some data that were collected in order to test the predictions.

RESEARCH DATA
Usable data were collected from 148 middle and lower level managers in five organizations. One of the organizations was a large manufacturing company; the others were small social service and welfare agencies. As determined from the demographic data collected from each manager, the sample was typical of other samples of middle and lower level managers, with one exception — 31 of the managers were female.

Two kinds of data were collected for each manager. Superior and peer rankings were obtained on two factors: (1) how hard the manager worked, and (2) how well the manager performed his job. Since a number of peers ranked each manager, the average peer's rankings were used for data analysis purposes. The rankings by the superiors and peers were in general agreement with each other, so the rankings met the requirements for convergent and discriminant validity. In addition to the superior and peer rankings each manager filled out an attitude questionnaire designed to measure his degree of satisfaction in five needed areas. This part of the questionnaire was identical to the one used in earlier studies by Porter.[14] It consists of 13 items in the following form:

> The opportunity for independent thought and action in my management position:
> (a) How much is there now?
>   (min)   1   2   3   4   5   6   7   (max)
> (b) How much should there be?
>   (min)   1   2   3   4   5   6   7   (max)

The answers to the first of these questions (*a*) for each of the 13 items was taken as the measure of need fulfillment or rewards received. The answer to the second of the questions (*b*) was taken as a measure of the individual's expected equitable level of rewards. The difference in answers between the second and first of these questions was taken as the operational measure of need satisfaction. That is, the larger the difference between 'should' and 'is now' in our findings, the greater the *dis*satisfaction.[15]

The 13 items, though presented in random order in the questionnaire, had been preclassified into five types of needs that have been described by Maslow: security, social esteem, autonomy, and self-actualization.

PREDICTIONS AND RESEARCH RESULTS
Let us now consider two specific predictions that our model suggests. The first is that an individual's degree of need satisfaction is related to his job performance as rated by his peers and by his superior. A second prediction is that this relationship is stronger for managers than for nonmanagers.

The basis for this second prediction can be found in the assumed connection between rewards and performance. It seems apparent that most organizations have considerably more freedom to reward their managers differentially than they do their often unionized rank-and-file employees (unless the latter are on incentive pay plans). Even in a nonunionized organization (such as a governmental unit), management jobs generally offer the possibility of greater flexibility in differential rewards, especially in terms of prestige and autonomy in decision-making. Management jobs also typically provide greater opportunities to satisfy higher order intrinsic needs. As the model shows, satisfaction of these higher order needs is more closely tied to performance.

Satisfaction and performance

Data collected from our sample of managers generally support the first two predictions. Job satisfaction (the sum of the difference scores for all 13 items) correlates significantly with both the superiors' rankings (r = .32, p < .01) and peers' rankings (r = .30, p < .01) of performance. Although the correlations are not large, they are substantially larger than the median correlation between satisfaction and performance at the level of rank-and-file workers (r = .14 as given in Vroom's review). It is possible that this higher relationship came about because we used a different measure of need satisfaction than has been typically used before or because we used a better performance measure. However, our belief is that it came about because the study was done at the management level in contrast to the previous studies which mainly involved nonmanagement employees. Neither our measure of job performance nor our measure of satisfaction would seem to be so unique that either could account for the higher relationship found between satisfaction and performance. However, future studies that use the same measure for both managers and nonmanagers are needed if this point is to be firmly established.

Satisfaction and effort

An additional prediction from the model is that satisfaction should be more closely related to the rankings obtained on performance than to the rankings obtained on effort. The prediction is an important one for the model and stems from the fact that satisfaction is seen as a variable that is more directly dependent on performance than on effort. Others have pointed out that effort is only one of the factors that determines how effective an individual's performance will be. Ability factors and situational constraints are other obviously relevant determinants. It is also important to note that if we assume, as many previous writers have, that satisfaction causes performance then it would seem logical that satisfaction should be more closely related to effort than to performance. Satisfaction should influence an individual's performance by affecting his motivation to perform effectively, and this presumably is better reflected by effort than by job performance.

The results of the present study show, in fact, a stronger relationship between the superiors' rankings of performance and satisfaction ($r = .32$), than between the superiors' rankings of effort and satisfaction ($r = .23$). Similarly, for the peer rankings there is a stronger relationship between performance and satisfaction ($r = .30$), than between effort and satisfaction ($r = .20$).

Intrinsic and extrinsic rewards
The model suggests that intrinsic rewards that satisfy needs such as self-actualization are more likely to be related to performance than are extrinsic rewards, which have to be given by someone else and therefore have a weaker relationship between their reception and performance. Thus, the satisfaction should be more closely related to performance for higher than for lower order needs. Table 1 presents the data relevant to this point. There is a slight tendency for satisfaction of the higher order needs to show higher correlations with performance than does satisfaction with lower order needs. In particular, the highest correlations appear for self-actualization which is, of course, the highest order need, in the Maslow need hierarchy.

Table 1   Pearson correlations between performance and satisfaction in five need areas

Needs	Rankings by Superiors	Peers
Security	.21[a]	.17[b]
Social	.23[a]	.26[a]
Esteem	.24[a]	.16[b]
Autonomy	.18[b]	.23[a]
Self-actualization	.30[a]	.28[a]

[a] $p < .01$
[b] $p < .05$

Overall, the data from the present study are in general agreement with the predictions based on the model. Significant relationships did appear between performance and job satisfaction. Perhaps even more important for our point of view, the relationship between satisfaction and performance was stronger than that typically found among blue-collar employees. Also in agreement with our model was the finding that satisfaction was more closely related to performance than to effort. The final prediction, which was supported by the data, was that the satisfaction of higher order needs would be the most closely related to performance. Taken together then, the data offer encouraging support for our model and in particular for the assertion of the model that satisfaction can best be thought of as depending on performance rather than causing it.

IMPLICATIONS OF THE FINDINGS

At this point we can ask the following question: what does the strength of the satisfaction-performance relationship tell us about an organization? For example, if a strong positive relationship exists we would assume that the organization is effectively distributing differential extrinsic rewards based on performance. In addition, it is providing jobs that allow for the satisfaction of higher order needs. Finally, the poorer performers rather than the better ones are quitting and showing high absenteeism, since, as we know, satisfaction, turnover, and absenteeism are closely related.

Now let us consider an organization where no relationship exists between satisfaction and performance. In this organization, presumably, rewards are not being effectively related to performance, and absenteeism and turnover in the organization are likely to be equally distributed among both the good and poor performers. Finally, let us consider the organization where satisfaction and performance bear a negative relationship to each other. Here absenteeism and turnover will be greatest among the best performers. Furthermore, the poor performers would be getting more rewards than the good performers.

Clearly, most organization theorists would feel that organizational effectiveness is encouraged by rewarding good performers and by restricting turnover to poorer performers. Thus, it may be desirable for organizations to develop a strong relationship between satisfaction and performance. In effect, the argument is that the less positive relationship between satisfaction and performance in an organization, the less effective the organization will be *(ceteris paribus)*. If this hypothesis were shown to be true, it would mean that a measure of the relationship between satisfaction and performance would be a helpful diagnostic tool for examining organizations. It is hardly necessary to note that this approach is quite different from the usual human relations one of trying to maximize satisfaction, since here we are suggesting trying to maximize the relationship between satisfaction and performance, rather than satisfaction itself.

One further implication of the model appears to warrant comment. It may well be that a high general level of satisfaction of needs like self-actualization may be a sign of organization effectiveness. Such a level of satisfaction would indicate, for instance, that most employees have interesting and involving jobs and that they probably are performing them well. One of the obvious advantages of providing employees with intrinsically interesting jobs is that good performance is rewarding in and of itself. Furthermore, being rewarded for good performance is likely to encourage further good performance. Thus, measures of higher order need satisfaction may provide good evidence of how effective organizations have been in creating interesting and rewarding jobs and, therefore, indirect evidence of how motivating the jobs themselves are. This discussion of the role of intrinsic rewards and satisfaction serves to highlight the importance of including measures of higher order need satisfaction in attitude surveys. Too often attitude surveys have focused only on satisfaction with extrinsic rewards, such as pay and promotion, and on the social relations which were originally stressed by the human relations movement.

In summary, we have argued that it is important to consider the satisfaction level that exists in organizations. For one thing, satisfaction is important because it has the power to influence both absenteeism and turnover. In addition, in the area of job performance we have emphasized that rather than being a cause of performance, satisfaction is caused by it. If this is true, and we have presented some evidence to support the view that it is, then it becomes appropriate to be more concerned about which people and what kind of needs are satisfied in the organization, rather than about how to maximize satisfaction generally. In short, we suggest new ways of interpreting job satisfaction data.

NOTES
1. Brayfield, A. H. and Crockett, W. H., 'Employee Attitudes and Employee Performance', *Psychological Bulletin*, LII (1955) 396–424.
2. Ibid.
3. Kornhauser, A. and Sharp, A., 'Employee Attitudes: Suggestions from a Study in a Factory', *Personnel Journal*, X (1932) 393–401.
4. Ibid.
5. Brayfield and Crockett, op. cit.
6. Herzberg, F., Mausner, B., Peterson, R. O. and Capwell, D. F., *Job Attitudes: Review of Research and Opinion* (Pittsburgh: Psychological Service, 1957).
7. Ibid., p. 103.
8. Vroom, V. H., *Work and Motivation* (New York: Wiley, 1964).
9. Georgopoulos, B. S., Mahoney, G. M. and Jones, N. W. 'A Path-Goal Approach to Productivity', *Journal of Applied Psychology*, XLI (1957) 345–53; Vroom, op. cit.; Lawler, E. E. and Porter, L. W., 'Antecedent Attitudes of Effective Managerial Performance', *Organizational Behavior and Human Performance*, II (1967) 122–43. See also Porter, L. W. and Lawler, E. E., *Managerial Attitudes and Performance* (Homewood, Ill.: Irwin-Dorsey, in press).
10. Vroom, op. cit., p. 246.
11. Maslow, A. H., *Motivation and Personality* (New York: Harper, 1954). According to Maslow, needs are arranged in a hierarchy with physiological and security needs being the lowest level needs, social and esteem needs next, and autonomy and self-actualization needs the highest level.
12. Lawler, E. E., 'Managers' Attitudes Toward How Their Pay Is and Should Be Determined', *Journal of Applied Psychology*, L (1966) 273–9.

13. Porter, L. W., 'A Study of Perceived Need Satisfactions in Bottom and Middle Management Jobs', *Journal of Applied Psychology*, XLV (1961) 1–10.
14. Ibid.
15. A third question about the importance of the various types of needs was also included, but the results based on it are not reported in the findings presented in this article.

19 Job Satisfaction and Turnover in a Female Clerical Population*

CHARLES L. HULIN[1]
University of Illinois

Job-satisfaction questionnaires were administered to a sample of 350 female clerical workers employed by a large firm located in Montreal. After a lapse of 5 months 31 girls had quit, 26 of whom had completed the questionnaire. These 26 girls reported significantly less satisfaction with their jobs than the 319 girls who remained on the job. An explanation of this finding in terms of the difficulty of finding a new job, economic pressures to remain on present job, and condition of the labor market in Montreal is offered. The relationship between satisfaction and turnover is not regarded as general. The study was continued for 7 more months. The data from the subsequent 7 months indicate that job-satisfaction scores continue to exhibit a significant relationship to turnover over a 12-month period. Even after a 12-month period the terminators had reported lower job satisfaction at the time of the assessment than those who were still with the company.

The relationship between job satisfaction and job behavior has been a source of dispute and controversy for several years. Herzberg (Herzberg, Mausner, Peterson, and Capwell, 1957) concluded in his review of the literature that high satisfaction and high productivity went together while Katzell (1957), using a more stringent criterion of statistical significance concluded that the published studies did not reveal such a relationship. The conclusions of Brayfield and Crockett (1955) and Vroom (1964) tend to support the position of Katzell.

A second aspect of job performance — job turnover — appears to have generated somewhat more consensus of opinion. Brayfield and Crockett (1955), Herzberg, Mausner, Peterson, and Capwell (1957), Katzell (1957), and Vroom (1964) all concluded that the published studies support the notion that the dissatisfied worker is more likely to leave his job than a

Journal of Applied Psychology, L [4] (1966) 280–5. Copyright 1966 by the American Psychological Association. Reprinted by permission.

satisfied worker. This finding and conclusion is theoretically appealing since one can expect that the job factors which lead a worker to like his job should be the same factors which lead him to remain on the job (see Vroom, 1964). The author (Hulin, 1963), however, concluded that the presence of such a relationship might be too dependent on situational characteristics and characteristics of the work force to be regarded as a general finding.

A careful analysis of the literature on the question of satisfaction and turnover indicates that only one of the studies deals with industrial workers, uses individual reports of satisfaction, and uses individual termination decisions. This one study, by Weitz and Nuckols (1953), was done on a mailed questionnaire basis on a sample of 1,200 life insurance agents. Weitz and Nuckols reported a 47% return of the questionnaires. The results indicated a .20 correlation (*p* < .05) between a direct measure of job satisfaction and subsequent survival as an agent and a .05 correlation between an indirect assessment of satisfaction and survival. Unfortunately, even in this study, there were two sources of bias: Significantly fewer of the terminators than the survivors returned the questionnaire and job survival and job performance are not independent variables in the case of insurance agents since they are paid on a straight commission basis. In this group of workers, low production leads to termination. Weit and Nuckols may have been predicting a combination of productivity and turnover.

The writer does not question the validity nor the rigor of the Weitz and Nuckols study. However, one could raise several questions regarding the generality of the conclusions of the reviewers who have generalized to all of industry on the basis of *one* study.

The remainder of the published studies bearing on this question are only tangentially related to the issue. Many of the investigators have used group analyses (Fleishman, Harris, and Burtt, 1955; Giese and Ruter, 1949; Kerr, Kopelmeir, and Sullivan, 1951) and related average departmental or group satisfaction scores and group turnover rates. There is always the problem that different departments, having different types of jobs, working conditions, and supervisors, will attract different types of workers. These other variables may be responsible for the obtained relationships between average departmental satisfaction and turnover levels. Several studies have used students or members of discussion groups or members of voluntary committees as subjects (*Ss*). While these latter studies are important, they do not answer the question of turnover and satisfaction in an industrial work force.

It should be evident that satisfaction is only part of the answer to the problem of turnover. Other factors such as the condition of the labor market (Behrend, 1953), the age of the workers, chances of obtaining another job, and financial responsibilities all contribute to a worker's decision to leave his job. While one might expect a relationship between turnover and satisfaction in general, it is possible that in certain situations this relationship would not be obtained because of the factors mentioned above.

The present study was carried out in order to obtain an indication of the generality of the hypothesized relationship between satisfaction and turnover.

METHOD

Research setting

The company involved in the research to be reported in this article is a large manufacturing company with its home offices located in Montreal, Quebec. During the past 3 years the turnover among the female clerical staff has been 30.3%, 30.0%, and 30.0%. The rate of turnover appears to be stable and has indicated no tendencies in either direction over the past 10 years. The company estimates by the use of a cost-accounting analysis that to hire and train one clerical worker costs approximately $1,000. At the present rate, turnover in the clerical staff alone is costing the company $130,000 per year. Voluntary turnover rate among 15 other large companies in the Montreal area averaged 18.4%, 20.2%, and 20.0% over the past 3 years. While labor market conditions may be contributing to the overall level of turnover in Montreal firms this particular firm seems to have more than would be predicted by the market conditions. This would indicate that a search for factors relating to individual turnover rates would be successful.

Subjects

The entire female clerical staff was asked to participate in a survey of job satisfaction which was to be conducted by the company. The workers were informed of this by their supervisors and by a letter from the personnel department. It was stressed that the company simply wanted to know what their clerical workers as a group thought of their jobs. They were told that the questionnaires were completely anonymous and their individual responses would never be revealed to the company. Of the 415 members of the clerical staff, 350 (86.3%) participated in the survey. (The largest percentage of the nonparticipants was either on vacation or ill during the testing period.) There was no apparent bias in the rate of participation between those who later quit and those who did not since 84% of those who quit had completed the questionnaires.

In addition to the survey of the present staff, questionnaires were mailed to the 129 clerical workers who had quit during 1963. Twenty-nine of these questionnaires (22.5%) were returned. These Ss were asked to describe in retrospect how they had felt about the company as a place to work.

Variables

The job satisfaction of these girls was assessed by means of the Job Description Index (JDI). The JDI is a cumulative-point, adjective check-list type of scale. It has been subjected to an extensive validation program and has been described elsewhere (Hulin, Smith, Kendall, and Locke, 1963; Vroom, 1964, p. 100). The JDI was constructed to measure five separate aspects of a worker's satisfaction: satisfaction with work done, with the pay, with promotional opportunities and policies, with the co-workers, and with the supervisor. A sixth, unvalidated scale constructed along the same general lines was added to the questionnaire for the purposes of this study. This sixth scale was an attempt to assess the workers' reactions to the 'atmosphere' of the company as a place to work. This added scale included such items as: friendly, everybody works together, helpful with personal problems, accept differences in cultural backgrounds, etc. This scale was intended to measure the workers' reactions to some of the general aspects of the company. As such it probably will have a lower degree of discriminant validity than the original five scales.

In addition to these six satisfaction variables, measures were also obtained of each worker's age, education level, job level (obtained by matching reported job title to the job-evaluation scale of the company), mother tongue, and marital status. All of the control variables were assessed by means of self-report. Measures of these six satisfaction variables and five control variables were obtained during the last week of June 1964 for each of the 350 workers who participated in the survey. By 15 December 1964, 31 girls had quit, 26 of whom had participated in the original survey. The same questionnaire was readministered to these 31 girls at the time of quitting to obtain a measure of their attitudes toward their jobs after the decision had been made to quit.

RESULTS

The averages of the satisfaction scores and the control variables which had been obtained in July from the 26 terminators were compared to the averages of the 319 girls who were still on the job on 15 December 1964. These data are presented in Table 1.

These data indicate that those who later quit their jobs reported less satisfaction in June than those who did not quit. They were also 8 years younger on the average. The major hypothesis of this study concerns the effects of satisfaction on turnover. Since age is positively related to certain aspects of job satisfaction the differences in age could have accounted for both the turnover and the differences in satisfaction levels between the two groups. Therefore, for every one of the 26 terminators two control *Ss* were drawn who were matched in terms of age, years of education, and mother tongue. The average satisfaction scores of these 52 controls and the 26 terminators are presented in Table 2.

Table 1   Characteristics and satisfaction scores of terminators and nonterminators

Variable	Nonterminators $n = 319$	Terminators $n = 26$
Satisfaction area		
Work	35.87	28.69
Pay	15.00	15.15
Promotions	10.90	9.35
Co-workers	41.13	37.40
Supervision	41.81	38.15
Atmosphere	34.78	32.92
Sample characteristics		
Age	32.04	24.23
Years of education	11.93	11.94
Job level	5.86	5.33
Percentage with English as mother tongue	25	26
Percentage unmarried	25	31

No significant differences in any of the control variables were observed between the control group and the terminators. The significance of the difference between the vectors of mean satisfaction scores obtained from the 26 terminators and the 52 matched controls was tested by means of Hotelling's (1931) T^2 analysis. The difference was significant at less than the .05 level. It should be pointed out that the T^2 analysis assumes random groups and in this case one is dealing with groups that have been matched on variables known to be associated with the dependent variables in question. For this reason the error term may be too large and the test will be a conservative one.

Column 3 of Table 2 gives the average satisfaction scores at the time of quitting of the 31 girls who quit between June and 15 December 1964. These scores were gathered originally for general information purposes. No

Table 2   Mean satisfaction scores from all groups of workers

Variable	Controls (June) $n = 52$	Terminators (June) $n = 26$	Terminators (at time of quitting) $n = 31$	1963 terminators $n = 29$
Satisfaction area				
Work	35.83	28.69	30.48	28.28
Pay	15.17	15.15	17.94	16.07
Promotions	17.16	9.35	10.10	10.72
Co-workers	41.44	37.40	40.48	39.10
Supervision	41.66	38.15	40.87	34.79
Atmosphere	35.52	32.92	36.48	31.72

predictions were made regarding the relative level of the scores as compared to the June scores. No tests of the significance of the difference between this vector of means and the vector of means obtained in June were made. The Hotelling T^2 analysis is not applicable since it assumes different groups and six t ratios done on correlated variables would seem to be inappropriate also. Column 4 presents the average satisfaction scores of the 29 girls who had quit during 1963 and who responded to the mailed questionnaire. Again, no predictions were made regarding this vector of means and no statistical analyses were done.

FOLLOW-UP STUDY

The company continued to record biographical data of the workers who quit from the fifth to the twelfth month of the study. These biographical data were used to identify the questionnaires completed at the beginning of the study. Twenty-three girls quit during the period from 15 December 1964 to 15 June 1965. Seventeen of these 23 had completed the JDI the previous June. For each of the 17 identified workers who had terminated employment, two control Ss matched in terms of age, years of education, and job level were drawn from the total group. The average scores on the satisfaction and biographical variables were computed for these two groups of Ss.

RESULTS

The results of this second analysis are shown in Table 3. The difference between the two vectors of means was tested for significance by means of Hotelling's (1931) T^2 analysis. This test resulted in a nonsignificant statistic indicating that the difference between these two vectors could reasonably be attributed to chance.

As an additional analysis an unweighted sum of the satisfaction variables was correlated with the turnover criterion. This Pearson correlation coefficient was $-.28$ $(p > .05)$. This latter correlational analysis merely supports the results of the T^2 analysis but it provides us with an estimate of the magnitude of the relation between the satisfaction variables and turnover. A similar analysis of the data from the terminators and their controls of the first 5 months resulted in a Pearson correlation coefficient of $-.26$ $(p < .05)$.

The two groups of terminators from the first 5 months and the last 7 months were combined and compared to the combined group of control workers $(n = 129)$. A comparison of the satisfaction scores of these two groups indicated a significant T^2 analysis $(p < .01)$, a multiple correlation of .34 $(p < .01)$, and a significant Pearson correlation between an

Table 3   Mean satisfaction and biographical variable scores from June 1964

Variable	Terminators (12/64 to 6/65) $n = 17$	Controls $n = 34$
Satisfaction area		
Work	31.41	35.85
Pay	15.94	16.38
Promotions	11.12	13.76
Co-workers	40.65	44.15
Supervision	30.82	41.97
Atmosphere*	33.24	36.97
Biographical variables		
Age	24.8	24.6
Years of education	12.6	12.5
Job level	5.9	5.2
Percentage with English as mother tongue	23	23
Percentage unmarried	35	21

*This last scale, 'atmosphere', was not part of the original JDI. It was constructed by the writer especially for the purposes of this study and was an attempt to assess the extent the workers regarded the company as a friendly place to work.

unweighted sum of the satisfaction variables and the turnover criterion of $-.27$ $(p < .01)$.

DISCUSSION

The results of this investigation indicate quite clearly that subsequent termination can be significantly predicted from a knowledge of the worker's job satisfaction in this sample of female clerical workers who are working in an area in which there is a labor shortage for clerical workers. This significant difference between the vectors of mean satisfaction scores for terminators and survivors held up both in the original analysis and after a matched control group was drawn. This seems to imply that workers on jobs whose characteristics are satisfying to them (for whatever reason) are likely to remain on those jobs. Vroom's (1964) analysis that job characteristics which lead to satisfaction also lead workers to remain in that situation appears to be correct for this sample of workers. It should be stressed that the writer is not concluding that these relationships will be obtained from all types of workers in all situations. To make such a conclusion on the basis of only two studies would seem to be premature. The generality of the results is still to be determined.

At the present time it seems best to ascribe a low value to the probability that these results would generalize to a large segment of the United States work force. Several factors in the present study undoubtedly contributed to these results. The *S's* were females. They have fewer economic reasons for remaining on any job they are dissatisfied with than would a comparable sample of males. They tend to be a young group (average age of 32 years) and they are relatively well-educated (average of 12 years of education). They tend to have marketable skills and live in an area in which there is a demand for these skills. Therefore, any decision they make regarding job termination can be regarded as being an easily made decision. They know that a new job can be obtained with a minimum of effort. There are few pressures which would tend to keep them in their present position if they are dissatisfied with it.

On the other hand, workers who are less able to find a new job and who have a number of economic obligations would have pressures on them to remain at their present job even if they were decidedly dissatisfied. It would be possible to postulate that there is a dimension of 'propensity to leave if dissatisfied' in the work force. At one extreme (high propensity to leave if dissatisfied) one would expect to find young, highly skilled workers, with few economic obligations, who are living in an area which has a demand for their skills. At the other extreme (no propensity to leave if dissatisfied) one would expect old, unskilled workers, who live in an area of substantial unemployment. It would seem to be unwise to conclude at this time that satisfaction and probability of termination are, in general, negatively related in the work force. The relationship would seem to depend on a great many factors.

The vector of mean satisfaction scores given in Column 3 of Table 2 while not tested for significance is interesting. These means represent the average response of the 26 terminators at the time of quitting. These 26 girls report more satisfaction in all areas at the time of quitting than they reported in June prior to quitting. Why this should be so is not immediately obvious. These results appear to be somewhat at odds with Festinger's (1957) theory of cognitive dissonance. The theory would hold that after these girls had reached their decision they would attempt to reduce any dissonance they may have felt by reporting *less* satisfaction. In the case of every one of the six satisfaction variables the mean score *increased*. While several post hoc explanations are possible this should probably be regarded as a regression to the mean effect until further replications have been attempted.

The final set of data reported in this paper is the mean satisfaction scores obtained from the mailed questionnaires which were sent to the girls who had quit during 1963. This sample of girls described (in retrospect) their jobs with the company in somewhat negative terms. The retrospective descriptions of jobs which these girls furnished appear to resemble the responses given by the terminators in June. However, since this is a cross-sectional comparison, any interpretation is on an unsound basis. The data are presented in the interests of hypothesis formulation, not hypothesis testing.

The differences in satisfaction scores between terminators and non-terminators appear to be small and, while they attain statistical significance, there may be some doubt about their practical significance. However, it should be remembered that the company estimates that it costs in excess of $1,000 to hire and train a new clerical worker. At this rate of cost the control of only 10% of the variance of turnover rates would become a very practical matter for many companies.

The nonsignificant T^2 statistic and the nonsignificant correlation between the satisfaction variables and the turnover measure in the group of workers who quit during the last 7 months of the study could be interpreted as evidence that the predictive power of a set of satisfaction variables has disappeared after a period of only 5 months. An explanation of these discouraging results would likely be centered around the notion that intervening occurrences can have substantial effects on the job satisfaction of the workers. Even though the termination decisions were related to the workers' job satisfaction at the time of quitting, their satisfaction at the time of quitting might bear very little relationship to their satisfaction at the time it was measured. This would be evidence neither for the lack of validity nor the lack of reliability of the JDI. It would be evidence for the lack of stability of job satisfaction itself.

It should be pointed out, however, that even though statistical significance was not achieved, the *magnitude of the relationship* between satisfaction and turnover has not changed from the first 5 months to the last 7 months. A comparison of the correlations between an unweighted sum of the satisfaction variables and turnover indicates this quite clearly. These correlations are −.26 for the early terminators (first 5 months) and −.28 for the late terminators (last 7 months). Further, the correlation of −.27 for the entire combined group cannot be said to be dependent on the existence of large differences in satisfaction between the early terminators and their controls since (to repeat) the magnitude of this relationship has not changed over the course of this study.

This degree of stability is regarded as both encouraging and surprising by the writer. It would be reasonable to expect that those girls who were extremely dissatisfied at the time of the administration of the JDI would be likely to quit shortly after the administration. That is, those who were most dissatisfied would be among the first to terminate; those who quit during the second and third months would have achieved higher scores on the JDI than those who quit first, etc. Thus, if one computed the mean June job-satisfaction scores for the groups of workers who quit during each of the subsequent months one would expect to find that these June scores exhibited a steady increase. Likewise, would be obtained a steadily decreasing validity for the prediction of turnover from satisfaction scores. An inspection of the month-by-month means indicates that this is indeed what is happening. The increase is not large enough to appreciably affect the validity of the JDI, however. In spite of these factors, the JDI exhibited significant validities for the prediction of turnover over a 12-month period.

One could infer from the results of this study that the JDI job-satisfaction scores possess a high degree of stability over time. Otherwise one could not achieve the long-term validities as was done. They would also demonstrate that the relation between attitudes and behavior is not a short-term transient phenomenon but can be expected to last for a considerable period of time (12 months in the case of satisfaction and turnover) and that valid predictions can easily be made during this period of time.

REFERENCES

Behrend, H., 'Absence and Labor Turnover in a Changing Economic Climate', *Occupational Psychology*, XXVII (1953) 69—79.

Brayfield, A. H. and Crockett, W. H., 'Employee Attitudes and Employee Performance', *Psychological Bulletin*, LII (1955) 396—424.

Festinger, L., *A Theory of Cognitive Dissonance* (Evanston: Row, Peterson, 1957).

Fleishman, E. A., Harris, E. F. and Burtt, H. E., *Leadership and Supervision in Industry* (Columbus: Ohio State University, Bureau of Educational Research, 1955).

Giese, W. J. and Ruter, H. W., 'An Objective Analysis of Morale', *Journal of Applied Psychology*, XXXIII (1949) 421—7.

Herzberg, F., Mausner, B., Peterson, R. O. and Capwell, D. F., *Job Attitudes: Review of Research and Opinion* (Pittsburg, Pa.: Psychological Service of Pittsburg, 1957).

Hotelling, H., 'The Generalization of Student's Ratio', *Annals of Mathematical Statistics*, II (1931) 360—78.

Hulin, C. L., 'Research Implications of Attitude Surveys in Large Organizations'. Paper read at the Illinois Psychological Association, Springfield, Illinois, 1963.

Hulin, C. L., Smith, P. C., Kendall, L. M. and Locke, E. A., 'Cornell Studies of Job Satisfaction: II. Model and Method of Measuring Job Satisfaction. Unpublished manuscript, 1963.

Katzell, R. A., 'Industrial Psychology', *Annual Review of Psychology*, VIII (1957) 237—68.

Kerr, W. A., Kopelmeir, G. and Sullivan, J. J., 'Absenteeism, Turnover, and Morale in a Metals Fabrication Factory', *Occupational Psychology*, XXV (1951) 50—55.

Vroom, V. H., *Work and Motivation* (New York: Wiley, 1964).

Weitz, J. and Nuckols, R. C., 'The Validity of Direct and Indirect Questions in Measuring Job Satisfaction', *Personnel Psychology*, VI (1953) 487–94.

NOTE
1 The author would like to express his appreciation to Sonia Plourde for her assistance in this study, and to the officials and workers of the company involved for their cooperation.

20 Employee Attitudes and Absences[*]

HELEN METZNER and FLOYD MANN
Survey Research Center, University of Michigan

SUMMARY

This study[1] was undertaken to test the relationship between absence rates and employees' attitudes for white and blue collar, peace-time workers. Satisfactions with the work situation were found to be inversely related to absence rates for white collar men working at low skill level jobs and for blue collar men, but not for white collar women or white collar men working at higher level jobs. The way a man feels toward his supervisor and toward his work associates were the two work situation areas related to absence rates for both white and blue collar men. Relationships between attitudes and frequency-of-absence rates were found to be higher than between attitudes and man-days-lost rates.

INTRODUCTION

Absence rates, along with turnover figures, scrap losses, and productivity, are frequently considered as objective measures of the relative efficiency of an operation. Organizations having high employee absence rates are commonly thought to be less efficiently managed organizations than those which have low rates of absence. It is also generally hypothesized that the attitudes and opinions of employees can be related directly to this objective measure of efficiency. Workers who are not particularly interested in their jobs or who are actually dissatisfied with their work situations would be expected to have higher absence rates than those who enjoyed their work and were satisfied with their supervision and with the opportunities their job provided for pay, self-expression, promotion, and associations with others.

While this relationship between employee work attitudes and absences is commonly assumed, it has not been quantitatively demonstrated very often. Only a few researchers have attempted to relate absence rates to employee attitudes, perceptions, and personal characteristics (Katz and Hyman, 1947; Noland, 1945). Most of the studies in this area have

Personnel Psychology, VI (1953) 467–485. Reprinted by permission.

229

attempted to explain the differences in absence rates between comparable work groups, departments, or plants on the basis of organizational differences in administration and policy (Covner, 1950; Fox and Scott, 1943; Mayo and Lombard, 1944). Differences in organizational policies have been searched out for groups having extremely high or low absence rates. Inferences were then made from these organizational differences and absence rates about employees' feelings and perceptions.

Most of these studies were investigations, growing out of the wartime problem of 'absenteeism'. This paper will present some post-war findings concerning the relationship between attitudes and absences using data obtained from white collar and blue collar employees in an electric light and power company. Our analyses were undertaken to test in the peace-time operations of a large hierarchical organization some of the hypotheses derived from blue collar, wartime studies.

HYPOTHESES
The general statement of the hypotheses that we were most interested in testing is as follows: Satisfaction with the work situation is inversely related to absence rate. Stated conversely in terms of dissatisfaction with specific aspects of the work situation, we predicted that—

Given similar physical conditions and the same general kind of work, employees in groups having high absence rates are characterized by feelings of:

1. low interest in the job itself or dissatisfaction with the kind of work;
2. dissatisfaction with the company's personnel practices;
3. dissatisfaction with wages and chances for promotion;
4. dissatisfaction with the supervisor and his supervisory practices; including the feeling that the supervisor will not listen to and understand personal problems;
5. poor team spirit or low pride in work group.

Still controlling on physical working conditions and type of work, other hypotheses which we tested were:

6. Absence rates are related to sex, women having higher rates than men. This relationship had been found in previous studies.

7. Absence rates are related to length of service; more employees with shorter service are in higher absence rate work groups, and employees with longer service tend to be in lower absence rate work groups. This was found in previous studies and was believed to be related to 'instability' among shorter service employees.

8. Absence rates are related to size of work group; the large work groups having higher absence rates. This was suggested in other studies and was associated with our fifth hypothesis. Larger work groups have been thought to be less conducive to the development of a group spirit. Group bonds cannot develop in large work groups as easily; concomitantly members in large groups cannot exert the same amount of social pressure

on fellow associates as people in smaller, close-knit work groups can. Nor are they likely to be as personally concerned about others around them.

THE POPULATIONS

These hypotheses were tested in two separate, though related analyses. The first was a study of 163 white collar men and 212 white collar women in the major accounting departments in a large electric power company. These employees prepared customer's billings, accounts, financial statements, and property and tax reports. The second analysis was of 251 blue collar men who worked at outside jobs involved in the construction and maintenance of overhead lines. About half these men worked at highly skilled electrical jobs, the remainder at tree-trimming and other supporting tasks. These two analyses were done separately because of the difference in physical working conditions and type of work. A work group absence rate rather than an individual rate was used because it was not possible to match absence and attitudinal responses for individual employees. Only those employees were included whom we could identify with a single work group, having one supervisor. Also only employees who had worked continuously in one work gloup for the entire six month's period of the study were included; that is, no new employees or transferees were part of the population studied.

THE ABSENCE RATES

For the white collar study two kinds of absence rates were constructed: a 'man-days lost' rate and a 'frequency of absence' rate. For the man-days lost rate, separate averages were computed for men and women in each work group of the number of days lost per month over the six month period just prior to the date the questionnaires were administered.

The frequency-of-absence rate was computed to get a different kind of information from that afforded by the lost days rate. One absence, in the frequency context, was defined as a minimum of a half day out or any longer period consisting of a series of consecutive working days. This rate minimized the effect of absences caused by prolonged illnesses. Averages of the number of absences per month over the designated six month period were computed separately for the men and women in each work group. The rates were grouped into the following categories:

For men
1 absence or less for the 6 month period
2 absences for the 6 month period
3 absences for the 6 month period
4 or more absences for the 6 month period

For women
2 absences or less for the 6 month period
3 absences for the 6 month period

4 absences for the 6 month period
5 absences for the 6 month period
6 or more absences for the 6 month period

In the blue collar study only the frequency of absence rate was used since, as will be shown later, it proved to be the most useful rate on the other study. The crew rates were grouped into the following categories:

3 absences or less for the 6 month period
4 absences for the 6 month period
5 or more absences for the 6 month period

The frequency-of-absence rates were tested for various characteristics before being grouped and used further.

1. The three distributions of the uncategorized group absence rates for the white collar men's groups, the white collar women's groups, and the blue collar men's groups were examined separately to see if they resembled normal distributions. The alpha measure of skewness was computed for each and was found to be so small as to lead us to conclude the distributions were close enough to normal to warrant the use of significance tests which depend upon normal distributions. We might have expected this, since, as mentioned, the rates are group rates or averages, and, distributions of averages generally tend toward normality.

2. Other studies have suggested that the proportion of people of the same sex in a work group is related to absence rates. To test this relationship, the work groups were divided into (1) all male, (2) more than 60 per cent male, (3) between 40 per cent and 60 per cent male, and (4) less than 40 per cent male. A similar grouping was made for females. Two F tests, one run for the male grouping and the other for the female grouping, showed no significant differences in the mean absence rates for these groupings. We, therefore, felt justified in disregarding this factor in further analyses.

3. Women's rates were found to be significantly different (at the .01 level) from the white collar men's rates using the *t* test of the significance of the difference between means. The mean difference was about one absence in the six month period, with women absent more frequently. Hypothesis six therefore was substantiated. This difference and the knowledge derived from the other studies that women's attitudes toward their work situations are different from men's dictated that we treat men and women separately in subsequent analyses.

4. When the frequency-of-absence rates for the white collar men were compared with those of the blue collar men it was found that the blue collar men had a significantly higher rate than the white collar men. The difference between the means was significant at the .05 level using the *t*-test. The difference between the two amounted to about one-half

absence for the six month period. The white collar men averaged almost three absences every six months, while the blue collar men averaged over three absences for the six month period. The time period for the accounting study was from December 1949 through May 1950, while that of the blue collar study was from July through December 1950. It is possible that the absence rates for the blue collar group might have been even greater if the time period had included as many of the winter months as were included for the white collar group.

5. Tests of significance (*t*-tests) were made to see if size of work group was related to absence rates (hypothesis 8). In both studies, work groups were arrayed in order of official size and all the groups falling in the lower half of the distributions were defined as small while those in the upper half of the distributions were called large. In the accounting study there were no significant differences either for men or women between the mean absence rates for 'large' work groups (12 or more) and 'small' work groups (under 12). In the blue collar study the mean absence rate of the large work groups (over 7) tended to be significantly greater (.10 level) than the mean absence rate of the small work group (under 7). From these two findings it is difficult to draw any positive conclusion about hypothesis 8. There are at least two possible explanations for the fact that the findings are not the same for the two studies. One is that we have not used the same absolute number of employees to mean 'small' or 'large' in the two studies; and the other is that the studies deal with two populations of men working under entirely different conditions at entirely different jobs.

We were not able to use the same absolute number of employees to mean 'small' and 'large' for both studies because of the marked difference in the size of the work groups in these two departments. All white collar groups had at least five employees, and half had over 12. Some of the blue collar groups had only two men, half had under seven and none had more than 10. When all the blue collar groups were taken together and compared with the men's rates of the 'small' groups in the accounting department (under 12 employees), no significant difference was found between the mean absence rates of the two groups. This suggested that for groups of under 12, white collar male employees did not differ from blue collar male employees in these studies. However, a more detailed analysis indicated further complications which seemed to be related to type of work. The following table shows the average absence rates for white and blue collar men in their respective 'small' and 'large' work groups.

White collar men
Small groups (under 12) 2.9 abs/6 months
Large groups (12 or more) 2.4 abs/6 months
Blue collar men
Small groups (under 7) 2.9 abs/6 months
Large groups (7 or more) 3.5 abs/6 months

The average absence rate for white collar men in small groups was larger (but not significantly) than the rate for white collar men in large groups. However for blue collar men, the average absence rate for small groups tended to be significantly smaller than the rate for men in large groups.

Not only were the findings from the two studies different with respect to significance but also with respect to direction of relationship of absence with size of group. It may be that the psychologically significant break between large and small groups lies at around five, six or seven employees, such as we used in the blue collar analysis, especially where the members of the group are highly interdependent for the performance of their jobs. Both of these conditions were met in the blue collar study. This size break was not met in the white collar analyses because of the small number of groups having under seven employees. Also, the members of the work groups in accounting units were not as dependent upon one another for the performance of their work as the members in blue collar crews were.

THE ATTITUDE MEASURES

The attitudinal measures were taken from the responses to a selected number of fixed-alternative questions included on longer questionnaires. In the final analysis, alternatives of each single question were combined so as to yield a dichotomy for that question — favorable and unfavorable. In the accounting study, an index composed of three questions concerning feelings toward the first-line supervisor was also computed and used. These three questions were found to form a unidimensional scale and were used together for the additional reliability afforded. The scores for the index ranged from 15 to 3, with 15 indicating maximum satisfaction and 3, maximum dissatisfaction.

The questions used to measure employees' attitudes towards the work situation were taken from the general areas of the job itself, the company's personnel policies, wages and promotions, supervision, the work group, and over-all feelings about the company and the job.

FINDINGS FOR MEN

Relationship between frequency of absence and attitudes

For white collar men our findings confirmed our predictions concerning the relationship between the frequency of absence and the attitudes which employees have toward the several aspects of their jobs. Men in work groups having an average absence rate of once in six months were in general more satisfied than men in work groups having an average absence rate of four or more each half year. Moreover when all four absence groupings were considered, absences and work attitudes appeared to be directly related. A progressively smaller proportion of the men in groups having increasingly higher average absence rates were satisfied with the various aspects of their work.

Of the 15 attitudinal measures related to absences, ten showed statistically significant relationships at the .10 level or better in the direction predicted by the hypotheses. For only one item was the trend different than predicted. For eight of the items the differences were significant at the five or one per cent levels. Table 1 shows the questions by area which were related significantly to absence rate groups.

The relationship between absences and attitudes toward the working situation for blue collar men is shown in Table 2. Of the 18 attitudinal measures related here, nine were significant at the ten per cent level or better; six at the five per cent level or better.

Since the questions asked in the accounting study were not the same as those asked in the blue collar study, only general comparisons by area were possible between the two studies. In the area of supervision both studies showed about the same degree of relationship between satisfaction and absence rate. In both studies the importance of good communication between supervisor and employee was suggested. Fewer white collar men in the high absence group felt very free to discuss important things about their job with their supervisors than men in low absence groups. Fewer blue collar men in the high absence group than in the low absence group reported their foremen usually or always had enough time to see them when they wanted to talk about something personal.

For white collar men, there were also significant relationships between absences and general satisfaction with immediate supervision and with intermediate levels of management. For blue collar men, there was a relationship between absences and the frequency with which the foreman involved his whole crew in discussions about things that concerned both him and the crew.

In the area of the work group, there appeared to be a greater relationship for the blue collar men than for the white collar men. For blue collar men, absences were clearly related to whether the men have a sense of belongingness and group pride. More men in the low absence rate groups than in the high absence groups felt they really were a part of their crew and that their crew was one of the best or better than most in getting the job done. Low absence men also had a greater feeling of team spirit and reported that *all* the men in the crew get along in a friendly manner. In the accounting study, there was a significant relationship between absences and group cohesiveness — the extent to which the men felt their group was better than others in sticking together to get what the group wants. One question showed an opposite trend from that predicted for the white collar men.

In the area of the job itself there was a marked relationship with absences for blue collar men only. The relationships between absences and attitudes for the wages and promotions and the company in general were more marked for white collar men than blue collar men.

Table 1   White collar men: relationship between frequency of absence and attitudes

	Men in work groups having an average absence rate for the men alone of:			
	1/6 months	2/6 months	3/6 months	4 + /6 months
Supervision				
Feel very free to discuss important things about my job with my supervisor. Sig: 1–4 (.01)*	69%	63%	57%	29%
Index of satisfaction with supervisor – mean scores– 15 = highest satisfaction 3 = lowest satisfaction Sig: 1–4 (.01)	12.25	11.54	11.02	8.22
The supervisors over my supervisor do a good job. Sig: 1–3 (.01)	82%	56%	41%	53%
Work group				
My group is better than others when it comes to sticking together to get what the group wants or wants to do. Sig: 1–4 (.01)	62	48	36	21
Wages and promotions				
Satisfied with my present wages. Sig: 2–4 (.01)	69	63	44	43
Satisfied with my chances for promotion. Sig: 1–4 (.05)	69	47	37	36
The company's personnel policies				
The company gives recognition for good work done by employees. Sig: 1–4 (.01)	94	74	61	54
The company makes an effort to place people in jobs that they can do best. Sig: 1–3 (.10)	50	34	16	25
The job itself				
Satisfied with the amount of responsibility I have in my job. Sig: 1–4 (.10)	62	53	50	35
Over-all satisfaction				
Satisfied with the company and my job as a whole. Sig: 1–4 (.01)	62	49	56	22
Number of men	16	57	62	28

*The information after the statement of the question indicates the major difference which is statistically significant for the specific item and the level of significance for that particular comparison. The other differences which are significant are not shown. Sig: 1–4 (.01) means that the difference between the percentages in columns 1 and 4 is significant at the 1% level. For the index items, the differences are between means.

Table 2   Blue collar men: relationship between frequency of absence and attitudes

	Men in work groups having an average absence rate for the men alone of:		
	1–3/6 months	4/6 months	5 + /6 months
Supervision			
My foreman usually or always has enough time to see me when I want to talk to him about something personal. Sig: 1–3 (.01)*	67%	65%	43%
My foreman practically never gets together with the whole crew to discuss things that concern both him and the crew. Sig: 1–3 (.05)	18	27	34
My foreman practically never takes time out to talk over how I'm doing on the job. Sig: 1–3 (.10)	46	49	61
Work group			
Yes, I feel I really am a part of my work crew. Sig: 1–3 (.05)	73	60	56
My crew is one of the best or better than most compared to other crews in getting the job done. Sig: 1–3 (.05)	57	64	41
My crew has lots of team spirit. Sig: 1–3 (.10)	62	55	48
All the men in my crew get along in a friendly manner. Sig: 1–3 (.10)	43	37	31
The job itself			
My job gives me a very good chance to do the things I am best at. Sig: 1–3 (.01)	27	16	6
I like the sort of work I'm doing in my job a lot. Sig: 1–3 (.05)	33	27	13
At the end of a work day I often (or always) get a feeling of accomplishment. Sig: 1–3 (.10)	74	70	59
Number of men	141	56	54

*The information after the question statement indicates the major difference which is statistically significant for the specific item and the level of significance for that particular comparison.

Relationship between frequency of absence and personal characteristics of men

The relationships found in the white collar study between absence rates and the personal characteristics of men were entirely different from the relationships found in our blue collar study. In the white collar study, the lowest absence group, as compared with the highest absence group, had significantly *smaller* proportions of men who were under 30 years of age, who had less than 5 years of service with the company, who were in the lower job grades and who earned up to $65 per week. In the blue collar study, the lowest absence group, as compared with the highest, had *larger* proportions of men who were in lower job grades and in the lower earnings category. High and low absence groups were not significantly different with respect to age or length of service. Hypothesis 7, which stated that low absence groups would be characterized by fewer employees with short service with the company, was substantiated by the findings from the white collar study and not by the findings from the other study. The differences between the two studies in the relationship of absence and personal characteristics may, however, have been due to the differences in the type of work done by the two groups and the departmental policies regulating absences and job and promotion policies.

In both studies, but particularly in the white collar study, there was a consistent pattern of relationships between absence and some personal characteristics which may be accounted for by the high intercorrelation among these personal characteristics. Previous studies indicated that these personal characteristics were also related to attitudes. The question was thereby raised as to whether the relationship between absence rates and attitudes was not partially or entirely a function of the relationship between absence and personal characteristics.

Relationship for white collar men between frequency of absence and attitudes with job grade controlled

From our other studies we knew that job grade was significantly related to a number of attitudes that workers hold toward their job situation. To answer the question raised above, it was, therefore, necessary to control on job grade by analyzing the relationship between attitudes and absence rate within categories of job grade. If the relationship between attitudes and absence for accounting men were simply a function of the relationships between job grade and absence, and job grade and attitude, controlling on job grade and thereby reducing its effect should cancel the relationship between attitudes and absence that we presented in Table 1.

In the white collar study seven questions were analyzed with job grade under control. We attempted to control the effect of job grade by grouping the white collar job grades into 'high' and 'low' skill level jobs. Low skill level jobs (jobs graded from one to eight) ranged from apprentice clerks and messengers to senior record clerks and advanced accounting machine operators; high skill jobs from senior special clerks to analysts and accountants. These seven questions showed high relationships with absence *without* the control on job grade. When job grade was controlled, and considering the lower skill level jobs only, there was a fairly consistent relationship in the expected direction between absence and attitudes (see Table 3). Not all relationships were significant at the .01 level or better, but for the extreme categories, all were in the expected direction.

For the high skill level jobs there was practically no relationship between attitudes and absence.

In our particular attempt to minimize any possible effect of job grade on attitude we recognize certain limitations. Since the number of men was small, we were forced to group the job grades into two categories. It is

Table 3   White collar men: relationship between frequency of absence and attitudes for men in job grades 1—8

| | | Men in work groups having an average absence rate for the men alone of: | | | |
		1/6 months	2/6 months	3/6 months	4 + /6 months
Free to discuss job prob-	Free	3	9	10	2
lems; Sig: 1—4, 2—4,	Not free	0	8	8	14
3—4**					
Satisfaction with wages;	Satisfied	2	11	3	6
Sig: 2—3	Dissatisfied	1	6	15	10
Company gives recognition	Yes	3	13	7	8
for good work, Sig:	No	0	4	11	8
1—3, 2—3					
Satisfaction with chances	Satisfied	2	7	3	5
for promotion	Dissatisfied	1	10	15	11
Group at sticking together;	Good	3	8	7	1
Sig: 1—4, 2—4, 3—4	Not good	0	9	11	15
Taking things as a whole;	Satisfied	3	10	7	2
Sig: 1—3, 1—4, 2—4	Dissatisfied	0	7	11	13
					*
Amount of responsibility;	Satisfied	3	11	7	4
Sig: 1—3, 1—4, 2—4	Dissatisfied	0	6	10	11
				*	*
	Number of men	3	17	18	16

*One 'no answer'.
**The information after the question statement indicates which distributions are statistically different from one another at the .10 level or better. The exact test was used to compute significances. Sig: 1—3 means that the distribution in column 1 is significantly different from the distribution in column 3.

possible that with a sufficient number of men and the ability to relate attitude and absence within *each* job grade, we would have had different results. However, within these limitations, there is good evidence that attitudes and absence are associated for men in the lower job grades. The question may still be asked whether this relationship was not a function of the remaining variables such as age, wages, and length of service. The number of cases, again, did not permit us to analyze the data in further detail controlling additionally on these other variables. However, the relationships between these variables and job grade were sufficiently high for us to feel that the control on job grade yielded substantially the same kind of information that a single control on any one of the other variables would.

This kind of analysis was not done on the blue collar data because there was not so definite a relationship between absence and several of the background variables.

Relationship between man-days lost and attitudes
A further analysis in the accounting study was made on the relationship of attitudes and absences using *man-days lost*. This operation was parallel to the one that used frequency as the absence measure. Some findings similar to those occurring with the frequency measure emerged, but the man-days lost rate provided fewer and less clear-cut consistent relationships of absence with attitudes than did the frequency rate. In addition, for every attitudinal question, the frequency rate was much more discriminating than the lost days rate.

FINDINGS FOR WHITE COLLAR WOMEN
None of the relationships between attitudes and absence which we found for men were found for women. An increase in the frequency of absence was not accompanied by any consistent change in the proportion of women showing favorable attitudes. Even the extreme absence groups showed little difference in the proportions of women with favorable attitudes.

In general, it can be said that none of our attitudinal hypotheses one through five were borne out by the women's data.

The relationship between women's personal characteristics and their absence rate groupings consisted mainly in the lowest absence group differing from the rest of the absence groups for some variables. There were significantly more women in the lowest absence group, compared with the highest absence group, who had short service and earned under $55 a week. The lowest and highest absence groups were substantially alike with respect to the other personal characteristics.

An analysis parallel to that done for white collar men was made for women. Women were grouped into high and low skill level jobs, and the relationship between absence and attitudes was then studied. Again no significant relationship was found. Nor did the use of the days lost rate yield any consistent relationship between absence and attitude for women.

SUMMARY AND INTERPRETATION OF FINDINGS
These studies suggest that there is no simple relationship between absences and work attitudes for all employees. The hypothesis that satisfactions with the work situation would be inversely related to absence rate was mainly substantiated for white collar men working at low skill level jobs, and for blue collar men — not at all for white collar women or for white collar men working at higher level jobs.

These findings raise problems about interpretation. Our general assumption was that if the totality of satisfactions that an employee obtains from the different aspects of his work situation were not enough to cause him to be willing to invest the extra energy occasionally required to get to the job, the employee would be absent from work. We postulated that some of the positive forces in the work situation which might result in a low absence record for an individual would include:

(a) wages or salary adequate to meet certain basic levels of living needs

(b) a type of job which provided a chance to utilize skills

(c) leadership which takes a personal interest as well as a job interest in the individual

(d) an intragroup relations work climate which offered both a sense of security and belongingness

(e) a set of organizational policies and mechanisms which evidenced the organization's concern for the placement and growth of the individual as a person.

While we had expected that the importance of these factors would vary from person to person, we had also thought they would be more or less relevant for all employees regardless of sex or type of work. Our findings from these two first analyses, however, suggest that these assumptions, derived in part from the non-quantitative studies of wartime absenteeism in factory and semi-skilled jobs, need further investigation.

The finding that there is no relationship between absences and attitudes toward *any* aspect of the work situation for white collar women raises basic questions. In view of the interim nature of employment for most young girls, it would not have been surprising to have found little relationship between their absences and their satisfactions with their promotional opportunities, use of skills, and wages. We would, however, certainly have predicted a relationship between their absences and their feelings towards their supervisor and particularly their work associates. Finding no association between attitudes and absences for either high skill or low skill level white collar women suggests one of the following: (1) our measurements, classifications, or attitudinal coverage is inadequate, or (2) that the absences for women are determined more by some other factor than feelings towards the work situation. It may be that work involvement for young girls (in contrast to that for young white collar men) is relatively low and that a particular girl's absence rate is more dependent upon factors related to her off-the-job activities (e.g. dating) than to work-centered factors. On the basis of this latter assumption we would expect (a) older women and (b) career-oriented younger women to meet our predicted pattern. This type of analysis is, however, dependent upon having absence rates for individuals, not groups as used in this study.

The fact that, in our study, absence is related to attitudes toward the work situation for white collar men at low skill level jobs but not for white collar men at higher level jobs presents a further problem of interpretation. Within the framework of our hypothetical formulation, the relationship should hold for both groups of men. Some explanation for this difference, however, may lie in the fact that men who are in higher level white collar jobs are also older and have greater length of service with the company. Men with considerable experience with the company may not see absence as an acceptable form of behavior except in emergency situations. The forces induced by a responsible job and a continuous pattern of attendance to the job in the same company may be strong enough to counter balance any negative forces of dissatisfaction with the working situation.

Our finding that men and women are significantly different with respect to frequency of absence is not startling and needs only to be mentioned in summarizing. We found white collar women averaging one absence more than white collar men over the six month period.

An important methodological finding deriving from these studies is that an absence rate based on actual days lost proved to be much less effective than the rate based on frequency of absence for showing a relationship between attitudes and absences for white collar men. Again this finding was not startling for it was suggested by the work of Mayo and his students. The Mayo school did outstanding work in emphasizing the importance of a measure of absences which minimizes the count of absences caused by illness, and maximizes the frequency of absences of persons whose attendance pattern is highly irregular. They did not, however, attempt to relate quantitative measures of workers' attitudes to this frequency of absence rate. The confirmation from our findings that this is a more effective measure strongly suggests that the frequency of absence rate should be the measure for further investigation into the concomitants of high absence.

REFERENCES

Covner, B. J., 'Management Factors Affecting Absenteeism', *Harvard Business Review*, XXVIII (1950) 42–8.

Fox, J. B. and Scott, J. F., *Absenteeism: Management's Problem* (Boston: Harvard Business School, Business Research Studies, No. 20, 1943).

Katz, D. and Hyman, H., 'Industrial Morale and Public Opinion Methods', *International Journal of Opinion and Attitude Research*, I (1947) 13–30.

Mayo, E. and Lombard, G., *Teamwork and Labor Turnover in the Aircraft Industry of Southern California* (Boston: Harvard Business School, Business Research Studies, No. 32, 1944).

Noland, E. W., 'Worker Attitudes and Industrial Absenteeism: A Statistical Appraisal', *American Sociological Review*, X (1945) 503–10.

NOTE
1. This is one of a series of studies and analyses of data collected in the Detroit Edison Company. John Sparling, Howard Ritter, and Carol Ridley of the Personnel Planning Department of the Company, and Anne Moldauer and Howard Baumgartel of the Survey Research Center worked closely with the authors on this particular project. This study,

like others in the Detroit Edison series, has drawn on the ideas and suggestions of S. F. Leahy, Blair Swartz, and Robert Schwab of the Company, and Theodore Hariton and Donald Trow of the Survey Research Center. This study was made possible by a research grant from the Detroit Edison Company to the University of Michigan.

21 Social Desirability as a Moderator of the Relationship between Job Satisfaction and Personal Adjustment*

CHRISTOPHER ORPEN
University of Cape Town, South Africa

There is general agreement in recent textbooks that a fairly high positive relationship exists between job satisfaction and personal adjustment: for example, 'there is considerable evidence that job dissatisfaction is often associated with generalized maladjustment of some kind' (Gilmer, 1966, p. 257) and 'the relationship between job satisfaction and life adjustment is a strong one' (Siegel, 1969, p. 361). These conclusions are based to a large extent on studies which have found significantly positive correlations between measures of job satisfaction and independent indicators of personal adjustment. In these studies job satisfaction has usually been measured by a questionnaire in which employees are asked to indicate their feelings towards their work situation as a whole, while personal adjustment has usually been assessed by an inventory in which employees are asked to report on incidences of poor mental health like headaches, feelings of anxiety, lack of self-confidence, etc.

Despite the commonly held belief that industrial workers are becoming increasingly more dissatisfied with their work, studies of the incidence of job satisfaction have consistently found that most respondents rate themselves as pretty satisfied. For instance, Robinson and Hoppock (1952) in a review article covering 191 studies report that only 18 per cent of all the subjects tested could be regarded as dissatisfied employees. Vroom (1964) and Parker (1967) claim that this figure should not be taken at face-value, since reporting a high level of job satisfaction is a socially desirable response which most people will give irrespective of their

Personnel Psychology, XXVII (1974) 103—8. Reprinted by permission.

actual feelings. In this respect Blauner (1964) argues that the tendency to report high levels of satisfaction follows from the fact that by demeaning his job (by reporting dissatisfaction) a subject is questioning his very competence as a person.

In a parallel fashion, despite the views of 'experts' regarding the prevalence of mental illness, most respondents obtain fairly high scores on the usual questionnaire measures of personal adjustment. For instance, although Srole et al. (1962) in an interview study with New York residents claim that fully 30 per cent of the population suffer from psychological problems which are sufficiently severe to interfere with their everyday lives, the mental health survey by Gurin et al. (1969), based on questionnaire replies, reports a markedly lower estimate for the incidence of mental illness. Edwards (1957) and Crowne and Marlowe (1964) claim that this discrepancy follows from the fact that it is socially undesirable to endorse items that reflect poor mental health. In this repect Vernon (1964) argues that it is a natural response for subjects to answer questions in such a way as to convey a picture of a 'good' personality, even if they are unaware of doing so.

Accepting that the usual ways of assessing job satisfaction and personal adjustment are both heavily loaded with social desirability, as suggested above, it is quite possible that a high correlation between the two variables may not be due to any 'intrinsic relation' but rather to the fact that it is simply socially desirable to give certain replies on the various scales. In short, social desirability is a possible moderator of the relation between job satisfaction and personal adjustment, especially when the latter two variables are assessed by questionnaires. It is, therefore, difficult to evaluate the results of studies into the relation between job satisfaction and personal adjustment, unless the effect of social desirability on the relation is explicitly taken into account.

The present study represents a first attempt to examine the relation between job satisfaction and personal adjustment, with the 'inflating' effect of social desirability partialled out. In the light of the argument presented earlier, it is hypothesized that the correlation between job satisfaction and personal adjustment will be reduced when the influence of social desirability is statistically removed. To test this hypothesis 91 white employees (50 males, 41 females) from different levels in a medium-sized manufacturing company were given two measures of job satisfaction, social desirability, and personal adjustment. Job satisfaction was measured by (*a*) the 18-item Brayfield-Rothe index of job satisfaction (BR), which has been widely used as an indicator of overall job satisfaction across diverse occupational categories (Brayfield and Rothe, 1951) and (*b*) a 7-point self-rating scale of overall job satisfaction, ranging from 0 (extremely dissatisfied) to 7 (extremely satisfied). Social desirability, or need for group approval, was measured by (*a*) the Crowne-Marlowe social desirability scale (CM), which has been shown to possess considerable

Table 1   Means and standard deviations ($N = 91$)

BR		SR		PIRT		PSI		CM		WP	
M	SD	M	SD	M	SD	M	SD	M	SD	M	SD
10.6	12.0	5.9	2.1	42.1	9.8	165.9	25.2	13.75	5.61	16.2	4.5

construct validity (Crowne and Marlowe, 1964) and (b) the combined judgment of three work-peers (WP) who were required to indicate the extent to which they regarded their respective subject as 'needing the approval of others' on a 7-point rating scale, ranging from not at all (0) to a very great deal (7), with scores for each subject given by the sum of the judgments of their three work-peers. Personal adjustment was measured by (a) the sum of the alienation, social nonconformity and discomfort subscales of the Psychological Screening Inventory (PSI), which have been shown to be highly related to the corresponding MMPI scales and to indicate the similarity of the subjects' profiles to criterion groups consisting of hospitalized psychiatric patients (alienation), incarcerated prison inmates (social nonconformity) and to classified neurotics (discomfort or anxiety) by Lanyon (1970) and (b) the self-rating version of the Personality Integration Reputation Test (PIRT), developed from Jahoda's positive mental health, which has been shown to discriminate sharply between subjects in terms of a number of independent indicators of personal adjustment (Duncan, 1966).

The mean score of this fairly typical South African sample on the Brayfield-Rothe index of job satisfaction did not differ significantly ($p > .05$) from that of their normative United States sample. The mean score of the sample also did not differ significantly ($p > .05$) from that of the United States normative sample on the three subscales of the Psychological Screening Inventory or on the Crowne-Marlowe scale of social desirability. However, their mean score on the self-rating version of the Personality Integration Reputation Test was slightly lower ($p < .05$) than that of the normative United States sample. Since these differences were generally insignificant, it seems safe to conclude that the reported levels of job satisfaction and personal adjustment are roughly the same as those of comparable United States samples.

An essential requirement for construct validity is that different tests of the same variable should be significantly correlated. This requirement is met for each of the three variables. From Table 2 it can be seen that the correlation between the Psychological Screening Inventory and the Personality Integration Reputation Test was significant at the .01 level, as was that between the Brayfield-Rothe index and the self-rating of overall job satisfaction, while the correlation between the Crowne-Marlowe scale and the work-peers' rating of social desirability was significant at the .05 level.

Table 2   Correlations between scales ($N = 91$)

	BR	SR	PIRT	PSI	CM	WP
BR	x					
SR	.36*	x				
PIRT	.28*	.21	x			
PSI	.31*	.23	.31*	x		
CM	.24	.21	.36*	.38*	x	
WP	.29*	.31*	.28	.35*	.23	x

*$p < .01$.

As predicted, the correlations between job satisfaction and social desirability were all positive. From Table 2 it can be seen that half of the correlations were significant at the .01 level and half at the .05 level. This indicates that those employees who had a high need for group approval tended to regard themselves as more satisfied with their jobs than those who had a low need for group approval. As predicted, the correlations between personal adjustment and social desirability were also all positive. From Table 2 it can be seen that two-thirds of the correlations were significant at the .01 level and one-third at the .05 level. This indicates that those employees who had a high need for group approval tended to obtain higher scores on the adjustment scales than those who had a low need for group approval. It is interesting to note that the mean correlation between the indicators of job satisfaction and social desirability, indicates that about seven per cent of the variance in job satisfaction scores can be accounted for by differences in social desirability. However, the mean correlation between the indicators of personal adjustment and social desirability indicates that as much as 12 per cent of the variance in personal adjustment scores can be accounted for in this way. In other words, it seems as if the measures of personal adjustment are more loaded with social desirability than are those of job satisfaction. This makes sense if one argues that it is less important for positive evaluation by others to admit to being dissatisfied with one's job than it is to admit to possessing traits indicative of mental ill-health. In this respect, it is perhaps easier to explain away job dissatisfaction rather than personal maladjustment as due to factors beyond one's control.

Given these positive correlations between the measures of both job satisfaction and personal adjustment and social desirability, it is not surprising that, in each case, the satisfaction-adjustment correlation was lower after the removal of the influence of social desirability. When the spuriously inflating effect of social desirability was removed by using the Crowne-Marlowe scores in the partial correlation equation, the resulting satisfaction-adjustment correlations were .21 (BR and PIRT), .15 (SR and PIRT), .24 (BR and PSI) and .17 (SR and PSI). When the work-peers' ratings were used in the partial correlation equation, the resulting satisfaction-adjustment correlations were .22 (BR and PIRT), .13 (SR and PIRT), .23 (BR and PSI) and .14 (SR and PSI). The fact that half of these partial correlations were insignificant ($p > .05$) indicates that the relationship between job satisfaction and personal adjustment is not uniformly high. Scatter diagrams of these correlations (Orpen, 1972) reveal that this is mainly due to the presence of a fairly large proportion of employees who are well adjusted in terms of the present measures, but who report that they are not highly satisfied with their jobs. The mean satisfaction-adjustment correlation across the different measures of .19 indicates that no more than four per cent of the variation in job satisfaction can be attributed to differences in personal adjustment. Given this figure, it is difficult to speak of the relationship as having 'considerable support' or of being a 'strong one', even though the correlations are all positive. It seems, in short, as if a failure to take the factor of social desirability into account has led some investigators to overstate the degree of relationship between job satisfaction and personal adjustment.

REFERENCES

Blauner, R., *Alienation and Freedom: The Factory Worker and his Industry* (Chicago: University of Chicago Press, 1964.).

Brayfield, A. and Rothe, H. F., 'An Index of Job Satisfaction', *Journal of Applied Psychology*, XXXV (1951) 307–11.

Crowne, D. P. and Marlowe, D., *The Approval Motive* (New York: Wiley, 1964).

Duncan, C. D., 'A Reputation Test of Personality Integration', *Journal of Personality and Social Psychology*, III (1966) 516–24.

Edwards, A. L., *The Social Desirability Variable in Personality Assessment and Research* (New York: Dryden Press, 1957).

Gilmer, B. von H., *Industrial Psychology* (New York: McGraw-Hill, 1966).

Gurin, G., Veroff, J. and Field, S., *Americans View their Mental Health* (New York: Basic Books, 1960).

Jahoda, M., *Current Concepts of Positive Mental Health* (New York: Basic Books, 1958).

Lanyon, R. I., 'The Development and Validation of a Psychological Screening Inventory', *Journal of Consulting and Clinical Psychology*, XXXV [2] (1970), part 2.

Orpen, C., 'The Relationship between Job Satisfaction and Personal Adjustment'. Unpublished manuscript, University of Cape Town, 1972.

Parker, S. R., 'The Subjective Experience of Work', in *The Sociology of Industry*, ed. S. R. Parker (London: Allen and Unwin, 1967).

Robinson, H. A. and Hoppock, R., 'Job Satisfaction Résumé of 1951', *Occupations*, XXX (1952) 594–8.

Siegel, L., *Industrial Psychology* (Homewood, Ill.: Irwin, 1969).

Srole, L., Langner, T., Michael, S., Opler, M. and Rennie, T., *Mental*

Health in the Metropolis: The Midtown Manhattan Study (New York: McGraw-Hill, 1962).

Vernon, P. E., *Personality Assessment* (London: Methuen, 1964).

Vroom, V. H., *Work and Motivation* (New York: Wiley, 1964).

Further Readings

PART I

Bockman, V. M., 'The Herzberg Controversy', *Personnel Psychology*, XXIV (1971) 155–89.

Dunnette, M. D., Campbell, J. P. and Hakel, M. D. 'Factors Contributing to Job Satisfaction and Job Dissatisfaction in Six Occupational Groups', *Organizational Behavior and Human Performance*, II (1967) 143–74.

Herzberg, F., Mausner, B. and Snyderman, B., *The Motivation to Work* (New York: Wiley, 1959).

Lawler, III, E. E. and Hall, D. T., 'Relationship of Job Characteristics to Job Involvement, Satisfaction and Intrinsic Motivation', *Journal of Applied Psychology*, LIV (1970) 305–12.

Lawler, E. E. and Suttle, J. L., 'Expectancy Theory and Job Behavior', *Organizational Behavior and Human Performance*, IX (1973) 482–503.

Locke, E. A., 'What is Job Satisfaction?', *Organizational Behavior and Human Performance*, IV (1969) 309–36.

Locke, E. A., 'Personnel Attitudes and Motivation', *Annual Review of Psychology*, XXVI (1975) 457–80.

Porter, L. W., Lawler III, E. E. and Hackman, J. R., *Behavior in Organizations* (New York: McGraw-Hill, 1975).

PART II

Hackman, J. R. and Lawler III, E. E., 'Employee Reactions to Job Characteristics', *Journal of Applied Psychology*, LV (1971) 259–86.

Hulin, C. L. and Blood, M. R., 'Job Enlargement, Individual Differences, Worker Responses', *Psychological Bulletin*, LXIX (1968) 41–55.

Maher, J. R. (ed.), *New Perspectives in Job Enrichment* (New York: Van Nostrand Reinhold, 1971).

PART III

Centers, R. J. and Bugental, D. E., 'Intrinsic and Extrinsic Job Motivations among Different Segments of the Working Population', *Journal of Applied Psychology*, L (1966) 193–7.

Porter, L. W. and Lawler, E. E., 'Properties of Organization Structure in Relation to Job Attitudes and Job Behavior', *Psychological Bulletin*, LXIV (1965) 23–51.

Pritchard, R. A. and Karasick, B. W. 'The Effects of Organizational Climate on Managerial Job Performance and Job Satisfaction', *Organizational Behavior and Human Performance*, IX (1973) 126–46.

PART IV

Gavin, J. F. and Ewen, R. B., 'Racial Differences in Job Attitude and Performance: Some Theoretical Considerations and Empirical Findings', *Personnel Psychology*, XXVII (1974) 455–64.

Lawler, E. E., 'Ability as a Moderator in the Relationship between Job Attitudes and Job Performance', *Personnel Psychology*, XIX (1966) 153–64.

Weitz, J., 'A Neglected Concept in the Study of Job Satisfaction', *Personnel Psychology*, V (1952) 201–5.

PART V

Argyle, M., Gardner, G. and Cioffi, I., 'Supervisory Methods Related to Productivity, Absenteeism and Labor Turnover', *Human Relations*, XI (1958) 23–40.

Brayfield, A. and Crockett, W., 'Employee Attitudes and Employee Performance', *Psychological Bulletin*, LII (1955) 396–424.

Porter, L. W. and Steers, R. M., 'Organisational, Work and Personal Factors in Employee Turnover and Absenteeism', *Psychological Bulletin*, XVIII (1973) 151–76.

Index